Cognitive Science

What is human nature? How does the mind work? What is consciousness? Is there a self in the brain?

Cognitive Science is a major new guide to the central theories and problems in the study of the mind and brain. The authors clearly explain how and why cognitive science aims to understand the brain as a computational system that manipulates representations. They identify the roots of cognitive science in Descartes – who argued that all knowledge of the external world is filtered through some sort of representation – and examine the present-day role of artificial intelligence, computing, psychology, linguistics, and neuroscience.

Throughout, the key building blocks of cognitive science are clearly illustrated: perception, memory, attention, emotion, language, control of movement, learning, understanding and other important mental phenomena. *Cognitive Science*

- presents a clear, collaborative introduction to the subject
- is the first textbook to bring together all the different strands of this new science in a unified approach
- includes many illustrations and examples to aid the student.

Daniel Kolak is Professor of Philosophy at William Paterson University in New Jersey, USA and an affiliate of the Rutgers Center for Cognitive Science (RUCCS). He originated the *Wadsworth Philosophers* series and is Series Editor of the *Longman Library of Philosophy*.

William Hirstein is Chair of the Department of Philosophy at Elmhurst College, Illinois, USA.

Peter Mandik is Associate Professor of Philosophy and Cognitive Science Laboratory Coordinator at the William Paterson University in New Jersey, USA.

Jonathan Waskan is Assistant Professor at the Neuroscience Program, University of Illinois at Urbana-Champaign, USA.

Cognitive Science

An Introduction to Mind and Brain

*Daniel Kolak, William Hirstein, Peter Mandik,
Jonathan Waskan*

Routledge
Taylor & Francis Group

NEW YORK AND LONDON

First published 2006
by Routledge
270 Madison Avenue, New York, NY 10016

Simultaneously published in the UK
by Routledge
2 Park Square, Milton Park, Abingdon, Oxon OX14 4RN

Routledge is an imprint of the Taylor & Francis Group, an informa business

© 2006 Daniel Kolak, William Hirstein, Peter Mandik, Jonathan Waskan

Typeset in Franklin Gothic by Keystroke, 28 High Street, Tettenhall, Wolverhampton
Printed and bound in Great Britain by Bell & Bain Ltd, Glasgow

Library of Congress Cataloging in Publication Data
Cognitive science : an introduction to mind and brain / Daniel Kolak . . . [et al.].
    p. cm.
  Includes bibliographical references and index.
1. Cognitiion. 2. Cognitive science. 3. Brain. 4. Psychology. I. Kolak, Daniel.

  BF311.C552322 2006
  153–dc22   2006002726

British Library Cataloguing in Publication Data
A catalogue record for this book is available from the British Library

ISBN10: 0–415–22100–5 (hbk)
ISBN10: 0–415–22101–3 (pbk)

ISBN13: 978–0–415–22100–9 (hbk)
ISBN13: 978–0–415–22101–6 (pbk)
ISBN13: 978–0–203–96893–2 (ebk)

Contents

Preface

We titled this book *Cognitive Science: An Introduction to Mind and Brain* because our focus is on basic, defining problems of the new discipline of cognitive science. A research discipline as such is unified by accepting a core set of problems and by agreed-upon techniques for solving them, however broadly that set of problems and techniques might range. Cognitive science has at its disposal a huge armamentarium of problem-solving techniques, from the PET scan of neurophysiology, to the stimulus–response techniques of the psychologist, to the conceptual analysis of philosophy.

One of the things our book accomplishes is that it brings the different subdisciplines of cognitive science together in stating and proposing solutions to these basic problems in a relatively seamless way. Thinkers interested in solving problems do not care what discipline developed the techniques which solve those problems, rather they follow their intuitive sense in selecting the techniques which seem most useful. If cognitive science is to flourish as a discipline, there must be a natural connectedness to its basic problems.

Cognitive Science: An Introduction to Mind and Brain is suitable for upper-level undergraduate courses in those universities which require students to take courses in the constitutive disciplines of cognitive science prior to synthesizing the disciplines in a junior or senior-level cognitive science course. The types of class which might use this book include:

- introduction to cognitive science courses
- lower and mid-level psychology courses
- introductory neuroscience courses
- lower and mid-level philosophy courses.

The core departments that now offer these courses are:

- psychology
- biology
- anthropology

- philosophy
- computer science.

One of the main differences between *Cognitive Science: An Introduction to Mind and Brain* and existing books is that ours is a text for the new discipline of cognitive science and not a set of mini-introductions for an old-style "interdisciplinary" course in psychology, artificial intelligence, philosophy, and so on. A base-level organization by existing disciplines defeats the purpose, power, and usefulness of cognitive science as a discipline. Instead of devoting chapters to the various constitutive disciplines, we devote chapters to basic mental capacities, such as perception, memory, action, and language, and present synthesized information from each of the disciplines *within* the chapters. The unifying model is that of *collaborative knowledge*. This means applying the various techniques, methods, and perspectives to the same problems in tandem, that is, in a coherent and unified manner.

There has been a corresponding shift in the textbook audiences, with an exponential increase in the neuroscience audience – witness the massive Society for Neuroscience meeting – at 20,000 people the largest professional conference in the country. We acknowledge this fact by beginning each chapter with sections on neuroanatomy and neurophysiology, followed by sections on neuropsychology and neurocomputing. In a sense we are letting the brain itself be the organizing framework for the diverse relevant information from the different perspectives.

Aside from these sorts of reasons, we find working from more concrete issues to more abstract ones to be preferable, largely because the abstract issues arise from problems encountered in giving an analysis of the more concrete ones, but also because it has been our experience in teaching cognitive science that students find it easier to learn this way. In the current framework, the six constituent disciplines can be arranged from concrete to abstract as follows: neuroscience, psychology, anthropology, neurocomputing and artificial intelligence, linguistics, and philosophy.

Cognitive Science: An Introduction to Mind and Brain is not just a collection of the right topics presented in the right order at the right level that can be used to introduce all students to cognitive science – though we hope it is that. It is a new paradigm that works and has already been applied, over the past four years at time of writing, with great success, at the authors' institutions – so much so that not only have other departments at our universities adopted it as part of their curriculum, but also other universities are seeking to implement the same model.

We thank all the people who have contributed to this project, especially: Jay Lombard, Melinda Campbell, Pat Churchland, Rick Grush, Brian Keeley, Portia Iversen, Thomas Natsoulas, John Searle, V.S. Ramachandran, Joel Thompson, Richard Wollheim, Joseph Salerno, Austin Burka, Daniel Dennett, and Jaakko Hintikka. William Hirstein and Daniel Kolak thank the many patients with whom we have worked and cannot mention by name, especially AA, LB, DS, RU and the 37 courageous children who took part in some of the studies mentioned in Chapter 5, and also their parents. We also thank our editor at Routledge, Tony Bruce, for his encouragement, foresight and patience.

This book was conceived and begun by Daniel Kolak and William Hirstein in 1998. Kolak and Hirstein invited Jonathan Waskan and Peter Mandik to join the project in the summer of 2000. Authorship of the various sections is as follows.

Jonathan Waskan authored the following sections and all subsections thereof (excluding text boxes): 1.2.1 – 1.2.3; 1.2.6; 1.3.1 – 1.3.4; 1.3.5.1 – 1.3.5.2; 2.3 – 2.5; 4.1 – 4.3 (excluding 4.2.1.1.2; 4.2.1.2.2; 4.2.1.3); 6.4.2 – 6.4.4 and the text box on The language of thought and the frame problem in Chapter 4. Sections 1.1; 2.2; 2.6; 4.2.1.1.2; 4.2.1.2.2; 4.2.1.3 were co-authored by Waskan and Kolak and/or Hirstein.

Peter Mandik authored the following sections and all subsections thereof: 1.4; 3.3 through 3.6; 3.9; 4.4; 5.3.2; 6.2 on the philosophy of language; 7.2.1; 7.2.2; 7.3.2 through 7.3.4. Additionally, Mandik authored the following text boxes: Mental rotation and mental imagery; Homunculus fallacies; Evaluating Cartesian skepticism; Popper's critique of confirmation; Rigid designation. Sections 3.7; 3.8; 5.4; 7.3.1 were co-authored by Mandik and Kolak and/or Hirstein.

All other sections were authored by Kolak and/or Hirstein.

Introduction

Cognitive science, as its name implies, is broadly defined as the science of cognition. It has emerged in recent years through the collaborative work of psychologists, neuroscientists, computer scientists, anthropologists, philosophers, and linguists whose combined research in these fields gave rise to a powerful new paradigm for unifying the study of the mind/brain.

This sort of development is hardly new. It has many grand historical precedents. Physics, for instance, came about as a result of the collaborative conjoining of the techniques of what was then called "natural philosophy" with mathematics, along with various other disciplines. Psychology came about as a result of the collaborative conjoining of what was then called "introspective philosophy" with biology and various other disciplines. Computer science emerged from logic, mathematics, automata theory, and engineering. There are many more such examples. In each case the emerging field required an integration of knowledge and methods under the rubric of one coherent and unified book. This is what *Cognitive Science: An Introduction to Mind and Brain* is designed to be.

Since 1990 the levels of understanding achieved in cognitive science have toppled traditional disciplinary paradigms and taken the academic community by storm. Courses have begun cropping up everywhere – in departments of psychology, biology, anthropology, neuroscience, computer science, philosophy, linguistics – showing cognitive science to be the premier field for the study of perception, language, attention, memory, control of movement, feelings, and consciousness. This all came somewhat as a surprise. "Interdisciplinary" had come to be little more than an overused buzzword among college administrators. Ubiquitous phrases like "knowledge across the curriculum" came to mean, not to the administrators who endorsed them but to the professors who had to teach them, a slew of watered-down courses with no real points of connection. Thus no one seemed to realize the astounding development until suddenly there it was staring everyone in the face: the real thing! Except cognitive science wasn't so much "interdisciplinary" as it was the birth of a truly new, *collaborative* discipline. It had all the epistemological and pedagogical benefits of a collaborative approach and none of the weaknesses.

All this may help in part to explain why there is such broad and unprecedented support for cognitive science at colleges and universities across the United States. Indeed, it has almost become a truism that if you want to get new funds – for programs, faculty positions, classes, laboratories, etc. – cognitive science is a sure bet. But it doesn't even begin to explain the revolutionary understanding of the mechanisms of the mind/brain that is at the core of cognitive science.

In general, researchers in cognitive science seek to understand brain processes as computational systems which manipulate representations. Toward this end, research often involves the construction of computer models of brain systems, models which ideally share input/output properties of the target brain system, and which behave similarly to the target system when "lesioned." The rapid growth of the number of universities offering degrees in cognitive science has been driven by the increasing necessity workers in the separate fields have seen for gaining information from other fields in order to solve their problems. A neuroscientist seeking to understand Broca's area, for instance, finds that she needs to learn more about linguistics; a philosopher working on the mind/body problem finds some of the new biological theories of consciousness relevant to his work; a psychologist needs to learn more about computer science in order to construct a more powerful computer model of her area of interest, and so on. Similarly, the neural networks, connectionist models, and neuromorphic systems of the computer scientist are designed to make use of the organizational principles used in the human brain, so that he finds the study of neuroanatomy rewarding. Thus – to give just one example – typical pre-cognitive science neural network models use binary computing elements (that can only be on or off). Biological neurons, however, as it turns out are not binary (they do not have only an on or off state as their output). Their outputs have *continuous* values – the neuron is more like a voltage-to-frequency converter that converts membrane potential into firing rate. That is why typical post-cognitive science neural networks designed to model the brain use outputs that can take a continuous set of values.

Indeed, since the mid-1990s the driving force in cognitive science has changed from artificial intelligence to neuroscience. Propelled initially by cell staining and lesion studies, and more recently by breakthroughs in neuroimaging, the neurosciences are making vast progress on many fronts. Artificial intelligence has tacitly admitted this by switching to approaches designed to mimic the activity of neuronal ensembles, such as connectionism and neurocomputation. And because it turns out that most of our complex functions – speech, language, perception – are carried out by the cerebral cortex, computer scientists have come to look at cognitive psychology as software that runs on a cortical computer; they have come to develop the organizational details of the output of artificial systems by studying how humans do it. They want to find out what kind of software runs best on neural networks by seeing what kind of software runs on us; cognitive science as practiced by computer scientists is viewed as a technique for reverse-engineering the software for a parallel computer. These are just some of the changes that are sweeping the field and with which our book hopes to inspire its readers.

One of the organizing principles of the book, and the theme behind the arrangement of the chapters, is the idea of the representational theory of mind. The basic related ideas are discussed in Chapter 1 "Beginning concepts," and the methods for their investigation are discussed in Chapter 2 "Windows on the brain and mind." The remaining chapters are organized around the role of representations in main faculties of the mind.

Sensory mechanisms transduce information into representations in perception (Chapter 3). Representations are stored in memory and processed in reasoning (Chapter 4), and ultimately inform our actions and emotional reactions (Chapter 5). Representations figure heavily in our comprehension and production of language which itself constitutes a means for representing the world (Chapter 6). Finally, mental representations structure our consciousness and our selves (Chapter 7).

1 Beginning Concepts

1.1 MANY PATHS TO THE SAME SUMMIT

The cosmos is a vast tumult of existential silence. For 15 billion years it has evolved, from the big bang to its present state, and, for all we know, it has remained entirely unconscious of itself until very recently. In our minuscule corner of this physical maelstrom there evolved beings with awareness – beings that wonder about their own existence. It takes enormous stars to illuminate the heavens, gargantuan engines of light that energize and animate the cosmos. But it is we creatures formed from the dust of stars in whom tiny sparks of consciousness have ignited. It is we who ask: "What am I? Who am I? Where do I come from? How am I able to be what I am?" Of all the wondrous things in the universe – from galaxies, quasars, stars and black holes to the one planet we know gives rise to life with all its myriad creatures – we are, as far as we know, the only beings capable of asking such questions.

As a human being you have much in common with other animals. You have a body, a brain, and internal organs, such as a heart that pumps blood, and lungs that bring oxygen into the blood. You were born, you eat, you may procreate, you sleep, and eventually you will die. Yet in asking such questions as "What am I?" you distinguish yourself in a radical way from all of the other species on this planet, maybe even from the rest of the cosmos. You can ask such questions of yourself, and you can think and reason and wonder about anything and everything. How is it that you are you able to do this? What is this thing that is aware of itself, wondering, asking these questions? Your hands may clench into fists or grasp dramatically in thin air, but your hands are not doing the asking. Your heart may be pounding in your chest, and although we may say figuratively that the heart wonders and feels, it is not the heart that is doing the asking. The heart only pumps blood, it is as unaware of itself as is blood or a star. It is a machine, an organic machine, but it is not the kind of machine that can become conscious of itself. Replace it with an artificial heart or with someone else's heart, and still you are there, still you are you, wondering, thinking, asking questions of yourself and the world. But who or what is doing the asking, and how is this being done, what makes it possible for this take place within you?

More than twenty-five centuries ago, the great ancient Greek philosopher Plato (428–348 BCE) wondered,

> Is the blood the element with which we think, or the air or the fire? Or perhaps nothing of the kind – but the brain may be the originating power of the perceptions of hearing and sight and smell and memory and opinion may come from them.
>
> (Plato, *Phaedo*, p. 481)

From our present perspective, it seems clear that the brain is what thinks. Indeed, according to our best theory, not only is thinking done by the brain, but so are reasoning, perceiving, feeling, willing, moving, attending, remembering, communicating, understanding, and choosing. And it is a theory. People sometimes say, "Such-and-such is just a theory," as if theories are, in contrast with things that have been proven, mere speculations. But formal proofs exist only in the domain of logic and mathematics, and empirical science must, as we shall see, proceed along many different paths to its summit. Not all of these paths are well worn, or even clearly marked; and it is never quite clear whether one has even reached the summit, or whether one will have to descend again before undertaking some treacherous new ascent. Therein, however, lies the thrill of the journey. Strictly speaking then, the point stands that the common-sense belief that our brains are most directly involved in cognition is, at bottom, only a theory.

It is worth taking a closer look at precisely in what sense this belief (i.e., that our brains are the locus of mental activity) is theoretical. To start with, notice that you can't see, just by looking, that these activities (e.g., thinking, seeing, and so on – activities going on within you as you are reading this) are the result of brain activity. In all likelihood, there are massive networks of neurons that are sending millions of electrochemical impulses to one another in order to make possible these mental activities. But when you consider, for instance, this book that you see and the sense of comprehension that you feel as you read these words, notice how neither looks or feels like neurons firing. They look and feel like things, words, and thoughts. If your awareness of these objects, words, and thoughts should turn out to consist of a sequence of neural events, then we will come to know this only through the activity of theorizing. This is the only way in which the brain can come to know that it is a brain that is doing the things that brains do, like theorizing that brains theorize.

Other animals are capable of wondrous deeds. Birds can fly and find their way over thousands of miles; deer can sprint through thick forest; fish can breathe under water; and lions can smell prey a mile away. Yet there is no evidence that any of these animals can engage in the very activity that we are presently engaged in, namely, thinking, wondering, and asking questions such as "What am I?"

But why not? These animals not only have hearts, lungs, and so on, but also have brains. Moreover, an elephant's brain is much bigger than ours, and so is a dolphin's. Like other animals, elephants and dolphins can see, they can respond to their environment, they can learn and adapt to changing situations. It is arguable that they even have feelings and emotions.

So what is it, then, that your brain has that none of these animals' brains have? What is it about your brain that enables you to wonder, "What am I?" There are, in fact, many further attributes that distinguish humans from the rest of the animals. For instance, of all the animals, humans have the most highly developed means of communication – we use a language that far exceeds, in complexity, expressiveness, and even variation, any of the languages used by beasts. We humans also have a well-developed capacity to remember, in great detail, the events surrounding our own lives. This may, in turn, enable an awareness of ourselves as beings that exist in time. If we lacked this awareness, we could never wonder about such things as whether we will always exist, or whether, instead, we will simply stop existing at some point. Another of our remarkable attributes is our ability to predict what will happen should certain possibilities become actualities. Should we, for instance, come across a disposable cup full to the rim with water, we can venture a pretty good prediction about what would happen were we to use a pencil to poke a hole through the side of the cup. We use this predictive capacity in order to generate plans concerning how best to achieve our heart's desires. We also have a capacity for tool use that far exceeds that of other creatures. Closely related to this is our unique ability to recognize what things like wrenches and light bulbs can be used for. Our thoughts are not, however, merely limited to concrete states of affairs. Our minds soar above this world of finite, changeable entities into the realm of things in their abstract and indestructible purity. As Plato noted, we don't just consider facts about this or that particular triangle (which are far from perfect and always finite) but eternal and immutable truths about triangles in general (what Plato called the form of triangularity). We also think about economics, the rules of chess, and quarks. We humans can even read minds – that is, we are able to represent the beliefs of one another and, somehow, keep those beliefs separate from our own. For this reason, it seems, we are able to understand one another and to predict one another's behavior to a remarkable degree.

What is more, these capacities do not exist in isolation. Instead, they interact in diverse ways, and the results are, to give ourselves the proper credit and blame, both magnificent and horrific. Thoughts of our own mortality seem to sow the seeds of religion. And shared beliefs, whatever their origin, enable groups of distinct individuals to enter into societies. So do shared languages. With the aid of shared beliefs and languages, we are able to cooperate in the execution of our shared goals. We can erect a skyscraper, score a touchdown, or coordinate an attack. In fact, we erect not only physical edifices, but social ones as well. We establish governments, universities, and committees. Science, too, depends upon memory, planning, communication, tool use, and even creativity (whatever that is). The list of uniquely human attributes and accomplishments goes on and on.

If we are ever to come to an understanding of how it is that we are able to ponder our own existence, solve problems, and wage modern warfare, a good place to start might be to gain a better understanding of the mental capacities just mentioned. Thus, in this book, we shall undertake an examination of the various forms of cognitive activity that make human beings stand out so starkly against the backdrop of other biological entities. We will try to figure out how it is that three pounds of specialized cells seated atop a relatively slow, weak, and clumsy frame gives rise to language, memory, forethought, tool use, abstraction, mind reading, and all of the other wonderful things of which humans seem capable.

Among scientists, there is no one accepted methodology for understanding these capacities. Rather, as noted earlier, there are many simultaneous and sometimes collaborative efforts to clear paths to this summit of all summits: self-knowledge. These paths have ominous names, such as: cognitive neuroscience, artificial intelligence, linguistics, philosophy, cognitive neuropsychology, cognitive psychology, and anthropology. Construed as a collaborative, interdisciplinary endeavor, these paths are collectively known as cognitive science. As we shall see, cognitive science is just the latest (and most fruitful) attempt to shed light on what seems at once the brightest and darkest corner of the universe. It is the most recent attempt by humankind to obey that ancient edict inscribed on the hallowed walls of the temple of Delphi: know thyself.

It is worth bearing in mind that science, as we know it, has been in existence for only a few hundred years. The art of observation, theory formation, and experimentation that Leonardo da Vinci described in the fifteenth century was first perfected and applied to bodies in motion (both terrestrial and celestial) by the contemporaries Galileo and Kepler in the sixteenth. Thereafter, attempts would be made to apply this method to all manner of phenomena. It would be some time, however, before people figured out ways to apply it to the study of human mentality. That is to say, the systematic testing of psychological hypotheses had to await methods, discussed extensively in the next chapter, that were developed only recently. Be this as it may, there has never been a dearth of theories about the nature of mentality.

1.2 THE ORIGINS OF COGNITIVE SCIENCE

Let us retrace our steps and see if we can come any closer to an understanding of ourselves. What is it that makes thinking possible? Why, it's your brain, of course. But why "of course"? How do you know it is your brain? You've never seen your brain. How do you know what your brain does and how it does it? Here, again, we notice something extremely peculiar. Your hand appears to you as a hand, and by looking at this appearance you can surmise what your hands are, what they are for, and how to use them. What makes the appearance and the recognition possible? Again, of course, it is your brain – but notice that nowhere does your brain appear to you as a brain! Indeed, if you start inquiring into the nature of your own existence, of what you are, it will not naturally occur to you to suppose that what you are (that is, what this activity of self-conscious awareness itself is) is a brain! Rather, what naturally emerges from such considerations is that this conscious activity consists of something very much different from all the rest of the physical universe, something that seems quite distinct from every other part of creation. According to many traditions, introspection reveals that the essence of you, what makes you *you*, is something non-physical, something mental, spiritual, or incorporeal. In other words, unlike your hand, which presents itself to you as a hand, your brain presents itself to you not as a brain but as something entirely other than what it is. It presents itself as a mind. So that we don't find ourselves reinventing the wheel, let us retrace the steps that others have taken in their quest for self-knowledge.

1.2.1 Philosophy and the mysterious mind

Considering the unique way in which the brain presents itself, it is no wonder that many who first asked the question "What am I?" invariably came up with answers such as spirit, soul, or mind. They did not see themselves as being made essentially of the same stuff as the rest of their surrounding environment. In becoming aware of itself, nature seemed to divide itself into that which was aware and that which wasn't – existence was bifurcated into physical and mental realms. This view culminated in the metaphysical dualism exemplified by the philosophy of René Descartes (1596–1650) and the famous mind–body problem that, under various guises, continues to perplex philosophers to this very day. Here is how Descartes so famously put it:

> From the fact that I know that I exist, and that at the same time I judge that obviously nothing else belongs to my nature or essence except that I am a thinking thing, I rightly conclude that my essence consists entirely in my being a thinking thing. And although perhaps . . . I have a body that is very closely joined to me, nevertheless, because on the one hand I have a clear and distinct idea of myself, insofar as I am merely a thinking thing and not an extended thing, and because on the other hand I have a distinct idea of a body, insofar as it is merely an extended thing and not a thinking thing, it is certain that I am really distinct from my body, and can exist without it.
>
> (Descartes 1970 [1641], pp. 151–153)

Descartes noticed that there is a great difference between our relation to our own minds and our relation to material objects. We can doubt the existence of extended (i.e., space-occupying) things, but we can't doubt the existence of our own minds; and, he went on to note, while the former are spatially divisible, the latter seem not to be.

Philosophers have been cataloguing these remarkable properties of the mental for hundreds of years. To mention a few more, notice that most of your beliefs about the world are, strictly speaking, dubitable (i.e., they may be incorrect). It is conceivable, for instance, that you are mistaken in believing that there are nine planets orbiting the sun. Perhaps, as you were reading this, a tenth planet was discovered. Even some of your most fundamental beliefs are dubitable, such as your belief that there is a book before your eyes. Perhaps you will wake up in a moment and realize that your experience was merely a dream. There are other beliefs, however, that are much harder (some would say impossible) to doubt – your belief, for instance, that every equi-lateral and equiangular planar figure with an even number of sides will have, for any given side, another side that is parallel to it. Some have held that beliefs of this sort differ from those mentioned earlier in that they are acknowledged by everyone (at least everyone who gives them any thought) to be eternal and indubitable. It is no surprise, then, that philosophers have long been preoccupied with explaining how it is that such universal and necessary truths might be grasped by the human mind. Theories have ranged from the fantastical (e.g., Plato's theory that we come to know pure geometrical forms that exist neither in our minds nor in nature but beyond space and time) to the downright mundane (e.g., Thomas Hobbes' theory that such truths are little more than a trick we are able to perform once we learn how to use language).

Another amazing property of mental states such as thoughts, beliefs, desires, fears, and so on, is that they are generally about something. When we think, we think about things and states of affairs – for instance, we think about our families, activities that we hope to accomplish, tasty foods, parallelograms, and so on. We wonder about the beginning of the universe. We have fears about death and taxes. The nineteenth-century philosopher Franz Brentano (1838–1917) con-sidered this *aboutness* of the mental to be something that defies physical explanation. We can think about things that are physically remote, like the far side of the galaxy; things that are physically impossible, like faster-than-light travel; and things that don't even exist, like Sherlock Holmes and the Easter Bunny. Following Brentano, we call this property the *intentionality* of the mental – though it remains an open question whether or not intentionality defies physical explanation. Sherlock Holmes and the Easter Bunny have what philosophers have called "intentional inexistence." We will discuss in section 1.4 on mental representation how intentionality and intentional inexistence might be explained by materialistic theories.

In addition to cataloguing and theorizing about the more mysterious aspects of our mental lives, philosophers have also engaged in speculation about the nature of such basic cognitive processes as perception, reasoning, and memory. For better or worse, this theorizing brought to light new philosophical problems. Galileo, for instance, noticed that when one feels the warmth of fire, one is tempted to conclude that the perceived heat is something that characterizes the flame. Yet, on moving one's hand closer, the heat becomes unbearable and painful. Clearly, says Galileo, we would not be tempted to conclude that the pain is a property of the fire. So why conclude that heat, which differs only in degree, is a property of the fire? Hence Galileo drew a distinction between the perceived properties of external physical objects that really are properties of those objects (namely, size, shape, and motion) and other properties (e.g., colors, odors, and heat) that are more ideal (i.e., mind-dependent) than real. Such properties are added to the perceptual equation by our minds. As Galileo explains,

> I cannot believe that there exists in external bodies anything, other than their size, shape, or motion (slow or rapid), which could excite in us our tastes, sounds, and odors. And indeed I should judge that, if ears, tongues, and noses be taken away, the number, shape, and motion of bodies would remain, but not their tastes, sounds, and odors.
>
> (Galileo 1954 [1623], pp. 719–724)

Of course, for Galileo and the naturalist philosophers inspired by his work, even minds were supposed to be physical. The universe was supposed to contain nothing but corpuscles (tiny bits of matter) in motion. So how, from the motion of the corpuscles in our heads, do such percepts as the color or scent of a rose arise? This conundrum of consciousness, discussed extensively in Chapter 7, remains one of the most vexing philosophical problems about the mind. Considerations of the workings of perception, where many of these conundrums first arise, are discussed in Chapter 3.

Another philosophical problem arising from this pre-scientific thought about the nature of perception is the seeming barrier that the apparent representation/represented divide poses for possibility of knowledge. When you see this text, there may be little doubt in your mind that this phenomenon, what you see before you, just is the book. Yet there are reasons to think that this phenomenon, the appearance of the book, is distinct from the book itself. For instance, as philosopher David Hume (1711–1776) once noted, as you move away from the book its phenomenal size seems to change – it becomes smaller. Yet, presumably, the book itself is not becoming smaller. Thus, appearance of the book (i.e., the mental representation of the book) seems to be distinct from the book itself. Regarding the natural tendency to assume the contrary (i.e., that the phenomena of perception are mind-independent objects), Hume (1977 [1777]) explains:

> But this universal and primary opinion of all men is soon destroyed by the slightest
> philosophy, which teaches us, that nothing can ever be present to the mind but an image
> or perception, and that the senses are only inlets, through which these images are
> conveyed, without being able to produce any immediate intercourse between the mind
> and the object.
>
> (Hume 1977 [1777], p. 152)

If this is a correct portrayal of our predicament, then difficulties arise concerning the possibility of ever establishing that our perceptions and thoughts about the world (our mental representations) accurately reflect the true nature of the world. Indeed, it becomes difficult to see how we could ever even know that a mind-independent world actually exists! Dealing with problems of this sort has been one of the central themes of epistemology (discussed in Chapter 4), the study of what knowledge is and how one goes about obtaining it.

Of course, if your concern is to discover what kinds of things humans can know, a reasonable first step might be to examine the instrument by which knowledge is attained. Thus, as a natural by-product of the epistemological concerns brought to light in the seventeenth and eighteenth centuries, philosophers became seriously interested in questions about the make-up of the human mind. Inspired by the remarkable success of Galilean (and later Newtonian) mechanics, philosophers attempted, from the philosopher's armchair as it were, to discover the underlying principles that govern human thought processes. A group of thinkers known as the Empiricists (whose ranks included such figures as Hobbes, Berkeley, and Hume) proposed that all of our ideas and thoughts about the world originate in experience and that our predictions about what will happen in the world under certain circumstances are the result of expectations borne of those experiences. For instance, my expectation that dropping an egg will cause it to break could, according to this view, be explained by my tendency to associate falling eggs with broken eggs – an association that has to be strengthened by repeated experience.

Another group of thinkers, the Rationalists, was unimpressed by this minimalist psychology. They would emphasize the importance, and novelty, of the human capacity to reason. This power, they thought, could not be accounted for by the associationism of the Empiricists. Indeed, the claim that the capacity for reasoning is what separates humans from beasts is a view that has, at least since the dawn of philosophy, enjoyed fairly widespread support. So, while the Empiricists were for the most part content to view human intellectual capacities as differing from those of animals in degree only, Rationalists supposed a more qualitative distinction.

For his part, G.W. Leibniz (1646–1716) believed that he had discovered a clear-cut qualitative distinction between animal and human psychology. He noted that animals may come to expect that certain actions will be accompanied by certain consequences, yet they seem incapable of grasping when exceptions to a given rule might occur. Expressing his opposition to the Empiricists' associationist psychology, Leibniz explains:

> It is, indeed true that reason ordinarily counsels us to expect that we will find in the future
> that which conforms to our long experience of the past; but this . . . can fail us when we
> least expect it, when the reasons which have maintained it change. This is why the wisest
> people do not rely on it to such an extent that they do not try to probe into the reason for

> what happens (if that is possible), so as to judge when exceptions must be made. . . . This often provides a way of foreseeing an occurrence without having to experience the sensible links between images, which the beasts are reduced to doing .
>
> (Leibniz 1996 [1705], p. 586)

As we will discuss in Chapter 4, the realization that we humans are easily able to recognize exceptions to rules has posed a difficult problem for those interested in creating rule-based computational models of human reasoning.

Another interesting fact about the human mind to which the Rationalists frequently drew attention was our capacity to apprehend certain necessary truths. How, they wondered, could an associationist psychology account for the human capacity to apprehend the seemingly eternal and immutable principles of mathematics? Rationalists accordingly took issue with the claim that all ideas are derived from experience. Instead, they maintained, some ideas must be innate – though they disagreed over the true extent of this nativism. As we shall see, the debate over whether or not human being and beast are, in terms of their cognitive capacities, qualitatively distinct and the debate over whether or not humans have any inborn cognitive gifts often go hand-in-hand. What's more, they have, in various guises, been revisited several times over the past hundred or so years.

Aside from attempting to describe what, psychologically speaking, underwrites the human capacity to reason, philosophers have also long been interested in understanding the norms of reasoning that one ought to obey. This line of inquiry was launched by Aristotle and has been directed, ever since, toward the end of specifying the principles that underlie good inferences, the bare form of cogent reasoning. To get a sense for how this form is revealed, notice how the connection between the two premises and conclusion of the inference below has the following peculiar feature: if the premises are true, then the conclusion must be true.

(1) Lulu is a cow.
(2) All cows chew cud.
(3) Therefore, Lulu chews cud.

The presence of this feature, known as validity, has, or seems to have, nothing to do with the particular items under consideration (i.e., it has nothing to do with cows or cud). Rather, the reason the inference has this peculiar feature, the reason why the conclusion must be true if the premises are, is that the inference has a particular logical form to it. Notice that the same connection holds between the premises and conclusion of the following inference:

(1) The moon is made of green cheese.
(2) All green cheese comes from Wisconsin.
(3) Therefore, the moon comes from Wisconsin.

The two inferences have the same underlying form, and it is this form that explains their validity (see also section 4.3 in Chapter 4). Philosophers have devised ways of representing the principles underlying valid inferences – that is, they have devised math-like notations (or formalisms). As we shall see, this project, which made great headway during the late nineteenth and early twentieth centuries, culminated in the creation of mechanical devices capable of manipulating these logical formalisms – that is, it gave rise to mechanical reasoning devices. This, in turn, precipitated the current revolution in information-based technologies, and it gave scientists new ideas and new tools for making sense of the mind.

While philosophical interest in human cognition is as old as philosophy itself, the scientific study of human cognition is comparatively new. Before we can gain a better understanding of the diverse experimental techniques currently being employed by those engaged in the study of the human mind (discussed extensively in the next chapter), it will help to understand some of the historical factors that conspired to give rise to this remarkable interdisciplinary endeavor.

1.2.2 Neuroanatomy and neurophysiology

The origins of neuroanatomy (i.e., the study of the structure of the nervous system) can be traced to the writings of Aristotle (circa 350 BC) and to Galen (circa AD 150). Galen's thoughts, in particular, were widely viewed as gospel until Galileo and his contemporaries got the engine of discovery up and running again in the seventeenth century. Galen believed the brain to be responsible for sensation and movement and that the brain's interaction with the body's periphery was hydraulic in nature. Nerves were viewed by Galen as a kind of conduit for carrying liquid to and from the ventricles (i.e., liquid-filled cavities) of the brain.

One major breakthrough for neuroanatomy was the invention of the microscope in the seventeenth century. On the heels of this invention came the realization that plants are made of cells – though there would be no conclusive evidence that all living things are made of cells until the mid-nineteenth century. Thereafter, the minute details of the nervous system were progressively revealed. Camillo Golgi, in particular, can be credited with uncovering many details of neural interconnections following his invention of a new staining technique. This method, involving the impregnation of nervous tissue with silver, enabled the visualization of the complete structure of neurons (the cells that comprise the brain and the rest of the nervous system). Somewhat ironically, because the nervous tissue he studied comprised an intricate network, Golgi disagreed with the contention that the nervous system is composed of distinct cells. Instead, he believed the nervous system comprised a single continuous network. Ramon y Cajal, a contemporary of Golgi, found a way to use Golgi's technique to stain single neurons. Thus he was able to refute Golgi's theory with Golgi's own invention.

In the early twentieth century, the study of neural cell types and neural density/distribution by Korbinian Brodmann revealed that the brain is divided into fifty-two distinct areas. Brodmann's classification of structurally distinct brain regions is still widely used nowadays (Figure 1.1).

He further theorized that areas of the brain that looked structurally different from surrounding areas were also functionally different. Thus, the detailed study of the anatomy of the nervous system began to merge with the study of the living functions of nervous tissue. That is, neuroanatomy and neurophysiology became complementary disciplines. It is worth taking a step back, however, in order to examine the origins of neurophysiology in its own right.

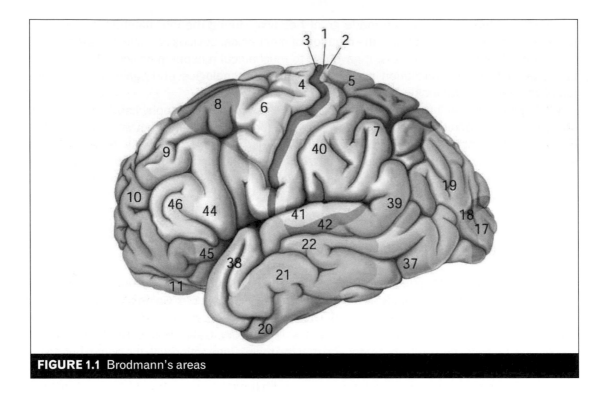

FIGURE 1.1 Brodmann's areas

One of the first major steps in neurophysiology (i.e., the study of the functioning of neurons and neural ensembles) took place in 1780. That was the year when Luigi Galvani (1737–1798) discovered that muscle cells produce electricity. By the middle of the nineteenth century, it was realized that neural activity is also electrical in nature and that neurons transmit electrical impulses that propagate from neuron to neuron. During this period, Hermann von Helmholtz (1821–1894) managed to clock the speed at which these impulses travel. He found that the rate of conduction was, despite the electrical nature of the process, actually quite slow. Indeed, it was found that the rate of conduction was not only slower than light (the suspected speed) but also slower than sound. In the early twentieth century, it would also be revealed that the electrical activity of neurons is largely an all-or-none process (i.e., there is a sharp divide between their active, or firing, state and their quiescent state) and that the firing of neurons involves the movement of ions (atoms that are positively or negatively charged as a result of having too few or too many electrons) across the cell membrane.

One of the first to try localizing cognitive functions to specific brain regions was Franz Josef Gall (1757–1828). Gall was an able anatomist and is widely credited with some fundamental insights about the structure of the nervous system. He is best known, and often ridiculed, for his now-defunct theory of phrenology. Gall noticed that people with bulging eyes tended to have good memories and speculated that other cognitive faculties might also give rise to visible external characteristics. Accordingly, he developed an entire system of reading skulls along with a phrenological map (Figure 1.2) divided into distinct regions – each of which was the

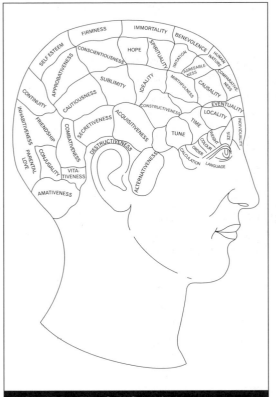

FIGURE 1.2 The Gall/Spurzheim map

supposed seat of a particular mental function. Gall theorized that enlarged areas meant greater abilities, and he would "read" the bumps on people's heads for clues to their mental abilities. Phrenology was soon adopted as a standard medical practice. Europeans were particularly enthralled by the new science of skull reading. It would not take long for Gall's theory to be tested experimentally. In 1824, on the basis of experiments involving the selective destruction of pigeon brains, Pierre Flourens proclaimed that cognitive functions could not be localized as Gall had speculated. Even after Gall's phrenology fell out of favor with the scientific community (it turns out, for the wrong reasons), phrenology retained its popularity. Skull reading salons persisted in Europe throughout the nineteenth century, and in the United States the phrenological analysis of criminals was considered admissible courtroom evidence.

Flourens' theory that cognitive functions are not localizable held sway until the early 1860s when Paul Broca discovered that the destruction of a particular part of the human brain (in the front of the left hemisphere) resulted in speech abnormalities. In particular, patients with lesions to this area typically speak very little, and when they do it is only with great effort – moreover, the speech they produce is often marred by grammatical errors. In 1874, in another classic localization study, Carl Wernicke discovered that a different kind of linguistic disorder resulted from the destruction of a more posterior part of the left hemisphere of the brain. In such cases, patients produced grammatical sentences quite readily, but their speech was remarkably devoid of content. Such individuals also had great difficulty with the comprehension of speech.

Thus, the stage was set for Brodmann's map of the structurally distinct areas of the brain. Though the debate over the possible localization of cognitive functions persisted into the twentieth century, the fundamental insight that physical differentiation parallels functional differentiation had been revived as a plausible hypothesis. Brodmann's map began to be used, and is still used nowadays, in order to correlate neural structures with cognitive functions.

Thus neuranatomy merged with neurophysiology. It had been revealed not only that the study of brains could shed light on the low-level functioning of neurons (e.g., the nature of the electrical activity that takes place within and between neurons) but also that it could provide insight into higher-level, cognitive processes. This merger gave rise to a new discipline, one christened by the publication of Wernicke's (1969 [1874]) study on speech disorders. The subtitle of Wernicke's paper read: "A psychological study on an anatomical basis" (Geschwind 1965). With Wernicke's paper the discipline of neuropsychology was born.

As we shall see in the next chapter, various forms of microscopy and staining remain the preferred method of data gathering for many neuroanatomists. Likewise, the study of the electrical properties of neurons continues to be a mainstay of much research in neurophysiology, and the correlation of brain function with structure through the study of impaired patients is still a very important source of evidence in neuropsychology. We shall also see that each of these fields has advanced greatly in the precision and number of different techniques utilized and that there has been a corresponding proliferation of important findings relating neural structure to cognitive function. In addition, emphases have shifted. For instance, neuroanatomists have been utilizing more advanced staining techniques in order to trace neural connectivity. They have also begun to capitalize on developments in genetics in order to determine with greater precision the structure of neurons. Neurophysiologists have, for their part, begun to recognize that tremendous importance is to be attached to the variety of chemicals on the basis of which neurons propagate signals between one another, and methods have been developed for studying, with tremendous precision, the levels of electrical activity over the course of a particular neural firing. Neuropsychologists have, for their part, begun to rely upon both sophisticated brain-imaging techniques and the experimental methods developed by psychologists. Let us turn now to psychology and see how this, one of the true cornerstones of inquiry into the nature of cognition, developed as an experimental discipline.

1.2.3 The origins of experimental psychology

The intellectual climate of nineteenth-century Germany was ripe for the development of experimental psychology for a couple of reasons. The first of these was the enduring influence of a gargantuan figure in philosophy, an eighteenth-century German philosopher named Immanuel Kant (1724–1804). As noted earlier, the Rationalists and Empiricists had differing views about the nature of the human mind. A theme that dominated among Empiricists in particular was the view that the reach of the human intellect (i.e., the determination of the kinds of things humans could ever lay claim to knowing) could be determined by analyzing the nature of the very instrument by which knowledge is attained, the human mind. According to the Empiricists, an analysis of mental faculties (which, recall, they believed to be associationist in nature) reveals that the extent of possible knowledge was highly circumscribed. Kant, for one, was not satisfied with either the minimalist psychology of the Empiricists or their conclusions regarding the kinds of things we can and cannot know. In particular, he felt that associationist psychology could not do justice to the human capacity for apprehending necessary truths. Nor, however, was he enamoured of the far-flung metaphysical speculations of the Rationalists. He therefore set out to provide a more accurate portrayal of the human mind, one that agreed both with the Empiricist proposal that experience plays a prominent role in our cognitive lives and with the Rationalist contention that human reasoning involves something more than associations between ideas. Details aside, his psychology was arguably the most intricate model of cognitive functioning yet proposed. Kant had a particularly strong influence on the German-speaking world – though it is worth pointing out that Kant was highly skeptical of the possibility that psychology could be a science.

The other factor that made the intellectual climate of nineteenth-century Germany conducive to the development of an experimental psychology was the state of the university system in Germany (Hearnshaw 1987). Early in that century, German universities began to look very much like the universities of today, which are not only of places of learning but the locus of much empirical research as well. Moreover, the German universities emphasized the importance of academic freedom. Faculty members were free to teach and conduct their research in whatever manner they desired. Elsewhere, the prospect of scientifically studying the mind provoked harsh reactions from theologians, who remained a powerful force in university administrations. Indeed, not only did German faculty members have great freedom, but also their research was sometimes supported by generous grants.

The stage was therefore set for the emergence of a science of the mind. In order to become a full-fledged science, however, psychology would have to exhibit all of the hallmarks of a science. That is, it would need a way of gathering and quantifying data, a methodology for testing competing theories, a way of controlling some experimental conditions while manipulating others, as well as replicability of experimental results. Precisely when all of these conditions were first satisfied is difficult to discern, but there were some clear milestones along the way, as well as several wrong turns.

One of the first steps toward quantified measurements, the use of controlled/experimental variables, and replicability was taken by Ernst H. Weber in the first half of the nineteenth century. Weber developed the method of just-noticeable differences (jnds) for studying the degree to which human subjects are able to discriminate between different sensory inputs. For example, he studied the ability of blindfolded subjects to discriminate between two weights or the difference between pairs of pressure points on the skin. The results were quantified and formulated as a law indicating that, in the case of weight discrimination, perceived differences vary as a constant function of the actual weight. This marked the beginning of what is aptly known as psychophysics. This line of inquiry was refined by Gustav T. Fechner (who coined the term "psychophysics"). One of Fechner's fundamental insights was that statistical analyses of data were warranted given that the outcomes of individual trials varied in ways that could not be controlled. As noted in the next chapter, statistical analyses are the backbone of much contemporary psychological research.

As it turns out, one of the developments in neurophysiology actually paved the way for another major step forward for experimental psychology. As was mentioned above, Helmholtz discovered that the rate of nerve conduction was quite slow. This meant that different mental processes might take differing, and measurable, amounts of time and that the time of cognitive processing might be reflected by the times it takes an individual to react to particular stimuli. Still, a method would be needed for measuring very short time intervals before this insight could bear fruit. A solution was found in the form of new technology developed, for military applications, in order to measure the velocity of projectiles at the time of launch.

The first two researchers to take advantage of this technology were Franciscus C. Donders and Wilhelm Wundt – friend and student, respectively, of neurophysiologist Helmholtz. As a way of capitalizing on new time-measurement technology, Donders developed an experimental technique known as the subtraction method. The essence of the subtraction method is to subtract the time it takes to perform a simple task from the time it takes to perform a more complex task, where the former is a component of the latter. For instance, as a simple task, Donders measured the reaction times of subjects who were charged with reacting to the lighting of a bulb by depressing a telegraph-style lever. For a more complex task, subjects were asked to press the lever only when one particular light from a display of five lights is lit. The complex task is much like the simple task except for the addition of a discrimination process. Thus the time of discrimination can be determined by subtracting the time of the simple task from the time of the more complex task.

Wundt and his students would adopt a modified version of Donders' subtraction method in order to study phenomena such as the temporal onset of apperception (i.e., conscious awareness and recognition). Wundt's laboratory at the University of Leipzig is widely recognized as the world's first full-fledged experimental psychology lab. It is generally said to have been established in 1879, though it seems to have developed over time rather than all at once. Wundt was a creative genius when it came to devising experimental apparatuses. Wundt also contributed to the advent of experimental psychology by founding scholarly journals and societies and by instructing a great many students, no small number of whom were Americans. When universities in the United States had, late in the nineteenth century, begun to conform to the German system, and as students of Wundt and émigrés from Germany began to arrive in the United States, psychology faculties and psychology laboratories began to sprout up across the country.

In content, Wundt's psychological theories had some commonalities with the associationist proposals of the Empiricists – though instead of relations between ideas, Wundt posited an actual synthesis of ideas. The structure of such mental processes could be revealed in part, Wundt thought, by careful introspection under controlled conditions. Indeed, introspection was an important component of much early psychological research. It was an essential component of psychophysics, and it also figured in reaction time-experiments concerning apperception conducted by Wundt and his students.

There were some, however, such as Carl Stumpf, who viewed Wundt's psychological theories as overly atomistic. Stumpf, a student of Brentano, was the father figure of what became a burgeoning early-twentieth-century movement known as Gestalt psychology. The Gestalt school took some inspiration from Kant's proposal that the mind does not passively receive sensory stimuli, but instead imparts order to the incoming sensory impressions. Gestalt psychology flourished until the rise of Nazism caused the dispersal of its most esteemed proponents. While this led, for a time at least, to the decline of the Gestalt movement, its central insights are still taken quite seriously by psychologists and neuroscientists alike.

Another important late-nineteenth-century development was the experimental study of memory and learning by Hermann Ebbinghaus, who devised a truly ingenious set of experiments using himself as a subject. He created a huge list of nonsense syllables (of the form consonant-vowel-consonant like "gek") which controlled for the effects of semantic content on learning and memory. As a measure of the level of retention, he would record the number of times the material had to be reviewed in order to have perfect memory of a given list (i.e., as indicated by his ability to perform one perfect repetition). Using these methods, over the course of about two years of painstaking research and replication, he discovered many important facts about learning and memory. For instance, he was able to conclude that the relationship between list length and learning was non-linear – the number of repetitions required to learn a list increased dramatically as the list increased in length. He also found that it would take fewer repetitions to learn a list if those repetitions were spread out over time, that memory was better for items near the beginning and end of a list, and that learning was greatly facilitated by the use of contentful material.

Philosopher and psychologist William James was one of the few non-Germans of the late nineteenth century to have a lasting impact on psychology. Though James did little to advance the techniques of psychological investigation, he did help to delineate important areas of inquiry that are constitutive of contemporary cognitive psychology. He was well versed in all of the latest developments in psychological research, including those discussed above, and he has even been credited with setting up the first psychology lab – though his was, unlike Wundt's, directed toward demonstration rather than research. In his landmark text, *The Principles of Psychology* (1890), James combined his own deep insights about the nature of mentality and the knowledge he had gained over the course of his visits to the leading German universities. Twelve years in the making, James' text continues to enlighten and inspire psychologists. Though he couldn't have foreseen where it would lead, James' emphasis on the study of behavior would sow the seeds for a radical shift in the nature of psychological investigation.

This shift began in Russia with the experiments conducted by physiologist Ivan P. Pavlov. The finding for which Pavlov is most famous concerns the amount of saliva secreted by dogs under various conditions (Yerkes and Morgulis 1909). As a normal reaction (the unconditioned response) to the taste of food (the unconditioned stimulus), dogs are known to increase their rate of salivation. This can be measured by attaching a tube to the salivary duct in the animal's mouth. What Pavlov found was that an increase in level of salivation can be elicited even when food is not present. If one repeatedly pairs the presentation of the food and a seemingly irrelevant sensory stimulus (the conditioned stimulus) such as a whistle, one can subsequently elicit the salivary response (which has thus become a conditioned response) merely by presenting the conditioned stimulus. The effect of the conditioned stimulus can be determined by measuring the amount of saliva secreted. Pavlov and his colleagues made other important discoveries about conditioning. They found, for instance, that the effect of the conditioned stimulus steadily diminishes when it is no longer paired with food.

The data from such experiments were neatly quantified and the results were easily replicated. Moreover, unlike psychophysics and the other popular research methodologies, the behaviorist methodology did not treat introspection as a datum. Data were reduced to observable stimuli and responses. Because objectivity is one of the hallmarks of scientific respectability, methodologies that relied upon introspection began to be viewed as departing substantially from this ideal. It is not surprising, then, that the behaviorists' careful quantitative analysis of observable stimuli and responses would begin to take hold in psychology. Also not surprising is the resemblance that behaviorist theory would bear to the Empiricists' associationistic psychology. Both emphasized habits and associations, and both downplayed the distinction between humans and beasts as reflecting a quantitative rather than a qualitative difference. In a classic exposition of the tenets of behaviorism, John B. Watson (1913) notes:

> Psychology as the behaviorist sees it is a purely objective experimental branch of natural science. Its theoretical goal is the prediction and control of behavior. Introspection forms

no essential part of its methods, nor is the scientific value of its data dependent upon the readiness with which they lend themselves to interpretation in terms of consciousness. The behaviorist, in his efforts to get a unitary scheme of animal response, recognizes no dividing line between man and brute.

The work of Pavlov and the polemic of Watson spurred a new generation of researchers to concentrate on the relationships between stimuli and responses.

Researchers in the behaviorist tradition varied with regard to how willing they were to, on the one hand, explain behavior solely in terms of relations between stimulus and response, and on the other hand, allow themselves to postulate the existence of cognitive intermediaries between stimulus and response such as goals, plans, and other representations. An example of research of this later kind is that of Edward C. Tolman, who used facts about stimuli and responses to support inferences about animal cognition, the inner workings of the animal psyche. He readily spoke of internal states such as goals and behavior-guiding structures such as cognitive maps. He even proposed that the new behaviorist paradigm would enable researchers to salvage many of the accurate, though methodologically suspect, proposals emanating from introspectionist psychology (Tolman 1922). For instance, inspired by anecdotes concerning the ability of escaped rats to locate food, Tolman (1948) examined the manner in which rats sought out food. In one experiment, he trained rats to run down a pathway which led, in a very indirect fashion, to an enclosure containing food (Figure 1.3).

He then presented rats with the setup depicted in Figure 1.4. Notice that, in addition to the path leading straight from the circular chamber (path 1), there are many other paths leaving the chamber at various angles. Notice also that path 6 leads in the direction of where the food had been located in the original maze. Tolman found that when path 1 was blocked, rats had a very strong tendency to choose path 6 over the other paths. Thus, concluded Tolman, rats were able to find the food chamber not only by following a programmatic series of turns, but also by consulting an internal representation of the relative location of the food (i.e., what he called a cognitive map).

The other kind of attitude toward behaviorism was exemplified by B.F.

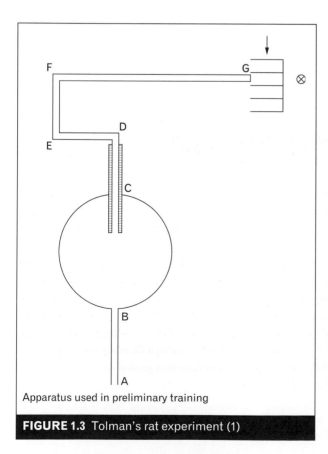

Apparatus used in preliminary training

FIGURE 1.3 Tolman's rat experiment (1)

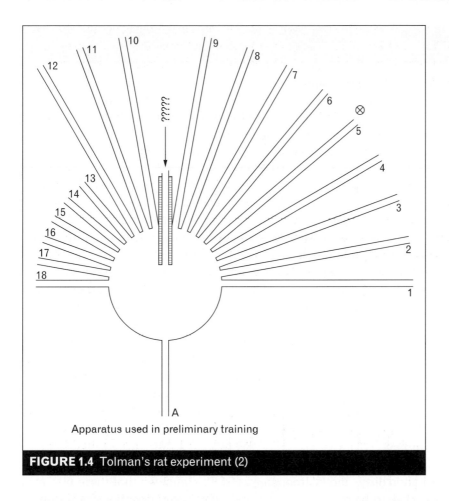

FIGURE 1.4 Tolman's rat experiment (2)

Skinner, who decried psychological theories that made reference to mental states. Skinner's great success can be attributed in part to his ability to gain control over animal behavior. While Pavlov's methods enabled him to elicit automatic responses such as salivation from various stimuli, Skinner's methods enabled him to elicit virtually any kind of behavior of which an animal was physically capable. He found that when something resembling a desired behavior was spontaneously elicited by an animal, this behavior could be reinforced with rewards such as food. In small increments, an animal's behavior could be molded to take on almost any desirable form. Unlike Tolman, who sought to salvage much of what had come before, Skinner advocated a fresh start for psychology. Like other behaviorists, Skinner severely downplayed the differences between humans and non-humans. During the middle of the twentieth century, American psychology would be dominated by behaviorism (see box on Philosophical behaviourism).

PHILOSOPHICAL BEHAVIORISM

Philosophers developed their own version of behaviorism, called logical, analytical, or philosophical behaviorism. Logical behaviorism grew primarily out of the philosophy of language, when the philosophers Wittgenstein and Ryle analyzed "mental" concepts such as thought, knowledge, memory, seeing, and understanding. They contended that the proper way to analyze these concepts was to look and see how we applied them in ordinary life. Since I cannot see inside your mind, I can only discern whether or not you are seeing, remembering, or understanding by your actions. Each of these mental concepts has certain actions or behavioral criteria which we employ in our use of mental concepts. For instance, with regard to the concept understanding, Wittgenstein notes, "Let us remember that there are certain criteria in a man's behavior for the fact that he does not understand a word" (Wittgenstein 1958).

Someone might object, however, that when I apply psychological terms to myself (e.g., I am in pain) I am clearly not going by my behavior. Wittgenstein's response to this was to argue that when I assert that I am in pain, I am not introspecting my state of mind, then applying a linguistic description to it, and finally saying this description out loud for others. Rather, we simply give voice to our inner states with the same immediacy and naturalness that children do when they cry out in pain. Whatever happens, it is not a process of picking out an inner entity and applying a linguistic term to it. Thus, he notes, "Words are connected with the primitive, the natural, expression of the sensation and used in their place. A child has hurt himself and he cries; and then adults talk to him and teach him exclamations and, later, sentences. They teach the child new pain behavior" (Wittgenstein 1958).

Behavioral analysis of mental concepts was something philosophers could still do without getting their hands dirty, and Wittgenstein and Ryle showed that there was a huge amount of close work to be done simply tracing all of the connections between concepts such as "believe," "think," and "see," and in sorting out exactly which situations the word was used appropriately in. It was also encouraging to philosophers that this project could be completed, as opposed to the goals psychology had set for itself, which seemed absurdly unreachable, at least to the unimaginative or the timid.

Psychology would finally come to resemble its current state in the second half of the twentieth century. The watershed event in this transition would be the devastating critique of the behaviorist program delivered by linguist Noam Chomsky (1964 [1959]).

1.2.4 The revolution in linguistics

In the 1950s, Noam Chomsky transformed the study of language by showing that the latest models of language processing could not account for the complexities of language comprehension and production. At the time of Chomsky's groundbreaking work, linguistics was dominated by structuralism, which had originated with the pioneering work of Swiss linguist Ferdinand de Saussure (1857–1913). Saussure had transformed the study of language by shifting the focus of linguistics to the analysis of existing languages and away from the study of the historical development of particular languages. Saussure's great contribution as a structural linguist was to further analyze the elements of language into *morphemes* and *phonemes*. Morphemes are the smallest units of meaning, sometimes corresponding to a single complete word, such as "dog," or a single letter, such as *s* when it is added to "dog" to make the plural "dogs." Phonemes, on the other hand, are the fundamental units of sound in natural language; "dog" contains three phonemes, *d* [duh], *o* [oh], and *g* [gh]. There is a certain degree of variation in any phoneme that does not change its identity or the identity of the word that it helps constitute. Subseqently, computational models of speech recognition required all phonemes to be first identified and then grouped into their appropriate morphemes, which in turn constitute words, phrases, and sentences. The underlying idea is that phonemes differ among the various languages, and that there are a small and limited number of phonemes in any language. Phonology is the study of the rules and principles for analyzing auditory stimuli into their constitutive sequences of phonemes.

For nearly two decades, in the 1940s and 1950s, the field was dominated by American linguist Leonard Bloomfield (1887–1949) and his disciples, who adapted these techniques for studying language to a behaviorist paradigm. They rejected the notion of cognitive processing internal to the brain or mind in lieu of discovery procedures that would provide an objective sequence of operations sufficient for establishing all the phonological and morphological elements of any given natural language. Working within the behaviorist agenda, they made startling leaps in the mechanization of these procedures, spawning a slew of machine translation projects in the early 1950s; hampered by the limitations of early computers, they joined forces with the growing influence of information theory, which used mathematical statistics to analyze speech and language. This structural approach to studying language, however, began to go in a different direction under the leadership of Zellig Harris, who not only had advanced discovery procedures and methods of phonology and morphology, but also began the quest for a full syntactic analysis of linguistic structures. Using transformations to normalize complex sentences by relating them to their simpler kernel sentences, he inspired a new generation of students, the most notable of whom was Noam Chomsky.

One of Chomsky's main innovations was to regard grammar itself as a generative system of rules for the construction of the entire infinite set of the grammatical (i.e., well-formed) sentences of a particular language. His fundamental question was to ask what sort of automaton, that is, what sort of computational system, would be needed in order to generate the sentences of a natural language such as English. He made explicit, detailed and devastating arguments to the effect that the current systems under consideration were grossly inadequate.

Chomsky proposed his own model that could explain the full range of grammatical sentences. His basic idea was that natural language sentences are generated through rule-governed transformations over inner sentence-like structures. That is, according to this model, all natural languages share the same deep structure – thus, our capacity to use language is, at the level of deep structure, innate. As Chomsky puts it:

> The child must acquire a generative grammar of his language on the basis of a fairly restricted amount of evidence. To account for this achievement, we must postulate a sufficiently rich internal structure – a sufficiently restricted theory of universal grammar that constitutes his contribution to language acquisition.
>
> (Chomsky 1972, pp. 158–159)

As noted above, Chomsky's views signaled the beginning of the end for behaviorism. Another important development in the history of the mind sciences was the use of computers to model and simulate human cognition.

Chomsky was mainly concerned with explaining linguistic behavior. But his proposals had important ramifications for psychology as well. Among Chomsky's concerns was the fact that human verbal behavior is not an inflexible consequence of environmental stimuli. In the presence of a given object, such as a painting, one and the same individual might exhibit any of a variety of verbal behaviors. In other words, there is something apart from the stimulus itself that determines the behavior that will be exhibited. Thus we have Chomsky's famous poverty of the stimulus argument. Since the stimulus is impoverished, there is, in short, something internal that is of great importance. Yet this is precisely what behaviorists wished to deny. Chomsky's persuasive critique forever altered the course of experimental psychology.

Another factor that contributed to the demise of behaviorism (and thus the emergence of a psychology that was more internalistic in its leanings) was the advent of the programmable computer. This not only created a new metaphor on the basis of which to explain the inner workings of the mind, but also supplied new tools and inspired some to undertake the project of creating an artificial form of intelligence.

1.2.5 The origins of artificial intelligence

In 1956, Allen Newell and Herbert Simon presented a startling and groundbreaking paper, "The logic theory machine: A complex information processing system." In it, they describe a device that was able to prove one of the theorems from Whitehead and Russell's (1910–1913) *Principia Mathematica*. It was nothing less than the first fully functioning artificial intelligence program. A year later, their General Problem Solver was able to solve a number of other problems in logic, mathematics, and chess. They created the program by identifying the techniques humans use in problem solving, obtained through introspective reports (called protocols) delivered by subjects as they worked on problem-solving tasks.

Within a few years, George Miller, Eugene Galanter, and Karl Pribram developed a theory of a basic cognitive mechanism based on the concept of feedback loops, which they called TOTE units (TOTE stands for Test-Operate-Test-Exit). As Galanter puts it,

> The aim, we all agreed, was to replace behaviorism (really our name for associationism) and trivial experimentation (the T-Maze and Skinner box) with the new insights and maybe even the new technology from computational logic, linguistics, and neurophysiology.
>
> (Galanter 1988, p. 38)

One of their goals was to realize Chomsky's grammatical principles and transformations using TOTES (Figure 1.5). The idea was that, within the brain, an initial test evaluates a given current state against a given goal. If they do not match, instructions are given to carry out an operation to reduce the differences until a match occurs through a series of repeating tests.

Throughout the 1960s and 1970s, there was a sudden proliferation of work in artificial intelligence. Because chess was seen as a game requiring intelligence and reasoning, many of these efforts were directed toward the construction of chess-playing computers. There were efforts directed toward modeling many other aspects of human reasoning as well.

One important strand of research involved the attempt to automate the kind of knowledge-based inference done by experts in particular fields. This was carried out through the use of some of the same general reasoning principles characterizing the General Problem Solver. The end result was the creation of systems, called expert systems, able to mimic (and in some cases even exceed) the performance of human experts. For instance, DENDRAL analyzed data from mass spectrographs to find the underlying molecular structures of organic compounds; MYCIN diagnosed infectious blood diseases; ANALOGY could solve visual geometric analogy problems; STUDENT could solve algebra story problems by translating ordinary English into manipulable equations.

It was also hoped that these artificial reasoning devices might supply the brains for robots. STRIPS, for instance, was the computational system used to guide one of the first robots, a wheeled contraption known as Shakey. Shakey used television cameras as input devices and could interact with a variety of objects. Other kinds of real and virtual interactions were modeled

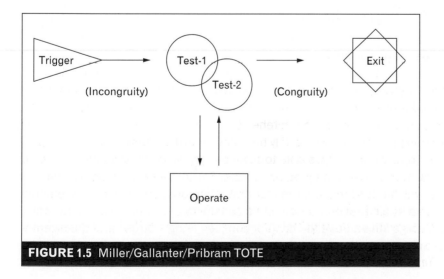

FIGURE 1.5 Miller/Gallanter/Pribram TOTE

as well. SHRDLU manipulated blocks in a virtual world displayed on a computer screen and could process sentences in order to answer questions about the blocks and carry out instructions. Developed by computer scientist Terry Winograd in 1972, SHRDLU did not use the earlier theorem-proving methods to achieve its goals but operated using a number of subprograms. Each subprogram could set up and achieve its own goal independently of the others, and control could shift from one subprogram to another. Soon, however, attempts to model intelligent interaction with environments ran up against a problem. The frame problem, as it was called, had to do with the difficulty of keeping track, with the aid of computational representations of the world, of the manner in which the world changes over the course of various alterations (see Chapter 4).

Another branch of research centered on the manner in which we humans are able to fill in information that is only implicit in a passage of text. For instance, if you are told that Bob has filled his car with gas, you can infer that he paid for the gas, that he parked the car, that he (unless he lives in Oregon or New Jersey) opened the gas cap himself, and so on. According to Roger Schank and Robert Abelson (1977), a knowledge structure in your head, called a script, contains information about certain kinds of events (e.g., filling your tank, going to the market, taking a course, and so on). It is this script that lets you make inferences such as the ones just described. Schank and Abelson were able to model these knowledge structures and the inferences they license with the help of SAM (Script Applier Mechanism).

1.2.6 The advent of connectionism

At the same time that research in artificial intelligence was taking root, some computer scientists and neurophysiologists were developing an alternate strategy for modeling cognitive phenomena. These researchers hoped to capitalize on the processing power that arises out of the inter-connections of many simple neuron-like structures. In 1943, neurophysiologist Warren McCulloch and a young logician named Walter Pitts demonstrated that such neuron-like structures (or units, as they were called) could be made to respect certain logical principles. They began by noting some of the basic findings regarding the functioning of neurons. They noted, for instance, that the activity of neurons has (as described above) an all-or-none character to it (i.e., neurons are either firing or they are quiescent) and that a certain amount of excitation from other neurons has to occur in order for a given neuron to reach its active state (i.e., a threshold must be exceeded). They also noted that some neurons are connected to others in an inhibitory fashion (i.e., the firing of one neuron can prevent the firing of another).

McCulloch and Pitts envisioned how networks of processing units that obeyed these principles might behave. They noted that, when configured in particular ways, networks of such units would behave in a manner that respected certain logical norms. For instance, one could imagine a network of three units which would respect the fact that a conjunction (i.e., two statements connected by "and") will be true if and only if both of its conjuncts are true. In such a network, one unit would represent the truth value of the conjunction (i.e., firing = "true" and quiescent = "false") and the other two units would represent the truth value of each conjunct. If each conjunct unit has an excitatory connection to the conjunction unit, and if only simultaneous excitation from both conjunct units will suffice to make the conjunction unit fire; the conjunct unit will fire only if each conjunct unit is firing. Other logical operations such as disjunction (i.e., two statements connected by "or") and negation can also be modeled through different configurations of units with the appropriate excitatory and inhibitory connections. McCulloch and Pitts showed, moreover, that if a properly configured network of units were to be supplied with memory (e.g., a tape containing a string of ones and zeros) and a means of altering the contents of memory, such a network would have the same computing power as a universal Turing machine (see box on Turing machines in section 1.3.2).

While such findings naturally led to a strengthening of the brain-as-computer metaphor, some researchers, McCulloch and Pitts among them, soon realized that the real potential of neural networks could best be tapped by using them in ways that had very little in common with the logic-machine tradition. Researchers began experimenting with different ways in which a unit might be made to respond to excitation and inhibition, and it would be recognized that the burden of encoding a piece of information (e.g., the truth of a conjunct) need not be borne by a single neuron. Instead, a piece of information could be encoded across a large number of units. This approach to encoding information enabled networks (unlike logic machines) to deal sensibly with a certain amount of noise and vagary. Moreover, the underlying redundancy of this scheme enabled networks (again, unlike logic machines) to maintain their efficacy even in the face of significant damage or imperfection.

Another major development occurred for connectionism on the heels of neurophysiologist Donald Hebb's proposal concerning the manner in which neural interconnections might be modified. Hebb proposed that the connection between two neurons might be strengthened (i.e., made more excitatory) when both neurons are simultaneously active. With the addition of this simple principle to the repertoire of modeling techniques, neural network models could be made to modify the strength of their connections on the basis of the kind of input they were receiving – in short, they could learn. The behavior of neural networks began to be modeled through the use of digital computers (which were, at the time, themselves a very new development).

Researchers also began to tinker with the manner in which neural interconnections are modified over the course of processing (i.e., the learning function). For instance, some added to the basic Hebbian learning rule a complementary rule which would weaken a connection between two neurons when one is firing and the other is not. Moreover, schemes were developed that would enable a modeler to train layered networks – that is, networks constructed with an input layer (e.g., to encode perceptual information) and an output layer (e.g., to encode motor commands). For example, imagine constructing a perceptuo-motor network with the goal of teaching it to exhibit one motor response (output unit 1) in the presence of flies (input unit 1) or grasshoppers (input unit 2) and a second motor response (output unit 2) in the presence of boots (input unit 3) and lawnmowers (input unit 4). Means were developed for configuring networks such that, in the presence of a particular input, the difference between the actual output and the desired output would determine the manner in which connection strengths (or "weights") were modified based on their contribution to the departure from the proper output values. For instance, if input unit 1 is activated and causes high levels of activation in output unit 2, the connection between them would be weakened a bit. If the same input failed to result in activation to output unit 1, the connection between those two units would be strengthened. By subtly modifying connections over the course of repeated presentations of inputs, eventually the proper configuration of weights will be achieved.

Such processes could be entirely automated such that a modeler would have only to specify the proper responses to a given input (i.e., input/output pairs) and let the model do the rest. Frank Rosenblatt (1961) soon demonstrated that such a procedure would always, if given enough time, result in the proper set of weights for a given task – so long as such a set of weights was in fact a possibility. Rosenblatt called devices like the one just described "perceptrons." By coupling the development of new learning procedures with the other tools in the connectionists' toolbox, it seemed possible to construct networks that could model a tremendous range of phenomena related to learning, recognition, and memory.

The exuberance associated with connectionism was soon tempered, however, as some of the shortcomings of perceptrons, and connectionist models more generally, began to be realized. In their book *Perceptrons* (1969), Marvin Minsky and Seymour Papert showed that there were certain input/output pairs for which no set of weights would suffice. At that point in time, it probably appeared to many as though the age-old cycle would again repeat itself. Just as the associationism of the Empiricists was not up to the task of explaining humankind's capacity to apprehend eternal mathematical truths, and just as stimulus–response psychology of the behaviorists was incapable of meeting the challenges posed by those who felt that there was a qualitative difference between humans and beasts, so too it must have seemed as though this new brand of associationism would fall prey to the new Rationalists (i.e., to those enamored of logical formalisms). Research continued, however, and ways of meeting the challenge set by Minsky and Papert would be devised (see Chapter 2). With hindsight, it was inevitable that this new research program, connectionism, would survive. After all, scientists were by this point in agreement that the operations of the mind depend upon the activity of the brain, and the brain is, after all, a vast network of interconnected processing units.

1.2.7 Joining forces

Throughout the middle part of the twentieth century, psychology, artificial intelligence (AI), and linguistics would join forces in order to develop a new cognitive theory that would incorporate some of the key insights of each into an integrated perspective. The emphasis of interdisciplinary cognitive research had, accordingly, a strong formalistic bent to it. Psychologist George Miller suggests that, as early as the late 1950s, there had emerged

> a strong conviction, more intuitive than rational, that human experimental psychology, theoretical linguistics, and the computer simulation of cognitive processes were all pieces from a larger whole, and that the future would see a progressive elaboration and coordination of their shared concerns.
>
> (Miller 1979, p. 9, in Harman 1993)

By the 1960s, psychology had, as a result of this collaboration, been irrevocably transformed into a science of the inner workings of the mind/brain. The discipline had been reborn. Indeed, just as Wernicke helped, with the aid of a provocative title, to usher in the new discipline of neuropsychology, Ulric Neisser christened a reborn discipline with his book *Cognitive Psychology* (1967).

> By 1964, it had come together in my head. In principle, I thought, one could follow the information inward from its first encounter with the sense organ all the way to its storage and eventual reconstruction in memory. The early stages of processing were necessarily holistic (an idea I borrowed from Gestalt psychology) and the later ones were based on repeated recoding (an idea borrowed, even more obviously, from George Miller). But the processing sequence was by no means fixed; at every point there was room for choice, strategy, executive routines, individual constructive activity. Noam Chomsky's linguistic arguments had shown that an activity could be rule governed and yet indefinitely free and creative. People were not much like computers (I had already sketched out some of the differences in a 1963 *Science* paper), but nevertheless the computer had made a crucial contribution to psychology: It had given us a new definition of our subject matter, a new set of metaphors, and a new assurance.
>
> (Neisser 1988, p. 56)

The alliance between cognitive psychology, linguistics, and artificial intelligence continued for some time. With the re-emergence of connectionism in the 1980s, however, and with the co-option of tools from cognitive psychology in order both to better understand the behavior of impaired individuals and to localize cognitive functions in intact subjects, connectionism and neuroscience became very active collaborators in the interdisciplinary endeavor that we now know as cognitive science.

1.3 BRAINS VERSUS PROGRAMS

Despite the inherently interdisciplinary focus of cognitive science, it is natural that practitioners in a particular discipline would view their own methods and findings as the best suited, in the end, to the task of explaining cognitive phenomena. In particular, those who study the brain directly and those who make inferences about the nature of cognition on basis of behavior have sometimes locked horns over the issue of whether or not theirs will be the discipline that supplies the answers. To give a bit of a caricature, the primary allies of the former have been traditional AI researchers, while the latter have counted among their allies the upstart connectionists. In philosophy, this underlying tension has manifested as an overt battle of ideologies. Thus, in philosophy, each of the various positions one might adopt has undergone extensive analysis.

1.3.1 The primacy of neuroscience: reductionism and eliminativism

One reasonable possibility is that the findings of psychology (i.e., concerning phenomena such as memory, attention, reasoning, and so on) will ultimately be explained by what we learn about neurons and their interconnections. Such an eventuality would be analogous to the manner in which one makes sense of the phenomena studied by chemists (e.g., concerning the various ways in which materials may be synthesized or distilled) by consulting the discoveries made in physics about the building blocks of matter and their interactions. If this is how things pan out in cognitive science, then, though cognitive psychology may remain, for all practical purposes, indispensable, neuroscience will nevertheless be able to offer a compelling argument that it is the fundamental discipline in cognitive science. This view is called reductionism because, to speak somewhat metaphorically, the higher level phenomena studied by psychology will have been reduced to the lower level goings-on brought to light in neuroscience.

An even more dire possibility for psychology is that its highly mentalistic framework will prove, in the end, to be an altogether wrong-headed (pun intended) conception of human cognition. If this is the case, then the constructs of cognitive psychology will have been eliminated altogether. Looking again to the history of chemistry for an illustrative example of theory elimination, the theory of phlogiston is a clear case in point.

In the eighteenth and nineteenth centuries, the theory of phlogiston was put forward as an explanation of combustion. According to phlogiston theory, combustible matter was thought to contain a substance, phlogiston, which was released during combustion. One piece of evidence which appeared to support phlogiston theory was the fact that the weight of material after combustion was found to be less than its pre-combustion weight, even when the moisture and particles constituting the smoke were weighed. The theory of phlogiston was, however, far from accurate. Towards the end of the nineteenth century it was discovered that combustion results not from the release of phlogiston, but rather from the addition of oxygen (i.e., oxidization). In other words, as it turned out, there never was such a thing as phlogiston. This particular theoretical construct, in other words, had been entirely eliminated from scientific discourse.

Contemporary cognitive psychology is itself rife with theoretical constructs. Many of them, in fact, overlap with the constructs of early introspectionist psychology. Indeed, constructs such as attention, memory, reasoning, and so on, date back millennia – we find mention of them in the philosophy and literature of all ages. They are part of our common-sense conception of ourselves – what some term "folk psychology."

Some philosophers, most notably Paul Churchland (2006 [1985]), claim that, as our scientific understanding of the brain is refined, the theoretical constructs offered by folk psychology will go the way of phlogiston. This would, of course, be a dire prospect for cognitive psychology insofar as many of its theoretical constructs look an awful lot like the ones put forth by folk psychology. Eliminativists thus view neuroscience as the fundamental discipline of cognitive science.

1.3.2 The primacy of computer science: the brain as computer

Computer scientists also have reasons for thinking that theirs is the fundamental discipline of cognitive science. In particular, many computer scientists endorse a view known as computationalism. Computationalism is defined in terms of effective procedures. Effective procedures, in turn, are explained in terms of formal notations.

One thing that makes a language or notation formal is the fact that it represents form (e.g., logical form) by abstracting away from content. Another feature of formal notations is that they include atomic elements. For example, one might construct a simple logic notation in which sentences are represented by letters. So the sentences, "Jose gets more money" and "Jose asks to be traded" might be represented by the letters M and T, respectively. These letters, or constants, can be construed as atomic elements in our formal language.

Another important feature of formal notations is the fact that there are, usually, multiple ways in which atomic elements can be combined into more complex structures (or molecular formulas). For instance, sentences M and T might be combined with the logical operation OR (symbolized with a v) to form a sentence that reads $M v T$.

A final important feature of formal notations is that they contain rules for manipulating atomic and molecular structures. For instance, according to one logical rule (known as disjunctive syllogism) it is permissible to infer from $M v T$ and $\sim M$ (where "$\sim$" means "it is not the case that") that T is the case.

Prior to the groundbreaking work of Alan Turing (1912–1954; see box on Turing machines), effective procedures were defined as the sorts of formal symbol manipulations that might be carried out by a human using only a pencil and paper and without any reliance upon insight or ingenuity. For instance, one can become proficient in formal logic even if one lacks any conception of what the various symbols mean. So long as they can follow the rules for manipulating the symbols, they will be able to make valid inferences. For instance, even if you had no idea what either "$\sim$" or v stand for, you would be perfectly capable of learning to infer T from the premises $M v T$ and $\sim M$. One of Turing's big insights was that this rather informal way of defining "effective procedure" could be recast in terms of Turing machine computability. His proposal, which now enjoys near universal acceptance, is that something is an effective procedure if and only if it is computable by a mechanical device – he even described what such a device would be like (a device which is now known as a Turing machine). The principles governing the operation of Turing machines have since been realized in the form of modern programmable computers. Thus effective procedures are the sorts of things that can be implemented in terms of a computer program.

TURING MACHINES AND THE MIND

We have seen various fruitful ways in which certain aspects of the mind and brain can be modeled on a computer. Of course nearly anything can be computationally modeled. According to the computational theory of mind, however, the mind and brain are essentially computational in nature. But what, then, is a computer?

A computer is a formal symbol manipulator. Symbols are tokens that stand for, or represent, things, concepts, words, names, ideas, images, etc. – in short, a symbol is a sign that carries or stands for information about something. Thus I can use pebbles to represent numbers, people, cars, or really anything I please. The word "formal" in this

continued

context refers to the uninterpreted, purely syntactic elements of the system rather than what they mean in some interpretation scheme – that is, independent of the semantic or intentional aspects of the computation process. A computer works by manipulating the syntactic structures of a formal language, independently of their meaning. A computer rendering of, for instance, a tiger is achieved by purely syntactic processes (involving the specification of positions, color saturation, and so on) which is entirely unaware that what is being represented is a tiger. This process, in turn, is made possible through the application of logic to circuits, which allows the manipulations to occur in an orderly and systematic way, independently of meaning, truth or reference. Mechanical devices can behave in either a discrete or a continuous manner. The latter (e.g., a fuel gauge) operate by a continuous variation among an infinite number of states. Computers, on the other hand, are discrete automatic devices which work by a series of step-by-step variations between a finite number of states. In the simplest possible case, a device has only two states and operates according to a yes–no (closed–open or on–off) principle, and can therefore be used to represent propositions which likewise can assume only one of two values (namely, true or false). It is this similarity between two-state discrete action devices and propositions – that both can assume only one of two values (states) that allows us to create networks of such devices in order to carry out logical computations.

Discrete action contact networks can be realized through electrical contacts which take one of two states, closed or open. In the closed state the circuit is completed through a contact mechanism, thus allowing the current to pass through. In the open state, the contact mechanism is not engaged, so current cannot pass through. In this way one can represent the meanings of disjunction, conjunction, and negation using circuits (recall, this is very much like the strategy used to model the norms of logic with the help of neuron-like units). For instance, the diagram shows the disjunction, A ∨ B.

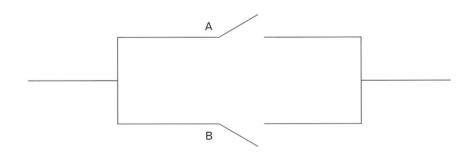

This is realized in a network of contacts, A and B, connected in parallel such that it is closed if and only if at least one of the contacts is closed. The conjunction A ∧ B (A and B) is represented by contacts A and B connected in series, such that it is closed if and only if both contacts are closed, as shown in the next diagram.

The negation, ~A, is represented by a contact that is closed when A is open and open when A is closed, as shown in the next diagram.

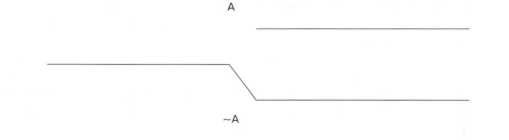

Because every function in the sentential calculus can be expressed using only disjunctions, conjunctions, and negations (using only the symbols ∧, ∨, and ~), one can assign to each sentential function a contact network of open and closed contacts using serial and parallel connections. These are called series–parallel networks, and they comprise the network realization of any given function. And given that sentences in English can be reduced, or translated, into logical symbols, this allows us to compute virtually all logical operations using automatic devices.

Consider, for instance, the three following inferences:

(1) If shape x is a square, then shape x is a parallelogram.
   Shape x is a square.
   Therefore, shape x is a parallelogram.
(2) If person x is a man, then person x is a human being.
   Person x is a man.
   Therefore, person x is a human being.

It is easy to see that in each case the step from the two premises to the conclusion has nothing to do with the meanings of the terms. The reasoning process in each case follows and is due to the shape, or form, of the sentences – a form that can be represented schematically as: "if A then B" and "A" therefore "B." This, in turn, can be expressed with the help of a formal notation as follows:

A → B
A
B

continued

These sentences can be translated into the symbols for negation and disjunction (since "p → q" is equivalent to "~p ∨ q"). Philosophers such as George Boole (1815–1864) and Gottlob Frege (1848–1925) transformed the study of logic into a true formal discipline, and this in turn set the stage for the pioneering work of Alan Turing, who developed a machine model of human reasoning that could carry out virtually any computation using symbols. This, in turn, led directly to the advent of the digital computers.

In his work, Turing described a mechanical system that we now know as a Turing machine. This hypothetical device had a controller that could read from, write to, and move backward or forward along an infinitely long tape. On this basis, it is able to carry out computations through a purely mechanical sequence of steps. Thus, the machine can engage in formal reasoning while being totally devoid of imagination, intuition, or creativity.

To understand how a Turing machine works, it is important to understand three related concepts, each of which, in turn, is related to the concept of an algorithm. These are computability, enumerability, and decidability. Turing machines work on computable (recursive) functions. A function, f(n), is computable if and only if there exists an algorithm such that for any value, n, there exists a uniquely associated function value, f(n), that can be found in a finite number of steps. Because the operation to determine a computable function is limited to finite steps, it is called a finite algorithm. If f(n) is thus a computable function whose domain is, say, the set of natural numbers, this gives the set M of f(n) the natural order, "f(0), f(1), f(2), . . . ," that generates the members of M (with possible repetitions). In other words, the function f(n) enumerates the elements of M in the order f(0), f(1), f(2), and so on.

Any such sequence of symbols is decidable if and only if it is possible to determine in a finite number of steps whether or not it can be derived from some given sequence of symbols using an algorithm. To solve any such problem, the Turing machine relies on its ability to write symbols down on its infinite tape. The tape, infinite in both directions, is divided into squares, each of which is either blank or else has a symbol from a finite alphabet written on it (see diagram).

This is called the computing tape. The symbols are part of a formal language, which consists of a finite alphabet of arbitrary symbols

$S_0, S_1, S_2, \ldots S_j$

that can be put together into various strings that are then scanned by a reading head, one square at a time. The Turing machine's action at any particular time is determined uniquely by a rule relating its internal states

$$q_0, q_1, q_2, \ldots q_n$$

to the scanned symbol S, such that it has four possible moves:

(a) change the scanned symbol
(b) move one square to the right
(c) move one square to the left
(d) stop.

The Turing machine is controlled by a sequence of instructions that can be represented in table form (the Turing table) in terms of a finite set of quadruples as follows:

	State	Scanned symbol	Act	Next state	
(a)	q_i	S_j	S_k	q_l	(replace symbol)
(b)	q_i	S_j	R	q_l	(move right)
(c)	q_i	S_j	L	q_l	(move left)

Because no two quadruples start with the same {state, symbol} pair, the machine operations are always finite, until a {state, symbol} combination is reached for which there is no corresponding quadruple. In other words, the machine starts by scanning a certain square of the tape, and the instruction might be, "If a square contains the symbol '3' follow instruction I_3 and then proceed to instruction k_1," or, "If a square contains the symbol '7,' obey instruction I_7 and proceed to instruction k_1."

For example, suppose I_3 states "Move the tape two squares forward." The Turing machine moves and scans the new square. Suppose instruction k_1 is "If the square contains the symbol '5,' follow instruction I_5 followed by instruction k_2." If I_5 is "Move the tape four squares back" and k_2 is "Print the symbol '8,' and then follow instruction I_8," where I_8 is "Stop," our Turing machine has successfully computed "3 + 5," to get the correct result, "8." In this way, the Turing machine begins with a given situation by scanning a square, carrying out the first step, and then using the symbols on the new square as a new starting square from which it carries out the second step, until it stops when it arrives at the required value of the function. For example, suppose that the Turing machine is in some state q_k, and it scans the square below:

We can represent this state, without the squares, as

$$\ldots S_{i0} \, S_{i1} \, q_k \, S_{i2} \, S_{i3} \, S_{i4} \, S_{i5} \ldots$$

continued

(where S_0 is a blank square). Let us now suppose that our Turing machine is bound by the following two sets of instructions:

(I_1): $q_1 S_1 L q_2$

and

(I_2): $q_2 S_2 L q_2$.

Let us also suppose that what is written on the tape is

$S_1 S_2 S_2 S_1 S_2 \ldots S_1$,

such that our Turing machine is in state q_1 and scanning the second S_1, which can simply be represented as follows:

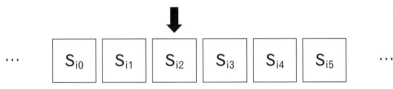

$S_1 S_2 S_2 q_1 S_1 S_2 \ldots S_1$.

At this point the Turing machine implements its first set of instructions, I_1, to create

$S_1 S_2 q_2 S_2 S_1 S_2 \ldots S_1$, followed by the second set of instructions, I_2, resulting in $S_1 q_2 S_2 S_2 S_1 S_2 \ldots S_1$. If this is then repeated, we get $q_2 S_1 S_2 S_2 S_1 S_2 \ldots S_1$.

Now, since there are no instructions that start with $q_2 S_1$, our Turing machine stops.

What has just been described is a simple Turing machine. But because even the tables for very simple computations can become very lengthy, a complex set of machines can be constructed to perform a number of computations. With proper arrangement of the suffixes of the q's, these machines can be linked together to perform extremely complicated computations. Today the notion of computability in computer science is typically defined in terms of such Turing machines that can calculate all functions following a step-by-step procedure.

If the brain is itself a computer, how is it able to carry out the computations necessary for the complexity of behavior and experience at the level of the human mind? Modeling logical operations using discrete-action networks and building Turing machines to carry out computations can help us to understand how it might be possible that other sorts of circuitries, such as are realized by networks of neurons, might be able to carry out such functions on a purely mechanical level. But what about computations over the complex representations of which the brain is obviously capable? The idea that the brain is, fundamentally, a computer, is itself predicated on the idea that the nervous system is representational, such that particular states realized at any given time by networks of neurons inside the brain can represent states of some other system, both elsewhere in the body (or brain) and in the external environment. Computation enters into the model at this level because the problem of explaining the obvious transitions that must occur from one state to another become essentially computational operations on representations. The mathematical theory of such computations is based on Turing machines, as discussed above, in which functions are executed using simple rules, which are encoded as a set of instructions, I, determining, for each state, "If you are in state q and have input S, then do X." Insofar as the brain is a complex network of neurons whose inputs and outputs can be modeled using complex mathematical functions, the brain itself can be represented as a Turing machine.

According to one version of computationalism (let us call it prescriptive computationalism, since it prescribes a particular course of action), cognitive theories ought to be expressed in terms of effective procedures. One indication that a theory has been formulated in these terms is that a computer program has been created that embodies the tenets of the theory – in other words, a computational model has been supplied. The computationalist prescription is motivated by the fact that, by formulating a theory in terms of effective procedures, it becomes much easier to determine the implications, in the form of explananda (that which stands in need of explanation) or predictions, of a theory. As Pylyshyn (1984) explains,

> One of the clearest advantages of expressing a cognitive-process model in the form of a computer program is, it provides a remarkable intellectual prosthetic for dealing with complexity and for exploring both the entailments of a large set of proposed principles and their interactions.
>
> (Pylyshyn 1984, p. 20)

If the principles constituting a theory are expressed in terms of a formal system, then explanatory and predictive implications can be determined mechanically by realizing that formal system as a computer program.

A closely related motivation behind prescriptive computationalism is that the formulation of theory in terms of effective procedures minimizes the need to rely upon intuition. Simply put, what is gained by formulating theory in terms of effective procedures is the capacity to determine whether or not the phenomena to be explained really do follow from theoretical assumptions. In other words, it can be determined through mechanical means whether or not a theory is up to the task of explaining the relevant phenomena (as noted in the next chapter, this condition has come to be known as the sufficiency constraint).

The prescription that all cognitive theory should be formulated in terms of effective procedures is independent of any assumptions regarding the degree to which cognition is itself a computational process. The prescription is taken to apply with equal force to all forms of scientific theorizing (e.g., plate tectonics, economics, astrophysics, etc.). There is a stronger form of computationalism, however, that is concerned with cognitive theory in particular. This latter, theoretical variant of computationalism generally presupposes the weaker prescriptive form and involves an hypothesis concerning the relation between the cognitive system and the explanatory formalisms invoked to explain it.

As suggested above, in order to arrive at effective procedures for modeling some system, a formal notation is needed to represent the states and state–state transitions of that system. Formalisms abound, and they range from the domain-specific (e.g., notations for expressing the product of chemical reactions) to those that have potential for more general applicability (e.g., predicate logic and arithmetic). In most cases of computational modeling, the system of interest is taken to be unlike the formalism invoked in order to express its principles of operation – that is, it is assumed that the system is not a formal system.

According to theoretical computationalism, on the other hand, the system of interest (i.e., the cognitive system) is taken to be like the artificial formalisms invoked in order to express its principles of operation. This stronger version of computationalism likens the mind to a computational device, and its origins can be traced back to the work of McCulloch and Pitts who, if you recall, showed that an appropriately configured network of neuron-like units can implement a Turing machine. If the brain is a computational device, then perhaps computer science has a legitimate claim to being the fundamental discipline in cognitive science.

1.3.3 The primacy of cognitive psychology: multiple realizability

The proposal that the brain might be a computational device has also given rise to the view that psychology has a legitimate claim to the throne of cognitive science. This is because there are various, some would say independent, levels in terms of which one can describe a computational device. Notice, for instance, that when a computer runs a particular program, it seems legitimate to characterize its operations in the terms of any of several explanatory vocabularies.

One such vocabulary corresponds to the highest or most abstract level of computational description, sometimes called the "algorithmic" level. Consider a program designed to output some proposition Q following any inputs consisting of statements $P \vee Q$ and $\sim P$. To describe the program in these terms is to give an algorithmic description – to specify an algorithm. The algorithm here corresponds to the natural deduction rule known as disjunctive syllogism. There are an indefinite number of effective procedures in terms of which to execute this algorithm. For instance, statements of form $P \vee Q$ might be translated into the logically equivalent form $\sim P \rightarrow Q$ and a mechanical procedure might be executed that outputs statements of the form Q in light of inputs of the form $\sim P \rightarrow Q$ and P. Algorithms are thus more abstract than effective procedures, because there is more than one effective procedure that can be utilized in order to implement an algorithm. That is to say, algorithms are multiply realizable with respect to effective procedures.

There are clearly many different programming languages (e.g., C++, BASIC, Lisp, etc.) capable of implementing the effective procedure just described. There are even many ways of implementing the same effective procedure within the same programming language. The encoding of an effective procedure in a particular language is a program. A description of a program will involve a slightly different vocabulary that includes, for instance, talk of function calls and executable statements. Effective procedures (and hence algorithms) are, therefore, multiply realizable with respect to the programming level. Programs, furthermore, may be implemented in many different sorts of computer architecture. A particular architecture, likewise, may be instantiated through the use of many different materials. These multiple-realization relations mark the independence of levels of description.

Where computational systems are concerned, there really aren't any hard and fast limits set on the number of applicable levels of description. There seems to be no upper bound to the number of levels, since there may be languages intervening between highest level programming language and the machine language into which a program is ultimately translated (i.e., compiled).

The idea that there are distinct levels of description that come into play when talking about computational systems may have implications for cognitive science – particularly if the brain is a computational system. On this conception, psychology might be construed as studying the mind's program and neuroscience would be viewed as studying the hardware that implements the program. If this is correct, then psychology would have a persuasive argument to the effect that it is the fundamental discipline in cognitive science. Because programs can be implemented by any number of distinct processing devices (e.g., neurons, transistors, water pipes and valves, and so on indefinitely), the study of neurons would, strictly speaking, be dispensable so long as we had a complete understanding of the mind's program. In other words, devices made of completely different materials might all count as cognitive systems in precisely the same sense. What they would have in common, that in virtue of which they are all cognitive, would be the same program. Thus, an understanding of the program (what cognitive psychology is trying to supply) would exhaust the study of cognition. Psychology thus has its own reason for viewing itself as the fundamental discipline.

1.3.4 The de facto unity of cognitive science

We offer no conclusions about which discipline, if any, will turn out in the end to provide the one true portrayal of human cognition. It is clear that all do, at present, offer theories and data that seem relevant to the problem of understanding the mind. It is worth pointing out, moreover, that there is another possibility that, perhaps because it doesn't raise many hackles, fails to get much press. It is possible that as the various disciplines approach the summit of self-knowledge, they will begin to converge. Perhaps that last mile will be traversed cooperatively and in unison. There is, in fact, some evidence that just such a convergence is taking place. As we shall see, most of the main problem areas of cognitive science are being studied from a variety of angles, and as we learn more conclusions are beginning to overlap.

1.3.5 The role of philosophers in cognitive science

Cognitive psychology, computer science, neuroscience, and linguistics seem to be sciences. Philosophy, however, is not a science. So what role, exactly, is philosophy supposed to play in cognitive science? Ever since Aristotle, questions about the nature of the human mind and its relation to the body and the rest of the world have, to a large degree, been the sole property of philosophers. Through Augustine, Descartes, Locke, Hume, Kant, Hegel, James, Wittgenstein, and Ryle, the participants in this debate have, so to speak, spent much time seated firmly in their armchairs. That is to say, they examined the mind primarily by thinking about the mind. Even when experimental psychology strutted onto the scene towards the end of the nineteenth century, the really deep questions about the mind remained the sole purview of philosophers. From the vantage point of philosophy, experimental psychology must have seemed like a motley collection of hypnotizers, dream interpreters, and animal abusers. Indeed, psychology did at one point entirely downplay the importance of explaining the mind. The only thing that mattered was behavior.

Yet drastic changes have taken place in the mind sciences in recent years. We (i.e., humankind) have begun examining the brain as it works, we have traced out pathways of processing in terms of both flowcharts and wiring diagrams, we are learning about the various kinds of processing information undergoes at various stages between sensory stimulation and behavioral output, and we have begun modeling every stage of this process – in short, the mind has become an object of scientific investigation.

This massive turf invasion has split philosophers into two groups. On the one hand are those who welcome the newcomers and eagerly wait to hear what they have to tell us about ourselves. On the other hand are those who bristle at the thought that the study of the mind is slipping from the grasp of philosophers. They worry that this might render an entire sphere of philosophical investigation irrelevant. In retort, some of these philosophers suggest that science can never decisively settle a genuinely philosophical problem. Philosophical problems, they say, are logical and not empirical; they are abstract rather than concrete; they are metaphysical rather than physical.

1.3.5.1 Separatism

Considering some of the mysteries of the mind mentioned earlier, this proposal is not without merit. It is difficult to envision, for instance, how an empirical theory could account for the human capacity to apprehend necessary truths, or how a description of the behavior of matter could ever explain why a particular color looks the way it does, or why the norms of logic are ones that we ought to follow. If we cannot gain insight into these problems about the mind with the aid of science, then perhaps philosophers have something important to contribute to the study of the mind after all.

Notice also that science, or at least the folk conception of science, seems to presuppose a number of things. For instance, science presupposes that there is a mind-independent material world to investigate. If science is to count as a respectable source of knowledge, this and other assumptions ought to be given some justification. Clearly they are not to be justified scientifically, so, the argument goes, it falls to philosophers to provide foundations for science. Indeed, if science is supposed to be our most trustworthy source of knowledge, it also falls to philosophers to investigate what knowledge is. If science presupposes that there is something that the term "knowledge" picks out, then perhaps science also needs philosophy to answer the question, "What is knowledge?" Metaphysics and epistemology are, according to this view, indispensable to the sciences, cognitive or otherwise.

With regard to this latter point, with regard to the sciences' needs for foundations, it is difficult to see how philosophy could be dispensed with. That is to say, what is needed is a discipline that does not justify its claims by appealing to the data delivered by the senses. How else, then, is a knowledge claim to be justified, if not through experience? In contradistinction to empirical claims, which are justified by experience, are (some think) a priori claims that are justified in some other way. Notice, for instance, that when you judge that a particular lawn is green, you seem to be bringing to bear a pair of concepts, your concept of lawns and your concept of green. You join the concepts together in a single judgment, and what justifies this synthesis is your experience. Notice, also, that a different form of justification seems to underwrite the judgment that bachelors are unmarried. Implicated in the former judgment are the concepts that you synthesize and the experience – which is what justifies the synthesis. In the latter case, only your concepts come into play. Your joining of the concepts in the form of a judgment is justified by the fact that one of the concepts is a constituent of the other. That is, what you mean by bachelor is, among other things, someone who is unmarried.

Insofar as you buy into this story, a story that was given its first adequate expression by Kant, one thing to note about the former, empirical judgment is that it could be mistaken. It could be that your green sunglasses tainted your perception of the grass (which is really brown), or it could be that you are dreaming and there is no lawn at all. The latter judgment, what Kant called an analytic judgment, seems a bit different. While you are generally prepared to admit that some evidence might come along that would falsify the empirical judgment, you may not be prepared to admit the same in the case of the analytic judgment. For instance, you are probably not prepared to admit that you might one day encounter a man who is, lo and behold, both married and a bachelor – that, in other words, you stand corrected because here, before you, is a married bachelor.

In sum, according to the Kantian viewpoint, when you join your concept of bachelor and unmarried in a judgment, the justification for so doing lies in the concept of bachelorhood itself. When you join your concepts of lawn and green together (as in the judgment above), your justification for so doing is something aside from an analysis of the concepts themselves. It is some experience.

Of course, sometimes you must direct a concentrated mental gaze at your ontology in order to determine exactly how it is that you divide the world up. For instance, many people think that a bachelor is an unmarried male, no more, no less. Yet, on being asked whether or not a priest is a bachelor, they come to realize that being eligible is another condition that must be satisfied in order to count as a bachelor – at least according to their conceptual scheme. Thus, as Kant would put it, through the analysis of a concept, that which is contained in the concept, albeit confusedly, is ultimately revealed.

Much of contemporary philosophy is concerned with the task of analyzing some of our philosophical concepts – for example, our concepts of understanding, consciousness, or intentionality. One of the tricks of the trade is the thought experiment. For instance, in order to determine whether or not talk of minds ultimately reduces to talk of neurons, you might consider whether or not something that lacks neurons might nevertheless have a mind. For instance, insofar as you are prepared to countenance thinking and feeling creatures that have a very different biological make-up than ours, what you mean by "mind" must not be the sort of thing that could reduce to talk of neurons (this is just the multiple-realizability argument again).

If this is a correct portrayal of the project that philosophers are currently engaged in, then there is a very real worry that this process will only deliver knowledge that is in some sense trivial. Conceptual analysis does not extend our knowledge in any significant way, it only tells us about our pre-existing concepts. If what we are learning is merely something about how we happen to conceive of things, where are we to look in order to discover how we ought to conceive of things? To use another well-worn philosophical turn of phrase, does our concept of minds carve nature at its true joints? Of course, we could not begin to answer such a question if we were not first clear on what our concept of mind amounted to. Thus, conceptual analysis does, if nothing else, serve the practical end of ensuring clarity within and between individuals, and this is a condition that ought to be satisfied before investigation proceeds any further.

Is there a third way in which concepts can be joined to form a judgment? Kant, for one, felt that there had to be. He noted, for instance, that our apprehension of certain principles of geometry seems to extend our knowledge beyond what is merely contained within a particular concept. For instance, as you follow a proof of the Pythagorean theorem, you seem to learn something new about right triangles, something about them that was not merely contained in your concept of a right triangle. At the same time, however, what you are learning seems not to be something about which you are prepared to be mistaken. Thus, Kant suggests, there is a third kind of knowledge, one that both extends our knowledge and is indubitable. If he is correct, then philosophy has a clear mandate to search for these precious truths, for no empirical discipline (since such disciplines deliver only empirical judgments) can possibly suffice. Moreover, if Kant is right, then philosophy might teach us something important about ourselves along the way. Notice that we know what justifies empirical judgments, and we know what justifies analytic judgments. What is it, though, that justifies this third sort of judgment? In answering this question, Kant thought we could learn something about our own minds – something that, once again, empirical science could never teach us.

1.3.5.2 Naturalized philosophy

The view just presented is, for the most part, highly optimistic about the potential role of traditional philosophical methods in the study of the mind. However, it also paints a picture whereby philosophers and scientists need interact very little. As with any philosophical viewpoint, there are many who find the proposal just described highly contentious. W.V.O. Quine, for instance, claims that there is no a priori knowledge. He points out, moreover, that philosophy has a dismal record of discharging its obligations to science. The foundations that men have been searching for since the advent of modern science have never been supplied. The question of what knowledge is, and, consequently, the question of how it is best attained, remains as open as ever it was. Thus, says Quine, why not look to psychology to see what answers it has to offer? Epistemology, after all, concerns the relationship between knower and known, and this is what psychology seems to be investigating as well.

Indeed, of all the thorny problems of mentality discussed above, it seems unreasonable to rule out, a priori, the possibility that science (namely, cognitive science) might one day supply some real answers. True, it is difficult to envision how an empirical theory could account for the human capacity to apprehend necessary truths, or how a description of the behavior of matter could ever explain why a particular color looks the way it does, or why the norms of logic are ones that we ought to follow. Yet there must have been many phenomena that seemed impossible to explain to those who lacked the appropriate theoretical framework.

For these reasons, many philosophers pay rapt attention to the latest research in cognitive science. Seldom, however, do they sit idly by and let the so-called "real scientists" dictate their beliefs to them. Rather, many philosophers hope to shape the course of this emerging field by imparting clarity (with the aid of the analytic skills discussed above), sharing their ideas about cognition culled from millennia of speculation, and testing their own hypotheses (particularly those with philosophical import).

1.4 THE REPRESENTATIONAL THEORY OF MIND AND THEORIES OF MENTAL REPRESENTATION

Some of the main foci of philosophy's involvement in cognitive science include cognitive science's vindication of and implications for the representational theory of mind – the age-old view that the mind is fundamentally a system of representations. The representational theory of mind works hand in hand with the computational theory of mind discussed above: the view that mental processes consist of the manipulation of representations in computations. According to the representational theory of mind, all of the various kinds of mental states and activities involve mental representations: knowledge, perception, memory, dreams, hopes, and fears (to name a few) all involve mentally representing something or other. As mentioned above, Brentano thought that the mind's ability to represent things showed that the mind stood apart from the physical and natural order – he boggled at the suggestion that a mere physical object or process could mentally represent anything. Contemporary philosophical orthodoxy is materialist and many contemporary philosophers have had a keen interest in spelling out, in materialist terms, what it takes for something to be a mental representation.

1.4.1 The representational theory of mind

Right now you are having a perceptual experience: you are having an experience of words written on the page of this book. You experience the blackness of the ink and the whiteness of the paper it is printed on. The experience itself, however, is neither black nor white. The experience itself is a state of your brain that represents the book, and represents it as having black words on a white page. Later, when you put the book down to do something else, you may conjure up a memory of the book – memories of what the book looked like, where you left off, etc. Like the percept, the memory is not the book itself, but a mental representation of the book.

In the history of philosophy the idea that the mind is in the business of mentally representing arises most acutely in considerations of perception and perceptual error. We will return to these topics at length in Chapter 3, but a sketch of them will be useful to us right now. When you pause to think about what perception is, it might not immediately occur to you that a representation of the thing perceived is involved in the process: there is just you and the thing perceived. It may seem that a representation need no more get in between you and the coffee mug that you see than a representation get in between your foot and the sock that it wears: there is just a direct, unmediated relation between you and the thing. But when we pause to reflect on the ways in which our senses may deceive us, the suggestion that perception involves mental representation becomes a more natural suggestion.

Look at Figure 1.6. Gray streets separate black blocks with white dots at the intersections. But your perception is systematically erroneous when you look at the figure, isn't it? You are seeing things that aren't really there – little spots that dance before your eyes. You will notice immediately that when you focus on any one of the white intersections, the adjacent intersections appear occupied by gray spots.

Shift your focus from one intersection to the others, and these gray spots elude your focus, flashing on and off in the process. At least part of what you perceive, then, is not really there on the printed page, but is supplied by the mind's representation of the external world.

Philosophical reflection on the nature of perceptual error has led many philosophers to the conclusion that all of what you perceive is due to mental representation. Descartes famously made much of the possibility of wholesale perceptual error – the possibility that everything you take yourself to be perceiving right now might be an illusion. How so? You could be dreaming. Dreams can be so vivid that you take yourself to be perceiving something that later, when you wake, you realize isn't really there. In a dream you stand before a waterfall, and see in exquisite detail the light reflecting off the spray, feel the moisture splashing on your face, and smell the clean freshness of the air. But you are not really interacting with an actual waterfall. You are tucked safe and sound in the coziness of your bed, where, we hope, you are warm and dry – not being sprayed by a mighty waterfall. Your dream of the waterfall was a mental representation of the waterfall. Dreams can be indistinguishable from perception of the real thing. This indistinguishability has led philosophers to the view that all of perception is a representational affair.

That all of mentality, not just perception, might involve mental representation, becomes apparent in consideration of what philosophers call the "propositional attitudes." In consideration of a wide variety of mental phenomena, philosophers have noted that so many of them involve an attitude toward a proposition. You open your refrigerator this morning and perceive that you

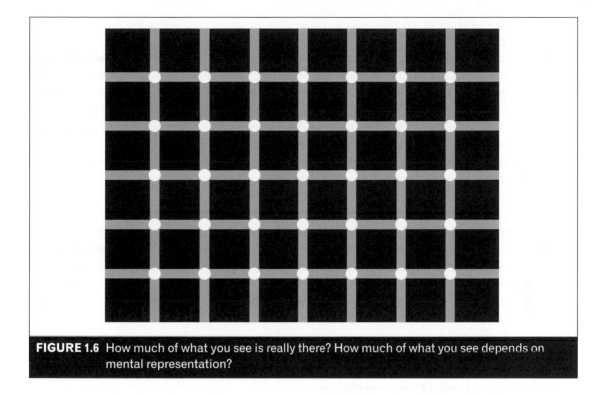

FIGURE 1.6 How much of what you see is really there? How much of what you see depends on mental representation?

are out of orange juice. Note what comes before and after the "that" in the previous sentence. Before the "that" is a word picking out a mental state: a state of perception. After the "that" is a propositional clause: a clause that by itself forms a complete proposition or declarative sentence. We can generate many more examples beyond those of perception. Here are a few:

- Mary believes that the world is round.
- Allen hopes that he gets paid today.
- Snoopy fears that he is out of puppy chow.
- Vivian remembers that St. Louis is not the capital of Missouri.
- Everyone thinks that the authors are handsome.

Many mental states, not just perception, can be thought of as propositional attitudes. And just as perceptions may portray things contrary to reality, so may other propositional attitudes. If you desire that tomorrow you win the lottery, the desire is about something that has not yet actually taken place. Someone may believe that the world is flat even though it is round. A drugged or drunk person may hallucinate that they are talking to a pink elephant when they are really just talking to a coat rack. The propositional clauses in the above descriptions are not picking out some actual states of affairs that the people are related to, but instead some non-actual states of affairs that they are mentally representing. The hallucinator is not relating to an actual elephant, pink or otherwise, but mentally representing the presence of a pink elephant. The representational theory of mind gives us a powerful philosophical grasp on these otherwise puzzling situations.

Not all propositional attitudes are about non-actual states of affairs like chocolate mountains and pink elephants. But the point of focusing on the non-actual cases is the way that it highlights the representational character of mentality. The fact that we get things wrong or contrary to fact makes apparent that what we are doing is representing. But sometimes we get it right too. If it is really the case that Jane knows that snow is white, then snow is white. Here, the propositional attitude of knowledge involves representing *correctly* the way things are: snow *is* white.

The representational theory of the mind is the view that mentality is fundamentally a representational affair: having a mental state involves having a mental representation, a representation that either accurately or inaccurately depicts the way things are. In this section we have sketched some of the philosophical reasons for thinking of mentality in representational terms. This whole book will constitute a collection of further reasons, both philosophical and scientific, for conceiving of mentality representationally. For instance, the chapters on memory and perception will describe the various roles of representations in those mental phenomena. One of the key topics in the chapter on consciousness is the relative success of representational theories of consciousness and whether there are aspects of consciousness – the felt quality of pain, the emotional tone of a depressed person – that elude a representational analysis. Thus is the relative success of cognitive science seen as a relative vindication of the representational theory of mind.

1.4.2 Theories of mental representation

Talk of mental representation already has figured and will continue to figure heavily in this book. But what are mental representations? What makes something a mental representation? The answers to these questions are far from settled, and continue to be debated. Here we sketch some of the major contemporary considerations.

1.4.2.1 *A minimal analysis of mental representation*

First, before describing the various and competing theories of mental representation, it will help to have a minimal analysis of mental representation: a short list of features of mental representations that pretty much all parties to the debate would agree to. In brief, a mental representation has the following features:

(1) it is a state of an organism
(2) that admits of a distinction between content and vehicle
(3) the content of which need not be of actual states of affairs

Items 1–3 thus constitute desiderata for any theory of mental representation. Let us briefly unpack 1–3 in order.

Regarding the first desideratum, that a mental representation be a state of an organism – not too much should be made of the word "organism," since many will want to hold that artificial creations such as robots can be the subjects of genuine mental representations. Thus, you should read "organism" as perhaps including artificial organisms if you like. The point of the first desideratum is to aid in distinguishing between mental and non-mental representations. A picture of a woman on a door is a sort of non-mental representation: it represents women, or perhaps it represents that the ladies' room is behind that door and not any other. Likewise, each sentence in this book is a non-mental representation: for instance "the cat is on the mat" is a linguistic representation of some cat's being on some mat. Additionally, individual written words and numerals themselves may be considered as representations – the word "red" represents redness; the numeral "2" represents two-ness or the number two; a globe represents the planet earth; a map represents the United States of America. You get the idea. These are all examples of representations, but not *mental* representations: they are not in anyone's head or mind. This is not to deny that they may *depend* on minds: whether "red" represents redness may depend on people interpreting it as such. But spoken words float in the air and written words are on pages and computer screens: mental representations in contrast, like your thought of red, or your idea of red or your experience or memory of red, are mental representations of redness, and part of what makes them mental representations is that they are states of you: they exist inside of you, inside of your mind, or, more materialistically, inside of your brain.

Regarding the second desideratum, that representations admit of a distinction between content and vehicle, this idea might best be introduced by way of analogy to non-mental representations. The word "red" may represent redness without itself being red. You could print the word "red" in red ink, but you don't have to. The words you are reading are printed in black ink, but their meanings – what they represent – do not change with changes of the color of the ink. The word itself, that which is printed on the page, is the representational vehicle. What it is a representation of – in the case of "red," redness; in the case of ":)," a side-ways smiling face – is the representational content. Just as non-mental representations admit of a contrast between content and vehicle, so do mental representations. When you remember that roses are red, and violets are blue, your memory itself need be neither red nor blue. Your memory is a state of your nervous system – probably a pattern of connection weights in one of your neural networks. Whether or not it makes sense to speak of the memory itself having a color, its color is quite irrelevant to determining what it is a representation of. The representational vehicle need not be blue to have the representational content of blueness. Your desire to go to the movies tomorrow exists today, and exists in your head, not in the movie theater. The point of the second desideratum is two-fold: first it asserts that all representations have contents, and second it asserts that the contents can be distinct from the vehicles.

Regarding the third desideratum, that representations may be representations of non-actual states of affairs, again we may illustrate our point in terms of examples of non-mental representations. A linguistic representation such as "Socrates lives on the moon" is false, but no less representational for being so. "Tomorrow I will eat breakfast" may very well be true, but the state of affairs it represents is not an actual state of affairs, at least, it is not actual yet. Salvador Dali's painting *The Persistence of Memory* has a melting watch draped over a tree branch in it: this also represents a non-actual state of affairs. Such sorts of examples have obvious mental analogues: imagine Socrates on the moon; visualize a watch melting. Note that it is not *essential* to mental representations that they represent non-actual states of affairs, but it is essential to them that they be able to. Something that was incapable of being about something non-actual could not count as a representation. Why have philosophers insisted on this point? The key motive is to distinguish representation from information. Both representation and information have aboutness, but only representation can be about non-actual states of affairs. A bone in the ground can carry information about dinosaurs, but only if there actually were dinosaurs. A ringing bell can carry information that Aunt Ethel is at the door, but only if Aunt Ethel really is at the door. Many philosophers use the word "information" in such a way that information is always about something that really happened. Further, they think that information exists wherever there is causal interaction. For example, if a leak in your ceiling causes a wet spot in the carpet, then the wet spot in the carpet carries the information that there has been a leak in the ceiling. Many people think that while causal interaction, and thus information, is quite abundant in the universe, mental representation is comparatively rare. Tree rings may carry information about the age of a tree, but few people take seriously the proposal that trees think, wonder, or fret about their age. Information is thus distinct from mental representation and the third desideratum helps draw out this difference.

1.4.2.2 *Resemblance theories of mental representation*

According to resemblance theories, mental representations resemble that which they represent and represent in virtue of this resemblance. Non-mental prototypes of such representations are pictures and photographs. A driver's license photo resembles the driver in some respects: the geometric arrangement of shapes and colors in the photo is the same as the geometric arrangement of shapes and colors on the driver's face. However, the second desideratum is not violated, since the photo does not resemble the driver in all respects: the photo is two-dimensional and small where the driver is three-dimensional and life-size.

Resemblance theories are perhaps the oldest theories of mental representation, and though they are relatively out of favor nowadays, they still have adherents. Through history, we may identify Aristotle as an adherent of resemblance theories. This view surfaces among many contemporary philosophers and scientists. It may at first seem like a natural suggestion that mental representations resemble their objects the way that pictures do. Look at this book. Now close your eyes and form a mental image of the book. You may imagine looking at an image of the book with your mind's eye: imagine looking at the book up close, then far away; imagine looking at its front and then its back. It is natural to say that what you are inspecting in imagination is the mental representation which is very similar to inspecting a book with your eyes open. Thus you might infer that the mental representation is similar to the book itself. But such an inference is unwarranted. All that is warranted is that the process of imagination is similar to the process of perception: the representations involved in perception are similar to the representations involved in imagination. This similarity does not warrant the inference that the representation itself is similar to that which is represented. Of course, this does not kill all hopes for the success of a resemblance theory, but resemblance theories are not without other problems either. One of the main problems is specifying just which resemblances are the ones crucial for representation. Everything resembles everything else in some sense or other. Pick any two things and it is an easy exercise to find something that they have in common. Take for example, Winston Churchill and the lint in the left pocket of George Bush's trousers. What do they have in common? Both have been in the White House, both are from the planet Earth, neither has been spray painted green by an angry elephant, and so on.

In spite of such problems, many researchers continue to think of representations in the mind/brain in terms of resemblance or isomorphism between the representation and the represented. One way of thinking along these lines is to construe representations in the brain as topographic maps. These maps represent adjacent portions of what is represented with spatially adjacent areas, the same way that a map of a country represents the fact that two cities are nearby by putting them near each other on the map. The somatotopic maps which represent the body generally have the same look and structure as the body itself, so that points of the body which are nearby are represented by parts of the map which are nearby. It has been shown that the maps can grow or shrink, roughly depending on the amount of use the part of the body they represent gets. So for instance, if you use one finger a great deal, the portion of the map which represents that finger will actually begin to grow, at the expense of the nearby portions of the map representing the other fingers. So sizes of the representations do not necessarily represent sizes of the corresponding organs, but reflect differences of use. The occipital lobe organizes much of its visual information into what are called retinotopic maps: this means that adjacent areas of the eye's retina are represented by adjacent areas on the map (see Kosslyn 1994).

Whatever role resemblance has in representations in the mind/brain, resemblance cannot be the whole story: you can mentally represent things that are much larger than your brain, that are different colors from your brain, and so on. And these points are supported by contemporary research, as Uttal (1973) points out with respect to representation in sensory systems:

> The essence of much of the research that has been carried out in the field of sensory coding can be distilled into a single, especially important idea – any candidate code can represent any perceptual dimension; there is no need for an isomorphic relation between the neural and psychophysical data. Space can represent time, time can represent space, place can represent quality, and certainly, nonlinear neural functions can represent linear or nonlinear psychophysical functions equally well.
>
> (Uttal 1973, p. 30)

Causal covariation theories may thus aid in fleshing out the story of how the mind/brain represents the world.

1.4.2.3 Causal covariation theories of mental representation

The gist of causal covariation theories is that what makes a brain state a mental representation of something is that there are crucial causal interactions that the brain state can enter into with that thing. Specifying just which causal interactions will do the trick is most of the battle in developing and defending these theories.

The origins of causal covariational theories come from philosophical reflection on perception. We have already discussed arguments that perception is representational. Your percept of a blue coffee mug represents the blue coffee mug that you are looking at. But why does it represent *that* blue coffee mug? There are lots of blue coffee mugs around the world, but your percept represents that one because that's the one that caused you to have that percept. Again, we may find non-mental representational analogues of such phenomena. A photograph of Joe resembles Joe about as much as it resembles Joe's identical twin brother Moe. But the photograph is a photograph of Joe, not Moe, because Joe, and not Moe, was a crucial link in the causal chain that led up to the production of the photograph.

The causal covariational view sees perception as functioning like detecting and measuring devices. The position of the needle on your car's speedometer causally covaries with the speed of your car thereby representing the speed of your car. The position of the needle on your car's fuel gauge causally covaries with the fuel level in your tank thereby representing fuel level. The ringing of your doorbell causally covaries with the presence of someone at the door and thereby represents that someone is at the door. Mere causal covariation, however, while constituting information, is insufficient for representation, since it violates the third desideratum from our minimal analysis of mental representation. Theorists have sought to solve this problem in several different ways, the most popular being to say that X represents Y not merely becauses it covaries with Y, but because it has the *function* of covarying with Y. Something can have a function without performing that function: hearts have the function of pumping blood, but sadly, sometimes they fail to perform that function. Eyes have the function of seeing, but in the blind, they have that function without performing it. The needle in your gas gauge represents fuel level, but can sometime misrepresent: the gauge may be broken and thus not performing the function it was designed to perform. Unlike cars, natural organisms were not literally designed, but evolved through the processes of natural selection. Thus, advocates of the kind of causal covariational theory of mental representation discussed here would say that X represents Y if X was naturally selected to causally covary with Y, and thus has the function of causally covarying with Y. But since something can have the function without actually always performing it, we have a way of seeing how mental representations can represent non-actual states of affairs. I push on my eye and see a bright spot in my visual field even though there is no bright light in front of me: I could be in a totally darkened room and get this effect. What I have done is activated something in the brain that has the function of indicating the presence of a light in my visual field: it has the function of causally covarying with a light, even though in this instance, it is not causally covarying with a light: it is causally covarying with mechanical pressure applied to my eyeball by my finger.

The neurobiological paradigms for causal covariational theories of mental representation are feature detectors. A feature detector consists in one or more neurons that are (1) maximally responsive to a particular type of stimulus, and (2) have the function of indicating the presence of a stimulus of that type. Neuroscientists have hypothesized the existence of detectors for stimulus types such as high-contrast edges, motion direction, spatial locations, and colors. Some have hypothesized that the nervous systems of frogs contain fly detectors. Lettvin et al. (1959) identified cells in the frog retina that responded maximally to small shapes moving across the visual field. The inference that such cells have the function of detecting flies and not just any small moving thing is based on certain assumptions about the diet and environment of frogs, thus satisfying (2) as well as (1).

The causal covariational view accommodates another kind of representation postulated to exist in the brain: motor representations (Mandik 1999, 2001). Representations in motor areas in the brain are discussed further in Chapter 5 on action and emotion. In the case of feature detectors, the brain state represents something that causes it. In the case of motor representations, the brain state represents something that it causes: a twitch of a finger, the raising of an arm. In both the motor case and the detection case, however, representation is equally a matter of causal covariation.

Like most theories, covariational theories have their detractors. We turn now to discuss some of the most prevalent considerations against such a view.

1.4.2.4 *Internal role theories of mental representation*

Causal covariational theories are a brand of externalism: they explain representations in terms of a relation between a state of the brain and something *external* to it. Internal role theories try to explain representation solely in terms of relations between items in the brain. The representational content of some brain state will be determined, on this view, by the various causal interactions internal to the brain that the state enters into. It is in virtue of playing a certain causal role that a particular brain state, the vehicle, has the content that it does. Thus, in contrast to externalism, internal role theory is a brand of internalism.

One of the main motives for holding such view is a curious combination of Cartesian skepticism and not-so-Cartesian materialism. Descartes' skeptical hypothesis was that, for all you know, you could be dreaming, or worse, the only things in the universe that exist are your mind and a deceitful demon pumping you full of illusory experiences. The materialistic analogue of this skeptical hypothesis is the supposition that for all you know, you are a brain in a vat. You could be a mere brain floating in an oxygenated nutrient bath, connected through wires to a virtual reality computer supplying you with illusory stimulations to the sensory regions of your cortex. This brain in a vat may have just popped into existence: it has never been in a body, it has no parents, no evolutionary history. But for all you know, you could be this brain in a vat. Regardless of whether you are a brain in a vat or not, one thing you do know is that you are mentally representing the *Mona Lisa*; you are mentally representing the Eiffel Tower; you are mentally representing polar bears, and all of this mental representing can go on even though, for all you know, you are a brain in a vat and there are no causal chains leading from states of your brain to the *Mona Lisa*, the Eiffel Tower, or polar bears. (We will discuss skepticism at greater length in Chapter 4, in section 4.4.1 on epistemology.)

Another consideration in favor of internalism involves the causal and explanatory work that mental representations seem to do in virtue of their representational contents. I have the desire for a beer and a belief that there is beer in my refrigerator. Because I have the mental states that I do, and because they have the representational contents that they do – contents concerning beer in the fridge as opposed to, say, contents about ice cream in the store down the street – I get out of my armchair and shuffle over to the refrigerator. The causes of my getting up and shuffling have to be internal to me. There is no action at a distance here: the beer does not exert a field of force that sucks me to it. Instead, events in my brain triggered events in my muscles and so on. If representational content is to have a similarly causal role in the explanation of why I did what I did, then representational content has to be similarly internal to me. If, however, some version of externalism is correct, it is very difficult to see how content can play a causal role in the explanation of behavior (though not necessarily impossible – many externalists have tried to work this out) .

So how do internal causal roles define representational contents? To see how this might work, it will help to start with the internal role theorists' paradigm cases: logical connectives like "and" and "or." It may not make sense to ask what the "and" *represents*, but it does make sense to inquire into what it *means* and meaning is at least closely related to representational content. As discussed in the box on Turing machines, the meaning of "and" can be given truth functionally: anything, like an electrical circuit, that maps two inputs onto a true output if and only if both inputs are true can mean "and." How about the meaning of other kinds of words and concepts, the mental analogues of words? What does the word "bird" mean? Here the internal role theorist will draw an analogy to dictionary definitions: the meaning of "bird" is determined by what other words it relates to and constitute a definition of it. "Bird" thus might have as a definition "warm-blooded animal with feathers" and thus, the meaning of the syntactic item "bird" is determined by causal, syntactic, relations that it enters into with other items, items like "warm-blooded," "animal," and "feathers."

Many have objected that internal role theory supplies only syntax. None of these syntactical relations, no matter how numerous or complex, can give rise to genuine semantics, that is, meaning or representational content. Consider the following analogy. Suppose you look up the word "halcyon" in the dictionary and you find it defined as "pleasingly or idyllically calm or peaceful: serene." Next you look up "serene" and find it defined as "lighthearted, carefree, having simplicity and charm." So then you look up "lighthearted" and "carefree" . . . and so on. Unless you're already quite familiar with a language, the dictionary will be quite useless. If you do not know English, familiarity with the chains of inter-definition in an English dictionary will never grant you understanding. Just knowing what marks are related to what other marks never supplies knowledge of the *meaning* or *content* of those marks.

A different, yet related problem with internal role theories is their failure to respect the truth conditional insight about representational content. The truth conditional insight is that in knowing the representational content of some representation, we thereby know the conditions under which it is true, or under which it contributes to truth. For example, in knowing that some symbol has as its representational content *rabbits eat carrots*, we know that the symbol is true if and only if rabbits eat carrots. In other words, if a particular theory of what the conditions determining content are is correct, then we should be able to *read off* from those conditions the circumstances under which the representation is true or under which it contributes to truth. Even the logical connectives, the paradigm cases for the internal role theorist, do not escape the criticism based on the truth conditional insight: the connectives are *truth* functions after all.

The problem with internal role theories of representation is that they define the representational content of a representation as being the relations that the representations bear to other states internal to an organism. Such states seldom enter into the truth conditions of the representation. For instance, none of the properties internal to my nervous system includes rabbits or carrots; nonetheless, I have brain states with the representational content that rabbits eat carrots.

Our sketch of the main theories of mental representation thus draws to a close. We have not described all of the current theories, nor attempted to adjudicate between the competing theories. It is worth mentioning, however, the possibility that there is a grain of truth in each theory, and that each theory has something to offer what might be the final, correct theory. Already researchers have dabbled with hybrids of the above theories. To mention just one kind of example, two-factor theories combine internal role factors and external causal covariational factors into a single account of how representational content is determined. As you read the rest of this book, keep an eye out for the different ways in which notions of mental representation are appealed to in philosophical and scientific explanations of cognition. Which theories of mental representation work best with which explanations of cognition? The ultimate answers to such questions will bring us closer to an understanding of what mental representations, and thus, minds, *really* are.

1.5 CONCLUSION: SEEING THE WHOLE ELEPHANT

There's a famous old adage about the six blind men and the elephant. Curious, they each set out to study the beast. The first, having encountered only the trunk, describes the elephant as being thick and soft and supple, snake-like. The second, having encountered only one of his legs, describes the elephant as being firm and steadfast, like a tree trunk. The third, having encountered only the tail, describes the elephant as thin and wavy, worm like. The fourth, having encountered only the torso, describes the elephant as a large, massive wall. The fifth, having encountered one of the tusks, describes the elephant as like a rock, sharp and smooth and pointy. The sixth, having encountered only his ear, describes the elephant as thin and flat and wavy, like a giant wing. When the six get together and compare notes they are flabbergasted and each cannot agree with or believe any of the others – surely they have not encountered the same beast?

The moral of the story is obvious. The elephant is not just one thing but many things, even though it is all those many things all at once. The six different theories about the whole elephant formed by the six blind men are each built out of elements provided by their experience, and their experiences differ depending upon which part of the elephant they happened to study. But now suppose that the six blind men try to create one unified theory of the elephant. They will have a hard time of it! Not only do their theories not fit one into the other, but also they blatantly contradict each other. Or, they may come to the conclusion that the elephant is a mysterious, amorphous beast capable of changing its form. Or, they may conclude that there is something wrong with one or more of the other blind men, that only one of them has the appropriate tactile apparatus for studying elephants. And so on.

What does all this have to do with cognitive science? Well, consider now that the question is not about what an elephant is but about ourselves. What am I? This age-old question has been asked since the dawn of human consciousness. From ancient times to the present, there have been a variety of often conflicting answers all of which have one interesting property in common. The terms in which the answers are given are determined by the terms set forth by the method of inquiry. Cognitive science is itself a new collaborative field that developed out of many different disciplines. One of its main aims is not only to facilitate an information flow between the different approaches by putting all the terms in which the various answers are given into one common framework, but to thereby create a new paradigm for understanding ourselves.

2 Windows on the Brain and Mind

2.1 WHAT ARE YOU?

You probably think of the brain as something you have. There is, however, another fruitful way to think about it. Rather than thinking of the brain as something you have, you can also think of it as something you are *in*. The word "you" is actually ambiguous. There is the sense in which "you" refers to a biological organism, a living, breathing, conscious human being engaged in the process of existing in a physical environment with others. This is an objective, third-person point of view of who *you* are. There is also a subjective, first-person view of yourself. You, in this sense, are a conscious being, situated in a space at a particular point in time, surrounded by the objects in your immediate environment. Our purpose in this chapter is to examine various third-person, objective, scientific perspectives of who you (and the rest of humanity) are. Nevertheless, we think it a worthwhile preliminary exercise to take a moment in order to examine this other, subjective perspective that you have of yourself.

Right now you are either holding a hard copy of this text in your hands or looking at a computer screen. In either case, the text is in front of you. You are probably sitting down in a room. Look at the room. Look at the text. Look at the hands rifling through the text or pressing buttons. Perhaps you see something that looks like Figure 2.1.

You see your arms, torso, knees, the text, and so on. What you *don't* see is equally important. You don't see your own head (although you can detect the end of your nose if you try). Your head is where you seem to be looking out *from*, much as a TV camera does not capture itself. The scene before you contains many objects, but neither your eyes nor your head are among them. You seem to be looking out of your head *through* your eyes, as if you are located at a place inside the head. This is where it gets tricky. If we choose to heed the philosophical pronouncements of the seventeenth and eighteenth centuries, the scene before your eyes is really just a brain event – it is to be identified with the movement of the tiny bits of matter comprising your brain. As we saw

FIGURE 2.1 What it looks like to read a book

in Chapter 1, there are other versions of materialism about the mental. Yet none of these, at least not any that we discussed, is incompatible with the thesis that the locus of a given phenomenon is the brain. In other words, the book you see, the hands holding the book, and everything in the room up to and including your body (which is, according to this way of thinking, not your body but your *body image*) are mental representations of a book, hands, a body, a room, and so on.

One way to think about your perceived environment is as a sort of virtual reality that your brain conjures up. Into this virtual environment is projected a representation of the machine that does the conjuring. Thus, according to this account, *you* are a self-representation inside of a brain. In that sense, it is not *you* who has a brain; rather, it is your brain that has *you*. The brain seems to be something we, as conscious selves, or egos, exist *in*, and not something we own. This may be surprising but really it shouldn't be too shocking once we remember how long it took us, as conscious selves, to realize what a brain is and that we may exist as events within a brain. We are, perhaps, just one part of the brain trying to understand the whole rest of the brain and ourselves within this entire neural array.

In this chapter, we will take an in-depth look at some of the most fruitful ways in which brains have gone about the task of trying to understand their *selves*. In particular, we will focus on techniques of experimentation and modeling that constitute our clearest windows on the structure and functioning of the human mind/brain.

2.2 INSIDE THE BRAIN

Investigating the various regions and subregions of the brain is not unlike generating maps of a particular geographical region. Regarding the latter, one's interests invariably dictate one's choice of data-gathering techniques. One might, for instance, have a broad interest in population demographics. The precise make-up of your demographic map will, of course, be determined by the particular characteristics of the population that you are investigating. Indeed, several complementary maps might be constructed that track such characteristics as lineage, language, and religion. Still further maps might be generated through the study of political boundaries, topographic boundaries, climate boundaries, and so on. Also worth noting is the fact that, whatever your criteria are for the demarcation of particular regions and subregions, the borders you discover will seldom be clearly demarcated. That is to say, more often than not, one area will fuse seamlessly into the next. In the end, when one compares the different maps that have been created, one will find that each map differs from all the others, sometimes subtly, sometimes drastically. Many of the same lessons apply to the study of the brain. There are many legitimate ways of mapping the various regions and subregions of the brain. One's interests will determine the techniques employed and, in turn, the precise details of the divisions that one discovers. One often finds, again, that one region will transition smoothly into the next.

2.2.1 Neuroanatomy

As noted in Chapter 1, through the study of the structure of neurons and their arrangement, Brodmann was able to divide the cortex into fifty-two distinct regions. His map of the cortex is still widely used nowadays. While this provides a useful tool for localizing cognitive functions to particular regions of the cortex, it tells us little about the manner in which the various regions are wired together. In order to study neural interconnections, one would like to know something about the extent and course of a particular nerve cell's projections (what we will come to know as the *axons* and *dendrites*). As these can be quite long (axons in the body can be as long as a meter), this is no simple feat.

One tried-and-true method for studying particular nerve cells, a technique pioneered by Cajal (see Chapter 1) and refined greatly over the past century, is to use stains that bring particular nerve cells and their projections into sharp relief when viewed through a microscope. It is not always easy to stain individual cells, however, nor is it easy to stain them in their entirety (axons have proven to be particularly troublesome). In order to chart the course taken by a particular axon, an alternative technique is to sever the axon from the rest of the cell (including the all-important cell body). Because degenerating axons stain differently than normal axons, the staining of degenerating axons gives one a pretty good idea of their reach and destination.

While these techniques tell us a great deal about the structure and connectivity of particular nerve cells, other techniques reveal the kinds of connections that exist between two or more neurons. One family of techniques involves injecting substances into the brains of live animals (e.g., rhesus monkeys). After exposing the cortex of an experimental animal, chemicals or live viruses are injected into the region one wishes to study. The animal might be made to engage in certain kinds of activity in the course of the next few days – preferably activity that taps the brain region being studied. During this period, the injected substances are absorbed by nerve cells, carried down the length of their long projections, secreted into the junction between nerve cells (the *synapse*, described below), and absorbed by the connecting nerve cells. The animal is then sacrificed and slices of the brain are examined under a microscope (in the case of the viral transport method, a stain is applied that reveals the presence of the virus). Combined with the use of electron microscopy, the various procedures noted above have yielded highly detailed wiring diagrams for the brain.

Another breakthrough in the study of neuroanatomy has been the development of sophisticated equipment for generating images of the large-scale structures of the brain. One such technique uses X-rays to generate images of the circulatory system following an injection of a radio-opaque material into the patient's bloodstream. This makes the blood vessels of the brain stand out sharply, allowing doctors to detect where the brain might have been damaged due to stroke, aneurysms, or malformed vessels. Determining the location and extent of brain damage (as discussed both in Chapter 1 and below) is important if one wishes to determine, on this basis, the functions that are carried out by a particular area of the brain.

Computerized tomography (CT) also uses X-rays, but the detection equipment is more sensitive than standard X-ray film. Moreover, instead of a single X-ray, many X-rays are taken from a variety of angles in order to display the density of particular areas of the brain. The result is a detailed image of the structure of the brain, one that even distinguishes between different types of nervous tissue.

Magnetic resonance imaging (MRI) reveals even more details than any of the standard X-ray based techniques (Figure 2.2). It allows researchers to clearly distinguish different types of brain tissue due to their different chemical compositions. The technique involves first directing a powerful magnetic field to the brain, which forces atoms in the brain into a different orientation. When the magnet is turned off, these atoms tend to return to the state they were in before exposure to the magnetic field, a process known as relaxation. Fortuitously, atoms in different types of brain tissue tend to return at different rates, and this difference registers on the final MRI.

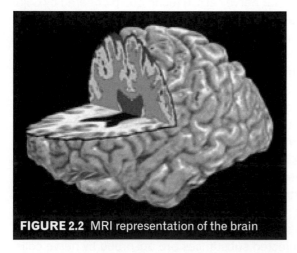

FIGURE 2.2 MRI representation of the brain

2.2.2 Neurophysiology

While the above practices have taught us a tremendous amount about the structure of the brain, still others are required in order to understand how the brain operates. One such technique (really a family of techniques) involves recording the levels of electrical activity exhibited by particular neurons. One way to accomplish this is to poke a tiny electrode through the membrane of a given cell. Paired with a voltometer, the result is an extremely sensitive device which can detect the most minute changes in a cell's electrical activity. Once the electrode is in place, the subject (usually a non-human primate) can be made to engage in certain kinds of activity. For instance, in one seminal study, Hubel and Wiesel (1959) recorded the electrical activity of individual neurons in an area of cortex believed (in light of, among other findings, the extensive projections from the retina to this region) to be implicated in visual processing. They discovered that certain cells in this area respond preferentially to bars of light (projected onto a screen in the animal's visual field) with particular orientations (e.g., |, /, -, etc.). That is to say, while one cell exhibits its most vigorous response (i.e., its highest rate of firing) in the presence of a vertical bar, another cell might respond selectively to a bar that is rotated away from vertical in a particular direction by a few degrees, and so on. The single-cell recording technique has been augmented in recent years in such a way that it is now possible to study the electrical activity of entire populations of neurons at the same time.

In addition to recording cell activity, it is also possible to stimulate neurons to fire (either individually or in groups). For instance, in a landmark set of experiments, Penfield (1958) stimulated different parts of the cortex in conscious human subjects. Sometimes the stimulation would evoke entire experiences, at other times it would cause the subjects to stop talking, make them laugh, make one of their legs move, and so on. Recently, a new technique, *transcranial magnetic stimulation*, has been developed that allows researchers to electrically stimulate parts of the brain directly through the scalp and skull. While the former technique is, given its invasiveness, used only on pathological individuals (usually to determine what parts of the brain *not* to remove during surgery), the latter can be used on normal volunteer subjects for purely experimental purposes.

There are two other important techniques for learning about the manner in which the brain functions. One uses advances in brain imaging technology and is known, appropriately enough, as *functional neuroimaging*. The other is an extension of the work begun by Broca and Wernicke. As both techniques involve a clear synthesis of neuroscience and psychology, we shall postpone discussion of them until after our excursus into the methods employed by cognitive psychologists.

2.3 COGNITIVE PSYCHOLOGY

The experimental psychologist is mainly concerned with discerning the manner in which information gained through the senses is dealt with by the cognitive system as it percolates through various stages of processing and gives rise, ultimately, to behavior. The experimental psychologist is not, however, directly interested in either neuroanatomy or neurophysiology. In fact, unlike neuroscientists, experimental psychologists never look directly at the organ whose activity they are studying. As a result, the challenge facing experimental psychologists is in many ways far more daunting than the one faced by neuroscientists. To get a sense for just how difficult the problem is that the experimental psychologist faces, consider the scenario in the box "The allegory of the interstellar dingus."

THE ALLEGORY OF THE INTERSTELLAR DINGUS

One day a large object enters our atmosphere and descends quite gracefully to the earth. Upon landing, it unloads a large number of boxes and immediately darts back into outer space. Each box contains what looks to be an identical device. About the size of a bowling ball, each device is composed of a substance that is both impregnable and opaque to our most sophisticated technologies. Each also comes equipped with a pair of what look to be sensors and a mass of tapered appendages.

A group of the world's best scientific minds is assembled to figure out what the mysterious devices are. One of the first things they discover is that the tentacles moved about when objects were placed in full view of the sensors. After observing the effects of presenting various stimuli before the sensors, varying the distance from the object, and covering, under each of these conditions, one or both sensors with any of numerous substances, it is concluded that one of the sensors responds to light (at any rate, the tentacles twitch more vigorously in the presence of light) and the other to sound.

The devices are each placed in well-lit containers within reach of any of a variety of objects. Of the many objects presented, only a few elicit from the devices any kind of response that seems at all purposeful. Specifically, the devices turn out to be quite effective at crushing and separating the meat of walnuts and pecans from the shells. It is announced to the world that the mysterious gift from the heavens was a shipment of the best nutcrackers humankind had ever encountered – clearly the work of a superior intellect!

Though many soon lose interest in the project, there are those who want to know how the devices, which really are quite deft, work. One thing they discover is that the devices are not equally deft. Some work better than others. In fact, some are more efficient at pulling the meat from regular walnuts, others are expert black walnut shuckers, and still others have a knack for dealing with pecans. With practice, however, the performance of a given device improves, though the rate of improvement also varies from device to device. In fact, even with extensive practice, some devices fail to measure up to the dexterity of others. Moreover, if a given device is used continuously for an extended period, performance begins to decrease. Performance is also affected by variations in lighting, temperature, and air pressure. How, from the meager evidence of the highly irregular responses exhibited by these devices in the face of various stimuli, can the scientists ever hope to discover their inner workings?

The task facing our hypothetical xeno-roboticists is a daunting one, to be sure. Yet it is child's play compared to the one facing the experimental psychologist.

Like the xeno-roboticist, the only data the psychologist has to go by are the responses exhibited in the face of various stimuli. And not unlike the alien artifacts, performance varies from individual to individual and is sensitive to any of a wide variety of factors. Unlike the alien nutcrackers, however, humans exhibit a tremendous range of behaviors, and the psychologist must figure out what cognitive capacities are brought to bear on any given task, the precise nature of those capacities, and the manner in which various capacities conspire to yield any of a tremendous variety of responses. Moreover, unlike the nutcrackers, the behavior of humans is not determined solely by the stimuli confronting them. As Chomsky famously noted, the behavior of humans is not stimulus bound. So how does the experimental psychologist proceed?

Generally speaking, experimental subjects are asked to perform a particular task while some measure is taken of their behavior. There are various sorts of behavior that can be measured. Two of the most popular are reaction times (RTs) and recall scores. To really get a sense for how cognitive psychology works, it will help to consider some concrete examples of how each of these measures is used in the testing of hypotheses.

2.3.1 Reaction times

Picture, if you will, a horse. By default, your imagined horse is probably facing in a particular direction and is upright. Now imagine what the horse would look like if it were upside down. Did you mentally rotate the horse 180 degrees around a particular axis or did the horse simply appear there? You may or may not feel that there is a clear-cut answer to this question. Fortunately, your own impression of the process is largely irrelevant. Gone are the days when such introspective reports are of much consequence to psychology. This is because psychologists have found, and are continually inventing, new ways of testing theories based upon quantified observations of behavior.

For instance, in order to decide between the competing theories just mentioned (i.e., continuous mental rotation versus instantaneous transformation), one approach would be to measure the time it takes to move a mental image through various degrees of transformation (e.g., 45, 90, 135 degrees, etc.). If it were found that it takes twice as long to decide what an image would look like turned 90 degrees than 45 degrees, and twice as long again to decide what it would look like turned a full 180 degrees, then we would have a pretty good reason for thinking that the transformation is continuous (i.e., like rotating a picture) rather than instantaneous.

Of course, one can't simply ask subjects when they have completed the various transformations. Indeed, in order to minimize the influence of subject expectations, it would help if subjects had little or no idea about the purpose of the experiment. Heeding this latter restriction has, of course, done little to alleviate the common conception of the experimental psychologist as a nefarious trickster. At any rate, what one might do, and what some have done (Shepard and Metzler 1971), is ask subjects to evaluate whether pairs of images depict the same object. For instance, a subject might be presented with one image on the left-hand side of a page (or computer screen) and an image to the right of it which is, aside from being rotated to some determinate degree, identical. Subjects can then be asked to evaluate whether or not the two images are identical and press a particular key or button in the event that they are.

If the instantaneous transform theory is correct, we would expect that reaction times would not be systematically influenced by the degree to which a duplicate has been rotated. If the continuous rotation theory is correct, on the other hand, we would expect the reaction time for comparison of slightly offset copies to be shorter than the reaction time for copies that are more offset. Shepard and Metzler (1971) discovered that there is indeed a linear relationship between reaction times and the degree to which a duplicate image has been rotated. The results of their experiment, in other words, favor the continuous rotation model over the instantaneous transform model and provide a beautiful illustration of the reaction-time methodology.

In this case, merely by recording and analyzing reaction times, an inference could be made about the inner (and quite possibly introspectively opaque) processes underwriting a particular cognitive operation. We now turn to a second popular technique for testing cognitive theories.

2.3.2 Recall scores

Recite, if you will, your phone number.

Are you finished? Good. Now think about all of the cognitive operations that might have figured in your execution of this simple instruction. For starters, you had to be able to read and understand our instructions; you had to be able to translate a neural representation of your phone number into an acoustic representation; in order to do that, you had to manipulate, quite precisely, the tremendous number of muscles controlling your vocal cord, tongue, lips, and so on; and you also had to *remember* your phone number.

Now have a look at this number: 723–3684.

Can you close your book (or turn off your monitor), walk to the phone, and punch the number into your key pad? Are some of the same cognitive processes brought to bear in the execution of this set of instructions as in the previous case? Which ones are the same, and which are different? More specifically, how is it that you were able to remember the number after the book had been closed, and is the same kind of memory used in this case as was used to remember your own number? One final question: what kind of experiment would you devise in order to answer the last question? Coming up with an answer to *this* question is no easy task, but it can be done.

To see how, try something else. Once again, we will present you with a number. This time, after you have closed your book and before punching in the number, count backwards from 15 as fast as you can. Here is your number: 537–9671. Now go to it.

How did you do? If you are anything like the rest of us, you probably had a bit of trouble. At the very least, it was probably harder for you to carry out this set of instructions than the previous set. That is, the task of counting backwards probably presented something of a distraction. How do you think you would have fared had you been asked to count backwards before dialing your own phone number? Intuitively, at least, it must seem as though your performance would hardly have been affected. Now we are getting somewhere, but we haven't quite achieved scientific respectability.

At around the time that behaviorism was on the wane and cognitive psychology was on the rise, a rather famous set of experiments was conducted (Postman and Phillips 1965; Glanzer and Cunitz 1966) using a set of instructions not unlike the ones we just gave you. The results of this set of experiments were, among other things, quantified, objective, and replicable. Specifically, subjects were presented with rather long lists of items (e.g., words, numbers, nonsense syllables, and so on), one item at a time, and after presentation they were asked to recall the items on the list. The results were then graphed out, and items near the beginning and end of the list were recalled more readily than items in the middle of the list. These phenomena came to be known as the *primacy effect* and the *recency effect*, respectively. The two effects happen to be separable – that is, it has been found that under certain conditions the former effect remains intact while the latter is severely diminished. For instance, when subjects are asked to perform some activity (e.g., counting backwards) in the interval between list presentation and recall, the primacy effect is undiminished while the recency effect all but disappears.

It has also been found that the length of the distraction period has a definite impact on the magnitude of the recency effect. It has been concluded on the basis of these and other results that two distinct memory mechanisms are being utilized in order to remember the list items (see Chapter 4 for more details). The first is a long-term storage mechanism. The early list items make it into this long-term store because one is able to repeat them to oneself a few times after they have been presented. When a large number of items has been presented, however, subjects are no longer able to repeat the entire list before the next item appears. Thus, once the list has grown beyond a few items, fewer of the items make it into long-term storage. The items at the end of the list, on the other hand, are thought to be held in a short-term storage mechanism. Items seem to remain in this mechanism for only a few seconds before they fade. They can be refreshed through repetition, but if something prevents repetition they are quickly lost. Thus, you may have difficulty dialing a strange phone number after being asked to count backward because you were not able to repeat the number to yourself, but counting backwards has no effect on your ability to remember your own number, which is in long-term storage.

As you can see, measures of recall provide another useful way of testing cognitive theories. The contemporary use of recall measures is, in fact, a direct offshoot of Ebbinghaus' technique of learning to criterion (see Chapter 1) and constitutes one of the most popular methods for investigating cognitive processes – particularly those associated with learning and memory.

Aside from illustrating the use of reaction times and recall scores for making inferences about the inner workings of the cognitive system, these examples show just how ingenious researchers have had to be in order to generate quantified, objective, and replicable data that will corroborate their theories.

2.3.3 Controls and statistics

Contemporary cognitive psychologists, many of whom take their cues directly from such historical figures as Wundt, Ebbinghaus, and Tolman, have undertaken, with great success, a project of reverse engineering with regard to the human cognitive system. They have done it, moreover, guided by little more than stimuli and observable behavior. The standard psychology experiment involves a comparison between the quantified behaviors of groups of individuals under various conditions. It is a common practice in psychology, as in other experimental disciplines, to examine the effects of one or more independent variables on one or more dependent variables. For instance, in the context of a mental rotation experiment, the dependent variable is the time it takes to judge that two images are identical. The independent variable is the degree to which one of the images has been rotated relative to the other. If you will recall, according to one hypothesis (the instantaneous transformation hypothesis) the independent variable should have no effect on the dependent variable, and according to the other hypothesis (the continuous rotation hypothesis) the independent variable should have measurable effects on the dependent variable.

What we have not yet discussed is how psychologists deal with the tremendous variability in the performance levels of individual subjects. In the case of mental rotation, for instance, the length of time that it takes one person to rotate an item 90 degrees might be less than the time it takes for another person to rotate an item 45 degrees; unless, that is, the former is not well rested, or is about to attend a job interview, or is too cold, and so on. What is needed is a way of controlling for variability or, failing that, a way of mathematically factoring out whatever variability cannot be controlled.

One way of controlling for variability is to see to it that there are few relevant differences between the groups. That is to say, on average, each group being studied should be of about equal intelligence, equal age, equally well rested, and equal on any other metric that might affect the outcome of the experiment. One way of guaranteeing equality on all of these dimensions is to use the same experimental subjects as both the control group and the experimental group. That is to say, sometimes it is possible to use what is called a *within subjects design* instead of a *between subjects design*. For instance, in the context of an experimental study of the recency effect, one might measure the behavior of the very same subjects under both normal recall and distraction conditions.

A remaining concern, however, is that the order in which the two tasks are carried out might have some effect on the results. In order to mitigate this worry, one might *counterbalance* the presentation of the two tasks such that half of the subjects are required to perform the distractor task (e.g., counting backwards) prior to the normal recall task and the other half are required to perform the recall task first, then the distractor task. These are just some of the techniques that experimental psychologists have amassed in order to counteract the inherent variability of human behavior.

Just as a perfectly normal coin can sometimes be flipped twenty times in a row and come up heads every time, so too is it conceivable that what looks like an interesting behavioral result turns out to be an anomaly. The results of behavioral measurements sometimes vary in ways that are beyond the experimenter's control. Consider, for instance, the finding that the recency effect is diminished when subjects are asked to perform a distractor task between presentation of the last list item and recall of the list. How big a difference between the slopes of the tails of the serial position curves would be enough to conclude that this experimental manipulation has had a definite effect? It is entirely within the realm of possibility that an observed difference between the two conditions is a mere anomaly. The task of figuring out whether or not the manipulation of an independent variable (in this case the presence or absence of a distractor activity) had an definite effect on the dependent variable falls to statistics.

If you will recall from Chapter 1, Fechner was one of the first to use statistics in order to deal with uncontrollable variability. The field of mathematical statistics has advanced greatly since Fechner's time, however, and the statistical analysis of behavioral data now constitutes a tool that is as reliable as it is indispensable.

The populace often takes a pretty dim view of statistics. While much maligned, the use of statistics in order to test hypotheses has nevertheless become an exact science. It seems worth the effort to consider briefly why the good name of statistics has been sullied so. Some of the blame might be attributed to the fact that statistics easily fall into misuse when causal relationships are being inferred on the basis of correlations. For instance, if one were to study the population of an urban center, one would find a positive correlation between the rate of ice cream consumption and the amount of violence – that is, as ice cream consumption increases, so does violence. Is this correlation a reliable basis on which to infer a causal relationship? Clearly not. In this case, ice cream consumption does not cause violent behavior, nor is the converse the case; rather a third factor (namely, summer heat) seems to be the cause of the other two. Coupled with the occasional erroneous poll result, the fact that correlation data sometimes lead (when proper care is not taken) to incorrect conclusions seems to have done much to tarnish the image of statistics in the eyes of the populace.

Be this as it may, there is little cause for suspicion concerning the use of statistics in psychology. Indeed, although correlation data sometimes play an evidentiary role in psychology, the most widely used statistical tools are those that enable one to determine whether or not one or more independent variables had an effect on one or more dependent variables in a controlled experimental setting. As described above, this is usually done by comparing measurements of performance, either within or between groups of individuals. Thus, unlike in the case of the ice cream correlation, statistics don't dictate theory to the experimental psychologist; rather, one of the main things statistics tell the experimenter is whether or not the difference between two measurements was merely an anomaly. While an extended lesson in psychological statistics is not feasible, we can convey some sense for how statistics work.

Consider the time it takes to judge whether or not two figures are identical. Statistical techniques enable one to determine, quite precisely, the probability that the difference between two groups of response-time measurements (e.g., the average response time for a 45-degree transformation and a 90-degree transformation) is just random variation. One may reasonably conclude that some other factor (presumably the independent variable) is involved, with a very low probability that random variation is accounting for the observed difference.

A bit of reflection reveals what the central factors are that need to be taken into account. To start with, if one were to find a difference between the two groups of reaction time measurements, and if the groups consisted of only three measurements apiece, such results wouldn't lend persuasive support to the mental rotation theory. On the other hand, such a difference would be more persuasive if the averages reflected 10,000 measurements per group. The number of separate measurements that figure in an average measurement is something that must be and *is* taken into account by modern statistical techniques.

Notice also that the degree to which measurements vary from the average measurement is of some importance as well. For instance, if every one of 100 people took exactly 0.5 seconds to determine that two images are alike when one has been rotated 45 degrees and exactly 1 second when one of the images has been rotated 90 degrees, we would have a pretty informative result. On the other hand, if the time to make such judgments varied from 0.1 to 0.8 seconds in the first case and 0.25 to 0.95 seconds in the second case, what we should conclude becomes far less clear. Thus, an informative statistical analysis must take into account the amount of deviation from the average as well.

With the help of equations that take into account these and other factors, one can determine quite precisely the probability that one's experimental manipulation had an effect. In most sorts of psychological studies, if your statistics reveal that the chance that your result is due to random variation is less than 5 percent, your hypothesis is taken to be affirmed. In such cases, the difference between the two groups is considered *statistically significant*. Of course, researchers are happier when the probability that random variation is responsible for their results is far less than 5 percent, and further support can be lent to a set of findings once they have been replicated.

With the help of statistics, psychologists have been able to make theirs an experimental science in the truest sense. In addition to objectivity, quantifiability, and replicability, they are able to manipulate independent variables (e.g., degrees of transformation, or the length of distractor period in our examples) and determine whether or not such manipulations have an effect upon a dependent variable (e.g., time to decide whether two images are alike, or the rate at which items toward the end of a list are recalled). Their ever-growing bag of tricks is giving experimental psychologists unprecedented insight into the inner workings of the human cognitive system.

2.4 COGNITIVE NEUROSCIENCE

One of the main areas of cross-fertilization and interdisciplinary synthesis in cognitive science lies at the intersection of psychology and neuroscience. Whereas psychologists have done a remarkable job of providing a functional breakdown of the cognitive system, and neuroscientists have been able to teach us about the micro- and macroscopic structure of the brain, the cognitive neuroscientist (who is usually a psychologist or a neuroscientist by training) is telling us how the cognitive functions revealed by psychology map onto the anatomical structures studied by neuroscience.

2.4.1 Neuropsychology

One age-old method for correlating cognitive functions and anatomical structures is through the study of individuals with some form of detectable brain damage (e.g., following surgery, stroke, excessive alcohol consumption, accidents, gunshot wounds, and so on) or some other pathology (e.g., schizophrenia, Parkinson's disease, autism, etc.). Contemporary neuropsychology is a continuation of the research program begun by researchers like Broca and Wernicke in the nineteenth century. Contemporary neuropsychologists, however, have at their disposal the additional tools of experimental psychology.

A common technique employed by early neuropsychologists was to group individuals into categories of pathology according to the family of symptoms they exhibited and to see what neural structures could be associated with these pathologies. The emphasis has shifted in recent years, however, from associating cognitive deficits with neural pathologies to *dissociating* particular cognitive deficits from one another (Ellis and Young 1988). This enables researchers to reach conclusions about the independence of various cognitive functions. For instance, if it were found that an individual or group of individuals suffered brain damage that resulted in their being unable to recognize faces (called *prosopagnosia*) while they remained fully capable of recognizing tools, we would have some basis for thinking that the two functions are carried out by separate neural mechanisms. This might be an erroneous conclusion, however, considering that recognizing faces requires more subtlety than recognizing tools. For instance, it is entirely possible that a person who had very low visual acuity would exhibit these same symptoms (e.g., such a person might be able to discriminate a hammer from a saw but not be able to distinguish Cary Grant from Humphrey Bogart).

What would make the case for functional independence stronger would be if the converse deficit were also observed. That is to say, the claim of functional independence would be more persuasive if some individuals had difficulty recognizing faces (and not tools) while others had difficulty recognizing tools (and not faces). While not infallible, instances of a *double dissociation* are generally viewed as providing compelling evidence that two cognitive functions are carried out by independent mechanisms.

In order to understand the precise nature of a functional deficit, one has to heed the clues offered by behavior. Neuropsychologists have thus either devised their own methods for studying cognitive functions or they have co-opted the techniques employed by cognitive psychologists. As an illustration of the former, imagine that you are studying two individuals who seem, on cursory examination, to suffer from some form of attention deficit. To study the precise nature of their respective deficits, you might employ as one of your tools the Rey figure (see Figure 2.3).

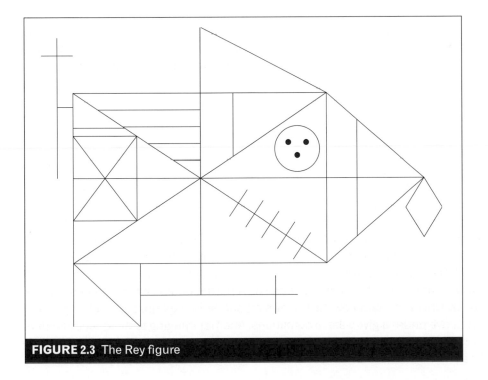

FIGURE 2.3 The Rey figure

When you ask the two individuals to copy the figure with the aid of pencil and paper, you notice that one is able to accurately depict the low-level features of the diagram while erring in terms of the spatial arrangement of these features. The other has the opposite propensity: she creates an accurate portrayal of the arrangement of the features while overlooking many of the details. On this basis, you might tentatively hypothesize that one is impaired in her ability to attend to local features of a scene while the other is impaired in her ability to attend to global features. The behavior of the latter might, however, stem from poor visual acuity, so a test of visual acuity might be administered to this individual. Likewise, in the former case, some other deficit might account for the poor global organization of the diagram. For instance, perhaps an impairment in short-term memory (discussed above and in Chapter 4) is responsible. Thus, for each individual, a battery of tests should be used in order to isolate the precise nature of her cognitive deficit. If, after this battery of tests has been administered, the original hypotheses remain credible, one will have thereby discovered an important double-dissociation (i.e., a double dissociation between global and local attention mechanisms).

Notice that there is a big difference between this kind of behavioral analysis and the kind carried out in cognitive psychology. Instead of using just a few behavioral measures to study a large group of individuals, a large number of behavioral measures is used in the study of single individuals. There are cases, however, where neuropsychologists adopt the former approach – in fact they borrow many of the techniques from cognitive psychologists.

The techniques of behavioral experimentation and statistical analysis pioneered by cognitive psychologists can be especially useful when one is interested in studying large, rather well-defined populations of pathological individuals. One application of the measurement techniques, controls, and statistical analyses supplied by cognitive psychology is to compare the performance of a clinical population with that of the population at large. For instance, a comparison of the serial position curve for Alzheimer's patients with the serial position curve of the rest of the population might reveal a statistically significant difference in the size of the primacy component between the two groups. Insofar as the recency component has been vindicated on independent grounds as an indicator of long-term memory functioning, one thereby has some reason to believe that these individuals suffer from an impairment to long-term memory. Moreover, one can also compare levels of performance between clinical populations in order to doubly dissociate cognitive functions.

2.4.2 Functional neuroimaging

Advances in imaging technology have made it possible to study the levels of neural activity in the brains of individuals as they carry out some task. Positron emission tomography (PET), for instance, distinguishes between different parts of the brain based on the rate of blood flow to particular regions. In general, blood flow will increase as a particular part of the brain becomes more active. Thus, by tracking blood flow, PET allows researchers a glimpse into what parts of the brain are most active under a given set of conditions. Another imaging technique, functional magnetic resonance imaging (fMRI), tracks changes in oxygen concentration, though the rationale is much the same as in the case of PET. One of the exciting new strategies employed by cognitive neuroscientists involves pairing these sophisticated imaging technologies with carefully controlled behavioral experimentation in order to correlate anatomical structures and cognitive functions. In particular, cognitive neuroscientists have come to place great reliance upon a technique pioneered in the nineteenth century by F.C. Donders: the subtraction method (see Chapter 1).

If you recall, the essence of the subtraction method is to subtract a subject's reaction times on a simple task from their reaction times on a more complex task of which the simple task is a component. As it is used in functional neuroimaging research, it is levels of neural activity that one subtracts instead of reaction times. Suppose, for instance, you were interested in determining what part of the brain is responsible for the comprehension of linguistic stimuli. Obviously, as the brain activity of subjects is being measured, you would have them engage in some kind of task that involves language comprehension. But sentence comprehension requires the contribution of several other cognitive capacities as well – for example, those that underwrite basic visual processing and the recognition of letters, words, and grammatical constructions. In order to distinguish the heightened brain activity that correlates with language comprehension from that which is associated with these other processes, one might have subjects perform a task that taps all of the relevant processes *except* comprehension and then subtract the levels of activity that are detected under this condition from the levels of activity registered during comprehension. For instance, one might have subjects read sentences that are grammatically well formed but which have little or no meaning. These might include sentences that are semantically anomalous (e.g., "The broom ate the ball to the window") or sentences that contain pseudo-words (e.g., "The dwardums glipped the actiphale"). Mazoyer and colleagues (1993) carried out a study along these very lines. After subtracting brain activity (measured with PET technology) during comprehension of normal sentences from activity measured while reading either semantically anomalous sentences or sentences containing pseudo-words, they found that a particular region of the brain was more active in the former cases than in the latter. This region, named for Carl Wernicke, had, for independent reasons, long been thought to play an important role in language comprehension (see Chapter 1).

Thus, in addition to providing a nice illustration of functional neuroimaging at work, this study also illustrates two distinct ways in which cognitive science is a collaborative endeavor. First of all, we find in this case that techniques from two distinct disciplines, neuroscience and psychology, have been combined in order to determine the anatomical locus of an important cognitive capacity. Second, this is an instance where evidence gathered through the use of two very different techniques has converged in support of a single hypothesis.

2.5 COMPUTER SCIENCE

Computer science is another important contributor to cognitive science. As discussed in Chapter 1, there is a broad division in computer science between logic-inspired approaches to modeling cognition (traditional artificial intelligence) and those that glean their data from neuroscience (connectionism).

The former research program does not always have as its explicit goal the construction of systems that should be viewed as models of *human* cognitive processing. Sometimes the goal in traditional AI is merely to design a system that can perform some task. IBM's Deep Blue is a perfect example of this. The goal set for Deep Blue is to defeat the world's greatest chess players, plain and simple. It is therefore of little consequence that Deep Blue happens not to play chess in a manner that mimics how a human plays chess. In such cases, there is only one condition that needs to be satisfied in order for the model to be considered a success – the model must meet the performance goals set for it. AI researchers refer to this as the *sufficiency constraint*; for example, beating the best chess player in the world, as it did recently, is sufficient for Deep Blue to have attained the goals of its programmers.

Oftentimes, however, those constructing a given computational system will have a more interdisciplinary goal in mind – that is, they are interested in modeling some aspect of cognitive processing. At one extreme of the modeling continuum are systems designed to model high-level cognitive processes like short-term memory, mental imagery, or language comprehension. At the other extreme are systems designed with the intent of modeling neurophysiological processes. While the former sort of model emanates from both traditional AI and connectionist camps, the latter (for obvious reasons) are usually of the connectionist variety. Indeed, any time connectionist systems are used in order to model what we are calling high-level processes, they do so in a manner that has at least the outward appearance of biological plausibility. For this reason, connectionism is viewed as one of the most exciting new developments in cognitive science – it attempts to bridge the gap between high-level and low-level explanations of cognitive processing.

The emphasis on plausibility brings a new set of constraints to bear on modeling efforts. That is, when attempting to model some aspect of cognitive processing, there are more restrictive success conditions than the mere sufficiency constraint. A given model must not only suffice to execute some task, but also enjoy either psychological or biological plausibility. Whether or not a model exhibits biological plausibility will depend upon the degree to which it incorporates known principles of neuroanatomy and neurophysiology. A good measure of psychological plausibility, on the other hand, will be the degree to which it behaves as a human subject would under various homologous conditions. Generally speaking, computational models are crafted in order to determine whether or not a particular theory is plausible – that is, whether or not it generates the kind of data that intuition says it should. In other words, many models are created in accordance with the tenets of prescriptive computationalism (see Chapter 1). Of course, to the extent that one considers the brain to be a computational system, such models might also be viewed in terms of the tenets of descriptive computationalism. While it seems a bit strange to force connectionism into this latter mold, there is nothing, in principle, to prevent it (see Clark 1990 for one such attempt).

Another class of models has been created with an interdisciplinary goal in mind, though the emphasis is not on biological or psychological plausibility, at least not in the empirical sense. That is to say, these models are designed in order to challenge purported a priori knowledge claims that some philosophers have advanced concerning such matters as whether or not a device that does not engage in formal (i.e., logic-like) processing can exhibit what many philosophers view as essential characteristics of mentality. In such cases, it seems to be the sufficiency constraint that once again holds sway.

Among proponents of the symbolic paradigm, the production system architecture remains one of the most popular modeling tools. In order, therefore, to provide a more in-depth look at the techniques of traditional AI, we turn now to a discussion of production systems.

2.5.1 Production systems and expert systems

Not unlike humans, production systems have a long-term and a short-term memory system. In short-term memory, production systems hold sentence-like representations of, among other things, the actual state of the world and the desired state of the world. They are able to evaluate the consequences of various alterations to the world through the application of certain inference rules (stored in long-term memory) and determine which of these alterations will bring them closer to their goal (Congdon and Laird 1997).

For instance, a production system might represent the positions of three blocks (let us call them A, B, and C) relative to each other and to a table. Specifically, it might represent, with the help of the following formulas, the fact that block A is on top of block B and that nothing is atop either A or C:

Ontop <A, B>
Ontop <B, Table>
Ontop <C, Table>
Empty <A>
Empty <C>

It might have as its goal the following state of affairs:

Ontop <C, A>

By applying certain operations, production systems can determine what sequence of actions will lead to a particular goal state. For instance, our hypothetical production system might have an operation called "Move <x, y>." "Move" is referred to as an *operator*; it takes two arguments (x and y) which, when applied, update the contents of short-term memory to reflect the fact that a block which has been moved is now on top of whatever surface it was moved to, that the surface from which it was moved is now vacant, and so on. Through repeated applications of the Move <x, y> operation, our hypothetical production system might determine the goal state can be reached by moving block B to the table and block C atop block A.

Whereas operations contain information about the consequences of alterations, a further set of rules, called productions, which have the form of "if . . . then . . ." statements. Certain productions enable a determination of which operations contained in long-term memory *can*, given the contents of short-term memory, be applied in a given situation. There are also productions that determine which of the licensed operations is the most appropriate to apply, and, on this basis, which shall be applied.

For instance, in the Dump <x, y> operation, the operator "Dump" might take as one of its arguments the name of a container and as the other argument the name of container's contents.

Thus, if there is no container represented in short-term memory, the *operator proposal* productions would not return the Dump <x, y> operation as one that can be applied in this situation. Of the (usually many) operations that can be applied, a further set of *operator comparison* productions determines, either through random choice or based upon some learned or programmed preference, which of these will be likely to bring the system closer to its goal. Indeed, one powerful feature of production systems is that they are able to remember which operations, or sequence thereof, brought about the desired result under similar conditions in the past. Finally, the *operator execution* productions implement the operation that was output by the operator comparison process.

In addition to reasoning forwards, from the actual state of affairs to the desired state, production systems are also able to reason backwards. This is important because the tree of possibilities tends to branch in myriad ways as one thinks forward in time. Thus, rather than searching each of the tremendous number of branching possibilities for one that leads to a goal, production systems are able to work in the opposite direction. That is, they might consider which actions would constitute an immediate cause of the desired state, which actions would bring about *this* cause, and so on until, to quote someone who described just such a process centuries earlier, "some cause is reached that lies within [its] power" (Hobbes 1988 [1651], p. 20).

Expert systems are one of the more highly regarded offshoots of the production system approach to modeling cognition. They are called *expert* systems because they embody, in the form rules which are the functional equivalent of operations, the knowledge of experts. For instance, an expert in auto repair might know that if a car is backfiring then the timing should be adjusted. This and countless other bits of knowledge can be encoded in the form of rules. After sufficient information has been incorporated into an expert system, this storehouse of knowledge can then be tapped (with the help of built-in reasoning mechanisms embodied by a set of production-like rules) by experts and non-experts alike. For instance, an auto repair expert system might prompt a user to enter a variety of facts with a set of questions like this one:

> Does the car start? *Yes.*
> Is there any loss of power? *Yes.*
> Does the engine backfire? *No.*
> Is there much smoke coming out of the exhaust? *No.*
> Is the end of the tailpipe oily? *No.*
> Have the wires, plugs, and distributor been replaced recently? *No.*
> Recommendation: Replace wires, plugs, and distributor.

Expert systems and other variations on the knowledge-as-rules approach have proven to be quite useful. As a result, they have been constructed in order to embody the wisdom of experts in any of a great many fields. In fact, a project to incorporate both common-sense and expert knowledge into one truly massive system (with millions of rules) has been undertaken by AI pioneer Douglas Lenat and his colleagues at Cycorp. The approach taken by Cycorp is to hire individuals (who are given the impressive title of Ontological Engineers) to add their knowledge to this truly massive system.

2.5.2 The return of connectionism

Recent advances in connectionist modeling have precipitated a new wave of modeling research. As noted in Chapter 1, in order to answer the charges leveled against connectionism by Minsky and Papert (1969), new learning algorithms had to be devised. One of the most powerful of these (indeed, the very backbone of much contemporary connectionist modeling) is the *back-propagation* learning algorithm. This algorithm enables the construction of networks that have one or more layers of units intervening between the input and output layers.

Back-propagation works like certain other learning algorithms in that connection strengths are modified based upon a comparison between the actual activation levels of the output units and the desired activation levels – a process that yields what is called an *error signal*. Earlier techniques modified the strengths of the connections between input units and output units as a function of this error signal. In other words, the contribution of each input unit to error signal for a given output unit was assessed and the connection strengths were strengthened or weakened accordingly. The back-propagation algorithm works in a similar manner, but with one major twist. As with earlier algorithms, the back-propagation algorithm enables an individual unit's contribution to the error signal to be assessed, and the result is a subtle strengthening or weakening of that unit's connections to the output layer. What is different in the case of back-propagation, however, is that the contribution to the error signal made by a unit once-removed, twice-removed, and so on, can be determined and the strengths of its connections to the next layer of units can be modified accordingly. That is to say, with back-propagation the error signal propagates back through multiple layers of units (the units intervening between input and output layers are known as *hidden* units) – hence the name *back-propagation*.

The back-propagation algorithm was, unlike its predecessor, found to be powerful enough to handle any input/output mapping that could be thrown at it. As a result, the 1980s saw the renewal of interest in connectionism and the proliferation of connectionist research in cognitive science. In addition, due to the complexity of the underlying causes of network behavior, the development of statistical techniques for analyzing the internal states and structure of trained connectionist networks has since become a science unto itself. This, in turn, has given rise to new ways of thinking about the mind.

2.6 THE BRAIN REVISITED

In the coming chapters, we will highlight some of the most important findings about human cognition that have been brought to light by the various disciplines that are constitutive of contemporary cognitive science. The next several chapters are each devoted to the inter-disciplinary study of such central cognitive functions as perception, memory, reasoning, action, and language. As we shall be referring throughout to a variety of anatomical stuctures, a bit of additional grounding in neuroscience should prove helpful.

2.6.1 Perception/action cycles

Try the following experiment. As you read this text, move your head around, forward and back, left and right. Despite the fact that your head is moving about, if you are anything like the rest of us, you have an amazing ability to compensate for this movement and thus keep your eyes focused on the text.

What, exactly, is going on in your brain as it engages in this kind of activity? The attempt to supply an explanation of the neural processes underwriting this ability happens to be one of the success stories of neuroscience. This is also a case in which the solution devised by mother nature is not unlike one that an engineer might come up with. A reasonable engineering solution would be to measure head movement and, on the basis of this measurement, calculate the precise eye movements that would need to be made in order to compensate. In humans, the hardware for measuring head movement is located in the inner ear and takes the form of three semicircular canals, each of which is neatly aligned along one of the three spatial dimensions. Each canal is filled with fluid that moves along its length in the direction opposite to that in which the canal is moving. The insides of these canals are also lined with sensitive hairs that connect to nerve cells. The nerve cells fire in a certain pattern depending on which way those hairs are bent by the moving fluid. These signals travel via two separate bundles of nerve cells (i.e., *nuclei*) before reaching the muscles which control eye movement. The nuclei determine which set of commands should be sent to the eye muscles in order to compensate for particular head movements. Taken together, the entire circuit gives rise to what is called the *vestibulo-occular reflex.*

To use the terminology of nineteenth-century neurologist David Hughlings Jackson, this entire circuit can be viewed as a *perception/action cycle* (see Jackson 1866, 1875a, 1875b, 1898, 1915). According to Jackson, these cycles supply the building blocks for cognition. Biological organisms are set up to sense their environment and react to it. Perception/action cycles can be as simple and inflexible as a knee-jerk reflex or as complex and improvisational as the trip to the market that follows the realization that one is out of milk. One seeming mark of so-called *higher* creatures like ourselves is that our behavior is governed by perception/action cycles that are more flexible than programmatic – though, to be sure, the more complex perception/action cycles will often depend upon the proper functioning of the simpler ones (e.g., the vestibulo-occular reflex).

This view meshes nicely with the widely accepted contention that the brain evolved from the inside out, rather like an unfolding flower. That is, the oldest parts of the brain seem to be buried mostly deeply beneath its surface. In general, the more automatic and pre-programmed functions such as the regulation of breathing and pulmonary activity are accomplished by the oldest, inner parts of the brain, while the most flexible determinants of behavior can be localized to the brain's outermost surface.

Thus, one way to functionally decompose the brain is through the study of these perception/action circuits, piled one atop the other. The frontal lobes, for instance, can be understood as supporting longer perception/action cycles by holding representations in short-term, or working memory. In concert with other mechanisms, working memory enables us to envision and react to hypothetical situations rather than reacting to the stimuli impinging on us from the immediate environment. It enables us to react to the future instead of just to the present. Suppose, for instance, you desire a raise. Before requesting one, you would probably consider various scenarios (e.g., demanding, begging, hinting, etc.). On this basis, you could determine which scenario would most likely to bring you closer to your goal of getting a raise.

Notice that the notion of perception/action cycles does not imply a clean separation between the two in time, so that we first perceive, then act. We are both perceiving and acting all the time, and we often act in order to perceive (when we direct our eyes, for instance) and perceive in order to act (e.g., when navigating through an unfamiliar space).

One nice feature of the perception/action-cycle framework for understanding the brain and nervous system is that it accounts for the ability of humans and other organisms to continue functioning despite severe neurological trauma. One might, for instance, suffer damage to those mechanisms that support planned responses while nevertheless remaining fully capable of recognizing and consuming food, directing eye gaze, regulating blood pressure and internal temperature, and so on. A limitation of this framework, however, is that it bites off a bit more than scientists can chew in one sitting. To study the circuit that gives rise to planned responses, for instance, one would have to study, among systems, those responsible for perception, memory, reasoning, language processing, and motor control. Thus, before we can understand how these systems collectively conspire to give rise to planned behaviors, we must understand each individually. In order to understand them individually, moreover, we may have to understand the contributions made by numerous subsidiary mechanisms (see Bechtel and Richardson 1993).

2.6.2 Localization of function

The project of breaking the cognitive system down into its functional components and identifying the neural loci at which these functions are carried out is, for the most part, continuous with a line of research instigated by Gall, Brodmann, and Broca (see Chapter 1). In the remainder of this chapter, we will introduce you to some of the basics of what has been discovered in the ensuing decades.

One part of the brain with which we are all familiar is its outermost surface, the cortex. This is the wrinkled gray sheet which covers the top and sides of the brain. The cortex itself is approximately 1.5 to 3 mm thick. Sheets of cortex can be divided into six cell layers, although some portions of cortex will have fewer. With the naked eye, one can see that the size and complexity of the cortex is something that sets humans apart from other animals – save for a few such as dolphins and killer whales. The grooves in this folded sheet of nervous tissue are known as *sulci* (singular: *sulcus*) and the raised parts in between the sulci are referred to as *gyri* (singular: *gyrus*). The human cortex is heavily folded, so it has far more surface area than it would if it were perfectly smooth.

The gyri and sulci of the brain are largely constant from one human brain to the next, although they can vary from individual to individual in terms of their precise spatial properties and relationships. The most prominent feature of the human cortex is its separation into two distinct halves, or *hemispheres*. Another prominent feature is the central sulcus, which runs in an almost vertical fashion through the top half of the cortex when viewed from the side (see Figure 2.4).

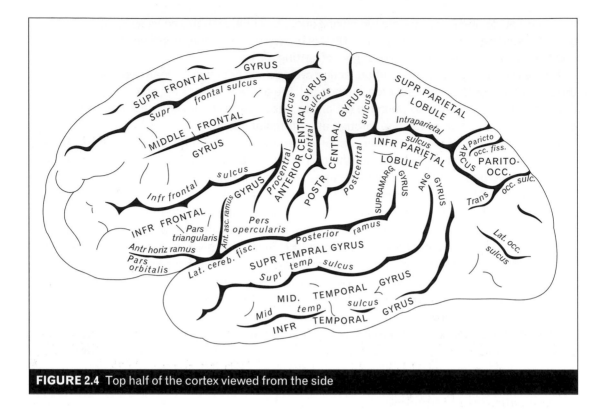

FIGURE 2.4 Top half of the cortex viewed from the side

As a rule of thumb, you can think of the central sulcus as the dividing line between the part of the cortex devoted mainly to perception (the rearward, or *posterior* part of the cortex) and the part devoted mainly to action (the frontal, or *anterior* part of the cortex).

The central sulcus and the other main sulci serve to divide the cortex up into distinct lobes (Figure 2.5), and each of these seems to have a particular class of functions associated with it. The occipital lobes, at the very back of the brain, are primarily devoted to visual perception. Anterior and superior to (i.e., upwards from) the occipital lobes we find the parietal lobes, which are devoted to representing the body and its relation to other objects in the environment (for more on perception, see Chapter 3). Just posterior to the central sulcus, for instance, are several maps of the body (discussed further below), each of which represents a different set of properties of the body (e.g., limb position, temperature, pain, and so on). Moving anterior and inferior (downward) from the occipital lobes, we find the temporal lobes, which are the main locus of such functions as memory, object recognition, and emotion. Particularly important for memory is the *hippocampus*, a structure buried beneath the surface of the lower part of the temporal lobe (for more on memory, see Chapter 4).

Directly anterior to the central sulcus is the motor cortex, which is responsible for executing bodily movements. Continuing to move forward from there, we find the prefrontal cortex, which is involved in the planning and execution of complex actions such as speaking (for more on action, see Chapter 5). The bottom part of the frontal cortex, known as the orbitofrontal cortex

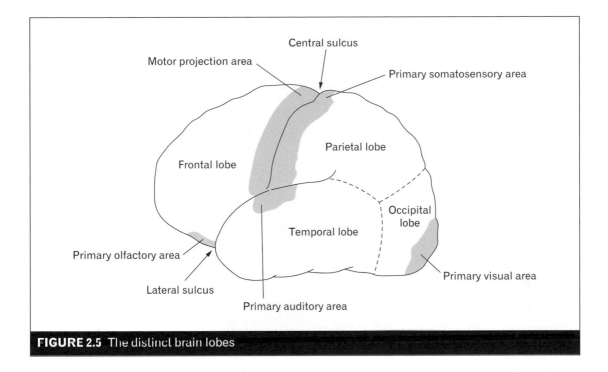

Central sulcus

Motor projection area

Primary somatosensory area

Parietal lobe

Frontal lobe

Occipital lobe

Temporal lobe

Primary olfactory area

Primary visual area

Lateral sulcus

Primary auditory area

FIGURE 2.5 The distinct brain lobes

because it lies just above the orbits of the eyes, seems to be important for the regulation of social behavior and for attaching emotional significance to particular actions or outcomes.

Another feature of the brain clearly visible with the naked eye is the *cerebellum* (Figure 2.6). This large structure is tucked beneath the occipital lobe and nestled against the brainstem. Initially the cerebellum was thought to be responsible for coordinating movements, since people with cerebellar damage seemed to lack coordination. Recently, the cerebellum has come to be viewed as a key player in the control of balance and the calibration of eye movement reflexes (including the vestibulo-occular reflex). Moreover, the cerebellum may even play a prominent role in higher cognitive functions (see Chapter 4).

Removing the two cerebral hemispheres and the cerebellum would reveal a pair of egg-shaped structures. These are the important bundles of nuclei known collectively as the *thalamus*. Most of the larger thalamic nuclei act as relays for information traveling from the sensory organs to the various areas of sensory cortex noted above.

2.6.3 Topographic maps

Several areas of the brain and spinal cord are organized in a topographic fashion. A simple example of this is the visual cortex. On the basis of single-cell recordings and functional neuro-imaging, it has been discovered that there is a neat mapping between the spatial relationships among cells in the retina (the sensory surface at the back of the eye) and cells that register input

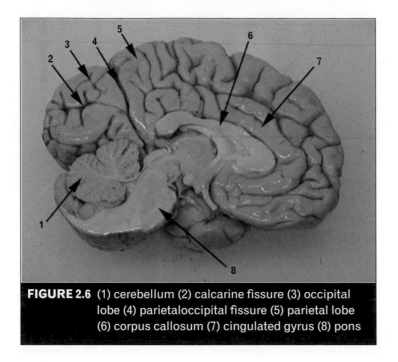

FIGURE 2.6 (1) cerebellum (2) calcarine fissure (3) occipital lobe (4) parietaloccipital fissure (5) parietal lobe (6) corpus callosum (7) cingulated gyrus (8) pons

from the retina – not unlike how a road map of a state preserves the relative spatial locations of cities. Thus, this part of the visual cortex has a retinotopic organization. Areas of the cortex that represent touch and limb position have what is known as a somatotopic organization. That is, the spatial relationships among parts of the body map onto spatial relationships among parts of the cortex that represent those parts of the body. There are also tonotopic maps in the auditory cortex of the temporal lobe. The motor cortex has a similar organization.

It was initially thought that these maps remained quite constant throughout the life of the individual. It has recently been shown, however, that parts of the maps can grow or shrink, roughly depending on the amount of use the corresponding sensory organ happens to get. For instance, if you use your toes a great deal (perhaps to feel for clams in the sand), the portion of the map devoted to processing sensory and motor information about the toes will come to occupy larger portions of the sensory and motor maps.

It is worth noting that connectionist systems have been constructed that also self-organize into topographic maps. Like cortical maps, these connectionist networks, called *Kohonen maps*, expand the portion of the map devoted to representing a particular kind of input depending upon the frequency with which such inputs are encountered. Kohonen maps are among the most biologically plausible connectionist systems in that they can be constructed using only a Hebbian learning function (see Chapter 1).

2.6.4 Neurons and how they communicate

The brain is made up of approximately 10^{11} individual cells, or *neurons*, which come in several varieties (Figure 2.7).

Differences aside, neurons have a few common features. The first is the cell body, where all the important metabolic activities take place. Branching out from the body are two different types of projection. There are *dendrites*, through which a neuron receives excitation or inhibition from other neurons, and the *axon*, which conducts an electrical (really electrochemical) pulse down its length and which terminates at the *synaptic terminal*. The terminal is where the axon meets the dendrite of another neuron, a junction known as the *synapse*. There is actually a minute space, or *cleft*, separating axon and dendrite. When an electrical pulse reaches the synaptic terminal, it generally responds by releasing chemicals (called *neurotransmitters*) into the synaptic cleft (Figure 2.8). When these chemicals are absorbed by the connecting dendrite, the corresponding neuron becomes either more positively or more negatively charged (depending on the type of neurotransmitter).

Because of their diversity and the important role they play in cognitive functioning, the study of neurotransmitters has become a discipline unto itself in recent years. One of the most important findings has been that abnormal levels of particular neurotransmitters seem to accompany certain forms of cognitive or motor dysfunction. Individuals with Parkinson's disease, for instance, have been found to have low levels of the neurotransmitter dopamine due to a loss of dopamine-producing neurons. Similarly, unusually low levels of the neurotransmitter serotonin may play a role in certain forms of depression. Schizophrenia, on the other hand, is thought to involve an excess of dopamine. Thus, one way in which these disorders have been treated is by altering either the amount of a particular type of neurotransmitter that is produced or the degree to which it is absorbed by neurons at the synapse. On a related note, another recent discovery about neurotransmitters is that certain mind-altering substances seem to work by altering neurotransmitter concentration or absorption. LSD, for instance, alters the absorption of serotonin, while cocaine effectively increases the concentration of dopamine.

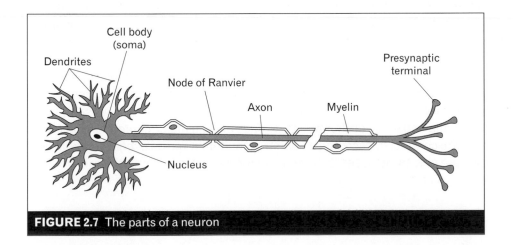

FIGURE 2.7 The parts of a neuron

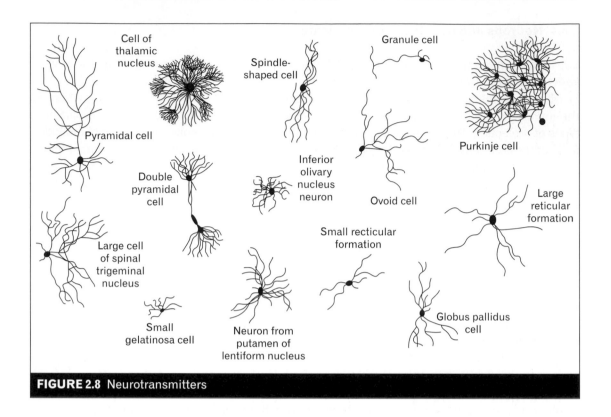

FIGURE 2.8 Neurotransmitters

At the interface with the environment are several different kinds of receptor neurons which connect, ultimately, to the sensory areas of the brain. Some of these, *mechanoreceptors*, respond to a particular sort of tissue distortion; others, *chemoreceptors*, respond to the presence of particular chemicals; and still others, *thermoreceptors*, respond to variations in temperature. Much of what we are aware of through the sense of touch is due to the activity of mechanoreceptors. There are mechanoreceptors, for instance, that respond to pressure on the skin, the stretch of a muscle (which provides information about limb position), or the movement of a hair (not unlike those in the semicircular canal discussed earlier). There are also various receptors which, when activated by extremes of temperature, tissue damage, or noxious chemicals, give rise to sensations of pain. Sensations of smell and taste depend upon the functioning of chemoreceptors, and the activity of photoreceptors (cells known as *rods* and *cones* that respond to the presence of light) give rise to visual sensations.

At the other side of the organism/environment interface are the motor neurons which cause the different muscles to contract by secreting a neurotransmitter known as *acetylcholine*. In general, motor neurons are able to increases the amount of force exerted by a muscle by increasing its rate of firing.

3 Perception

3.1 INTRODUCTION

Perception is the gateway to cognition. The first and most fundamental tasks of cognitive systems are to register, transform, and act on sensory inputs. Furthermore, many cognitive functions are continuously regulated by the sensory consequences of actions. In a very real sense, an understanding of cognition depends on an understanding of the sensory processes that drive it.

In the context of modern cognitive science, it is easy to overlook the formidable tasks faced, and so effortlessly mastered, by sensory processing. The task of sensory systems is to provide a faithful representation of biologically relevant events in the external environment. In most cases, the raw signals transduced by receptors seem woefully inadequate to this task and far removed from the complex structures in the world that give rise to them. Yet our sensory systems all contrive, by subtle and complex operations, to create efficient and informative representations of that world.

The study of perception in cognitive science involves the study of the contributions of the cognitive system in generating the way the world appears to us. It is a gross mischaracterization to say that we simply open our eyes and take it all in; what we are in contact with is a constructed product of many different brain processes. This chapter explores issues concerning the contribution of cognition to the creation of the perceptual appearance of the world.

3.2 THE NEUROPHYSIOLOGY OF THE SENSES

The nervous system meets the world with a diverse array of sensory neurons, light-sensitive cells in the eye's retina, pressure-sensitive cells in the ear's cochlea, motion-sensitive cells in the vestibular system. These cells accomplish something called "transduction," that is, transferring energy from one form to another, usually for some purpose. The tiny hair cells in the vestibular canals transduce simple mechanical friction (the movement of the fluid against the cell) into the brain's favorite form of energy: electrochemical signals. The cone cells in the retina transduce light energy of certain wavelengths into another kind of neural signal. Other, temperature-sensitive, cells transduce heat energy into neural firings. These receptor cells have evolved over time to be maximally sensitive to their special physical parameter, whether it is light, pressure, or certain chemicals, in the case of taste and smell. Our brains can receive information only about those properties of the world that causally impinge upon its transducers. We lack, for instance, cells that are capable of transducing light in the ultraviolet frequency range. Transducing receptor cells sensitive to other properties in the world might produce a different sort of higher-level cognitive structure, and would certainly produce a different sort of mental life from the one we now have.

3.2.1 The neurophysiology of vision

Light enters the cornea then is focused by the lens and projected to the back of the eye, where it contacts the eye's sheet of receptors, the retina. The lens inverts the incoming image, so that it is upside-down when it strikes the retina, the image is reinverted by higher visual processes so that we do not see the world upside down. The retina contains photoreceptors that transduce the incoming light energy into electrical signals that are then sent up the optic nerve to higher brain centers that eventually produce the image that we experience (see Figure 3.1).

There are two types of photoreceptors in the retina, called rods and cones because of their shape. Cones are responsible for our color and daylight vision, and are concentrated in the fovea, the part of the retina that produces the high-focus center of our visual field. Cones are also primarily responsible for our ability to perceive form. Rods on the other hand are specialized for night vision and are located mainly around the periphery of the retina, and hence are responsible mainly for peripheral vision (see Figure 3.2). The output of the rods and cones eventually reaches retinal ganglion cells, which are the output cells for the retina. Their axons form the optic nerve, which exits the back of the eyeball, transmitting information to higher brain centers.

Our field of vision contains an area where the fields of view of the two eyes overlap, known as the binocular zone, along with areas on either side of it that are seen only by one eye, the monocular zones (see Figure 3.3). For instance, at the far right of your visual field is the right monocular zone, which is seen only by the right eye. Each eye's field of view has a blind spot, caused by the fact that there are no rods or cones at the place where the axons of the retinal ganglion cells converge, forming the optic nerve. In section 3.4 we discuss the question of why we do not perceive a hole or dark spot in our visual field where the blind spot is and examine some of the scientific and philosophical issues this question raises.

The primary pathway of the axons of the ganglion cells leaving the eye enters the lateral geniculate nucleus (LGN) of the thalamus. There are two types of ganglion cells: small parvo cells whose axons enervate the upper layers of the LGN, and large magno cells whose axons enervate the lower layers of the LGN. From there, processing moves to the cortex at the back of the brain, the occipital lobe. This cortical area has been subdivided by anatomists into several

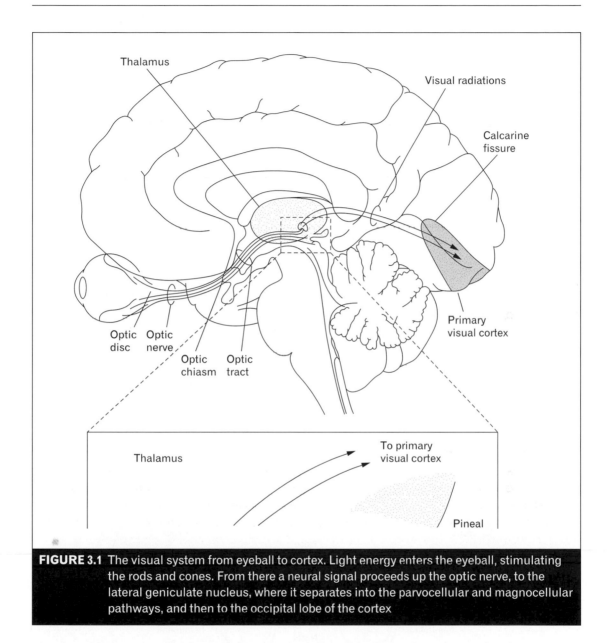

FIGURE 3.1 The visual system from eyeball to cortex. Light energy enters the eyeball, stimulating the rods and cones. From there a neural signal proceeds up the optic nerve, to the lateral geniculate nucleus, where it separates into the parvocellular and magnocellular pathways, and then to the occipital lobe of the cortex

functional areas, known as V1, V2, V3, V3a, and V4 (see Figure 3.4). These visual areas are retinotopically organized, which means roughly that they are maps of the retina. More informatively, it means that adjacent neurons in, say, V1 are receiving information from adjacent areas of the visual field. Area V1 seems to be specialized primarily for the detection of edges of objects. Research on what tasks each of the other cortical visual areas performs is under way at present. There is some evidence that V4, for instance, specializes in color vision (Zeki 1993).

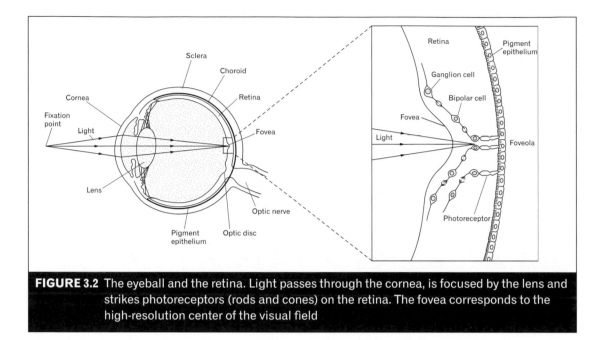

FIGURE 3.2 The eyeball and the retina. Light passes through the cornea, is focused by the lens and strikes photoreceptors (rods and cones) on the retina. The fovea corresponds to the high-resolution center of the visual field

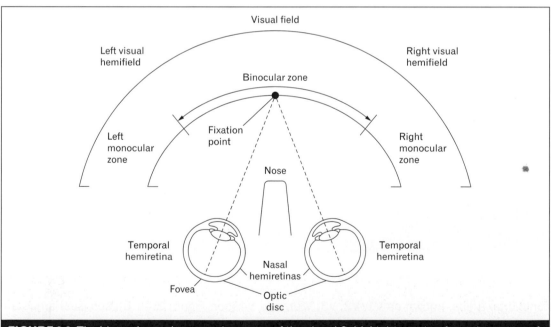

FIGURE 3.3 The binocular and monocular zones of the visual field. Light coming from the center of the visual field strikes the retinas of both eyes, whereas light coming from the edges of the visual field is detected only by a single retina. Light coming from the right side of the monocular zone strikes the left sides of both retinas

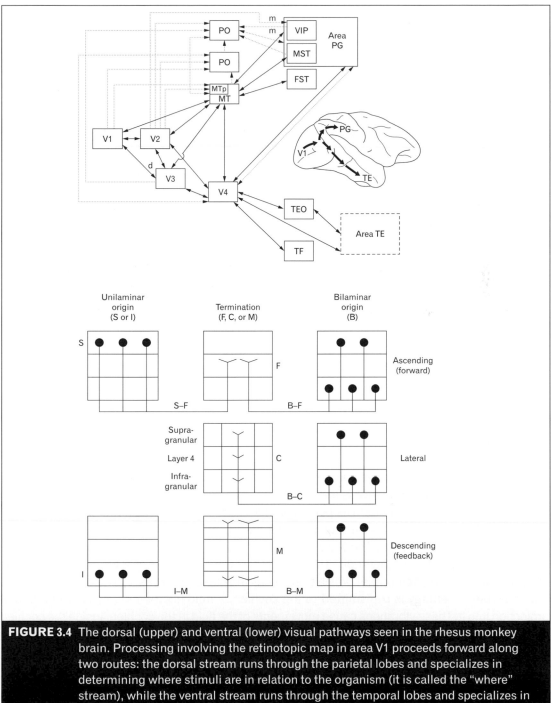

FIGURE 3.4 The dorsal (upper) and ventral (lower) visual pathways seen in the rhesus monkey brain. Processing involving the retinotopic map in area V1 proceeds forward along two routes: the dorsal stream runs through the parietal lobes and specializes in determining where stimuli are in relation to the organism (it is called the "where" stream), while the ventral stream runs through the temporal lobes and specializes in the identification of objects (it is called the "what" stream). (See the box on "The what and where streams" on p. 86.)

When all of these areas are understood, however, a daunting problem still remains: what we are visually aware of is the combination of the work done by all of these areas. How does the brain recombine the output of all these areas into a single, coherent visual scene? This is a version of what has come to be called the binding problem; see Chapter 7 on Consciousness for a fuller discussion of it.

THE WHAT AND WHERE STREAMS

One of the most important and well-documented findings of recent years has been the presence of two separate routes of visual processing leaving the occipital lobe, where visual information first enters the cortex (Ungerleider and Mishkin 1982). These routes have been called the "what" stream and the "where" stream; the "what" stream primarily serves the function of object identification, while the function of the "where" stream is to represent the agent's nearby visual space, for purposes of navigation, reaching, and so on (see Figure 3.4). The what route runs ventrally from the rearmost portion of the cortex into the temporal lobes. Damage here can result in inability to visually recognize familiar objects, including people. The where route leaves the occipital lobe and runs in a dorsal direction, toward the parietal lobe, where damage can produce neglect of one's nearby personal space: people with neglect will simply ignore objects on the neglected side, usually the left. They may eat only the food on one side of their plate, and so on.

3.2.2 The neurophysiology of hearing

The ear is divided into three parts, called the outer, middle, and inner ear (see Figure 3.5). Sound is produced by vibrations and travels through the air in the form of pressure waves. The frequency of these waves (the number of waves per second) determine what we experience as the pitch of the sound. Normal human ears are sensitive to sounds in the frequency range from 20 to 20,000 waves per second (or Hertz). The loudness of the sound is determined by the height of the pressure waves, or their amplitude. These pressure waves contact the brain's receiver, the eardrum (or tympanic membrane), which transduces the pressure waves into mechanical energy. This mechanical energy is transmitted to the cochlea, a fluid-filled canal, by vibrating a long projection into it. These vibrations cause movements of the fluid in the cochlea. Inside the cochlea rows of tiny hair cells move when vibrations are transmitted into the cochlea. These cells are a type of transducer, translating mechanical displacement of the hair into neural firings. These signals arrive eventually at the auditory cortex, which organizes its information in the form of tonotopic maps. In this case, the mapping is from frequency to space: sounds which are near in frequency are represented by spatially adjacent cortical areas.

Have you ever heard a door with rusty hinges slowly closing in such a way that you hear clicks, then as the frequency of the clicks increases, they seem to merge together to form a low-pitched

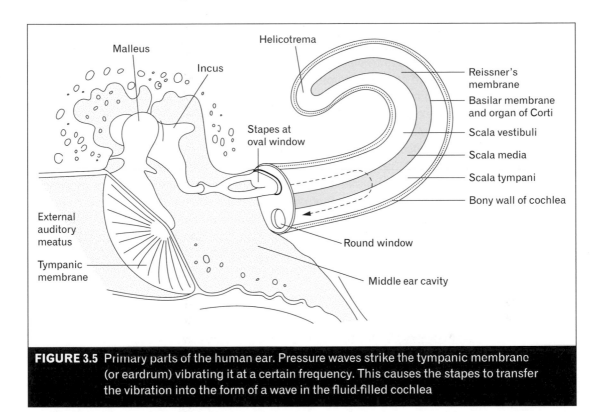

FIGURE 3.5 Primary parts of the human ear. Pressure waves strike the tympanic membrane (or eardrum) vibrating it at a certain frequency. This causes the stapes to transfer the vibration into the form of a wave in the fluid-filled cochlea

sound? One can observe the same phenomenon with the use of a computerized sound-generating system. Simply have the system start at a few clicks per second, then gradually increase the frequency until (somewhere around 20 clicks per second) you begin to hear the output of the speakers as a low sound rather than as a set of clicks. This phenomenon, known as the auditory merge frequency, may hold important clues as to the nature of conscious human perception. Why, for instance, has nature seen fit to cause us to experience clicks faster than 20 times a second as tones, rather than simply giving us the equipment to continue to hear the sound as faster and faster clicks? Dolphins come to mind as a species that seems to communicate with very fast clicks, so perhaps their brains are structured according to this other principle, something that may explain why we are having such a difficult time understanding the nature of their intelligence. The same question applies to vision. Why did nature see fit to equip us with color vision, rather than simply increasing the acuity of our black and white vision so that we could better distinguish all the shades of gray? The answer to this question will no doubt shed light on the question of what the function of conscious perception is, and what advantages it gives us over the different varieties of unconscious perception.

The very notion of somatosensation, or perception of one's own body, challenges certain ways of thinking about perception. Perception cannot always involve the human being taking in information from outside itself, since somatosensation is a type of perception, yet it involves the taking in of information from inside the perceiver's body. This information arrives at the brain from two separate routes, known as the dorsal column–medial lemniscal system and the anterolateral system. The dorsal column system transmits primarily information about touch and about the position of the arms, while the anterolateral system primarily transmits information about pain and sensations of heat and cold. This information passes through different brainstem nuclei, through the thalamus, to its ultimate destination: a set of somatotopic maps located in the parietal lobe of the cortex, just behind the central sulcus, known collectively as the primary somatic sensory cortex.

The primary somatic sensory cortex is divided into four different somatotopically organized areas, Brodmann's areas 1, 2, 3a, and 3b (see Figure 3.6). Each of these areas has a somewhat different specialty. Most of the inputs to area 1 are from a type of receptor located in the skin known as rapidly adapting cutaneous receptors, used for identifying stimuli by touch. Area 2 receives input primarily from deep pressure receptors; area 3a receives input primarily from muscle stretch receptors that function to transmit information about limb position. There are

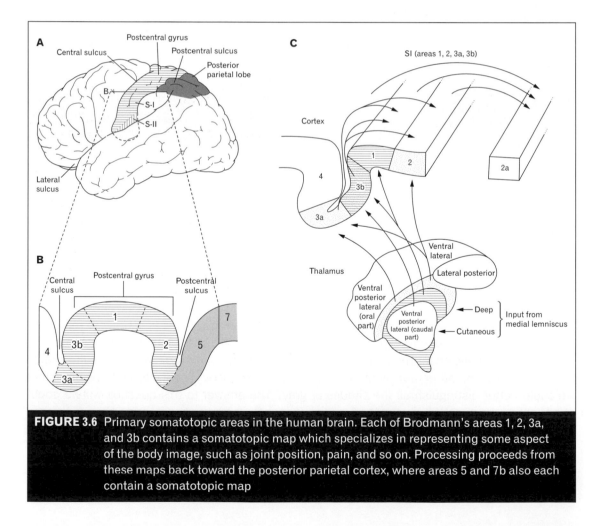

FIGURE 3.6 Primary somatotopic areas in the human brain. Each of Brodmann's areas 1, 2, 3a, and 3b contains a somatotopic map which specializes in representing some aspect of the body image, such as joint position, pain, and so on. Processing proceeds from these maps back toward the posterior parietal cortex, where areas 5 and 7b also each contain a somatotopic map

higher-level somatosensory areas which receive input from the primary somatic sensory cortex, including the secondary somatic sensory cortex, located just below it, and Brodmann areas 5 and 7b located just posterior to it. All of these areas, and others, work together to produce both our conscious body image, and to supply motor areas with the information needed to execute complex movements. As with vision, the same question applies about how the brain is able to merge the functions of several of these maps to produce a single, unified body image. For instance, if one of the somatotopic maps signals pressure while another signals limb position, how is it that we are aware only of a single body that has both of these properties? Notice also, in the Penfield homunculus (Figure 3.7), that the amount of cortex devoted to representing a body part seems to correspond to the vividness of that body part in our body image.

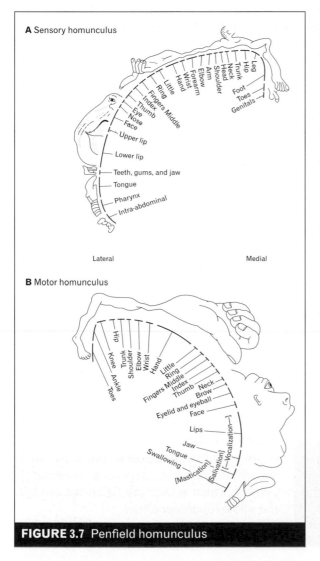

FIGURE 3.7 Penfield homunculus

3.3 SENSORY MEMORY IN VISION AND AUDITION

The portion of the visual scene that you are able to focus on at any particular instant is surprisingly limited. To verify this for yourself, randomly select a card from a deck of playing cards. Without looking directly at the card, hold it out at arm's length in your visual periphery. You cannot see whether it is a face card or even what color it is. Slowly move the card toward the center of your field of view – the fovea, where visual information is most acute. Note how small the fovea is and how close to center the card has to be before you are able to tell what color it is or whether it is a face card. To compensate for the poverty of information delivered by this small fovea, your eyes are constantly darting about in a collection of brief sharp movements called "saccades." It may seem mysterious, however, that the visual scene seems like a large stable array of objects. If your eyes are constantly jumping around the scene, and only able to take in tiny parts of the scene at any particular instant, how does your brain assemble this information to give rise to the way the scene appears to you? Part of the answer will involve reference to the concept of visual sensory memory, also called "iconic memory." Light goes into the eye, is transduced into visual information, and then goes into sensory memory.

One instance of visual sensory memory is *visual persistence*. You may have had the experience of seeing a bright flash in the dark, as in the case of seeing lightning at night or a night time display of fireworks. Alternately, you may be in a darkened room and briefly switch a flashlight on and then off again. You will see an afterimage that persists after the stimulus has subsided. After the flash of lightning you continue to see a bright jagged shape similar to the shape of the lightning bolt.

Sperling and his colleagues conducted one of the classic studies on visual sensory memory (Sperling 1960). Subjects viewed brief presentations of arrays of letters: three rows of four letters each, as in Figure 3.8.

The array was shown for 50 milliseconds (i.e., 0.05 seconds – a very brief time) followed by a blank screen. Then the subjects heard a tone indicating that they were to give a report on what letters they recalled. In a condition called the "whole-report condition," subjects were instructed to recall as many of the twelve letters as possible. Subjects averaged about 4.5 letters correct (37 percent). In a different condition called the "partial-report condition," the tone prompting a response would be played in one of three pitches corresponding to the three rows of letters in the visual stimulus array. The high pitch signified that the subject should report on the letters in the top row, the medium pitch corresponded to the middle row and the lowest pitch corresponded to the bottom row. The tones were played only after the presentation of the array ended. Subjects in the partial-report condition were to report only on letters in the row indicated by the tone. Partial-report condition subjects averaged about 76 percent correct.

The difference in accuracy between the whole-report and partial-report conditions supports the following conclusions about the nature of visual sensory memory. The amount of information about the stimulus array that is stored is much larger than the 37 percent that is indicated by consideration of the whole-report condition alone. Since 76 percent of any randomly cued row could be reported, researchers inferred that at least 76 percent of the information about the whole array remained. But this information soon fades. The rate at which the information available in visual sensory memory fades may be tested by varying the time between the offset of the stimulus array row-cueing pitch. When the pitch is immediately after array offset, the accuracy of recall is about 76 percent. But as the interval between array offset and pitch increases to about one whole second, the accuracy diminishes to about 36 percent, which is near the figure obtained for the whole-report condition.

Studies show that there is auditory as well as visual sensory memory. Auditory sensory

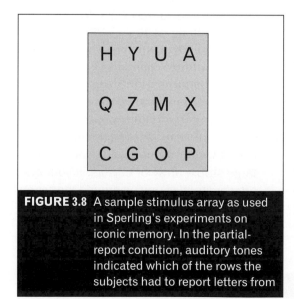

FIGURE 3.8 A sample stimulus array as used in Sperling's experiments on iconic memory. In the partial-report condition, auditory tones indicated which of the rows the subjects had to report letters from

memory – also called "echoic" memory – is postulated to be crucial for our perception of auditory stimuli, especially spoken language. As Neisser (1967) points out, sound is spread out in time, and in order to perceive that an entire word or an entire sentence has been uttered, there must be some storage of information about events spread out in time.

To test the duration and capacity of echoic memory researchers devised tests similar to Sperling's (1960) whole- and partial-report experiments (Darwin et al. 1972). These researchers employed the "three-eared man" procedure in which subjects heard three different stimuli simultaneously through headphones: the first stimulus (a spoken series of three letters or numbers, e.g. "5X9") was heard only in the right ear, the second stimulus only in the left ear, and the third stimulus heard in both ears so that the sound was localized in the center of the head – the "third ear." Subjects were thus exposed to nine auditory stimuli within about one second: three stimuli to each of the "three ears." As in the Sperling study, there were both whole-report and partial-report conditions. In the whole-report conditions subjects had to report as many of the nine items as they could remember and they averaged about four items. In the partial-report condition, a visual cue indicated which of the three ears the subjects should attend to. When the visual cue was presented immediately after the auditory stimuli, subjects averaged above 50 percent, thus indicating that about five out of the original nine items persisted in echoic memory. Even after a delay of four seconds, performance on the partial-report condition was superior to the whole-report, although it did degrade over time.

3.4 VISUAL OBJECT RECOGNITION

We humans must recognize visually presented three-dimensional objects with only two-dimensional projections on the retina as our guide. Somehow, we are able to recognize objects seen from unfamiliar viewpoints, that is, based on unfamiliar projections onto our retinas. Recent theories of visual object recognition divide into two camps: viewpoint-independent theories and viewpoint-dependent theories. Viewpoint-independent theories have been most recently and prominently championed by Irving Biederman and his colleagues (e.g., Biederman 1987, 1995; Biederman and Gerhardstein 1993). The opposition is led by Michael Tarr and his colleagues (e.g., Gauthier and Tarr 1997; Tarr and Bülthoff 1995; Tarr and Pinker 1989; Tarr et al. 1997).

3.4.1 Viewpoint-independent theories of visual object recognition

Viewpoint-independent theories postulate that the memorial representations supporting object recognition are specifications of the three-dimensional structure of objects. On these theories, recognition consists in the abstraction of a structural specification of the object perceived and a match of that specification to a memorial specification. Such theories are called "viewpoint-independent" because they predict that, as long as the crucial structural information can be abstracted from the percept, then there should be no variation in recognition speed and accuracy across unfamiliar rotations of the presented object (where rotations are either in depth or along the picture plane).

Many studies, however, have shown that the above predictions are not borne out and have found instead evidence of viewpoint-dependent recognition performance (e.g., Tarr and Pinker 1989). Such evidence has motivated the formulation of viewpoint-dependent theories of object recognition. According to these theories, the memorial representation of an object is one or more encoded views that store only two-dimensional information based on previous retinal projections. Recognition of familiar objects seen from unfamiliar viewpoints involves a match between a stored view and the perceptual view via a *normalization* mechanism. Normalization is a generic term for any hypothesized mechanism by which spatial representations are to be compared (e.g., Bülthoff and Edelman 1992; Shepard and Cooper 1982; Ullman 1989). For example, such a mechanism might be a mental rotation of an image (Shepard and Cooper 1982). According to viewpoint-independent theories, the representations that facilitate object recognition are specifications of the three-dimensional structure of seen objects abstracted from the two-dimensional array of the retinal image. While the most prominent recent formulation of this kind of theory is due to Biederman, we begin with a classic formulation of this theory due to Marr and Nishihara (1978). At the core of Marr and Nishihara's account is their proposal regarding the format of information about three-dimensional object shape in memory. They postulate that objects are represented in a coordinate system that is centered on the parts of the objects themselves, not on a coordinate system relative to the viewer. The object-based coordinate system is based on axes centered on major parts of the object. Each of the major parts of an object is represented as differently sized volumetric primitives, namely, cylinders. Further, the object representations are thought to have a hierarchical structure. Thus, a person is represented as six main cylindrical shapes, one for each of the limbs, the head, and the torso. A limb is represented by smaller cylinders, for example one each for the upper and lower arm and one for the hand. The hand itself is represented by still smaller cylinders, for example one for each of the fingers.

The important point is that objects are represented in terms of their major axes of elongation as cylindrical parts centered on those axes. Such a model supports a prediction that recognition performance will be equivalent across different views as long as information about the major axes of elongation of the objects is retrievable from those views.

A related theory is Biederman's view. The primary difference between Marr and Nishihara's view and Biederman's is that where Marr and Nishihara postulated only one kind of volumetric primitive, the cylinder, Biederman postulates 36 volumetric primitives called "geons" (see Figure 3.9).

Biederman came up with the 36 geons based on combinations of what Lowe (1985) calls "non-accidental" features of objects. According to Lowe, objects have many aspects that remain constant even when seen from different distances and points of view. For instance, in many different projections of a book, the parts that correspond to the book's edges remain parallel. Also, symmetrical objects look symmetrical despite widely varying changes in distance and angle. A coin seen from different angles may project sometimes a circular and sometimes an elliptical image (and sometimes a thin rectangular image) but either way, the images retain the symmetry of the coin. Lowe defined about a half-dozen of such non-accidental properties of visually presented objects. Based on these non-accidental properties, Biederman devised his system of geons, examples of which include cylinders, cones, and prisms.

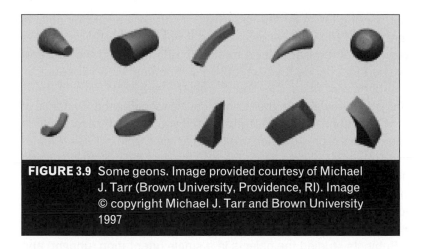

FIGURE 3.9 Some geons. Image provided courtesy of Michael J. Tarr (Brown University, Providence, RI). Image © copyright Michael J. Tarr and Brown University 1997

A coffee mug, then, would be represented as two geons, one larger cylindrical geon for the body of the mug; one curved smaller geon attached to the larger one's side for the handle. The mug is recognized by the extraction of features from the retinal array that activate geon representations and the relations between them forming a perceptual representation that is matched against a geon-specified memorial representation.

Biederman and his colleagues predict that as long as such geon information is recoverable from a view of a previously seen object, different rotations of the object should not affect recognition. Thus if, for example, you had seen a coffee mug for the first time, successive views of the mug would facilitate recognition equally as long as both the body and handle geons of the mug were extractable from the retinal array. Biederman predicts that, as long as the handle is in view, rotational deviations from the original presentation will not affect recognition. Thus the theory is a viewpoint-independent theory of visual object recognition. Many studies, however, have demonstrated viewpoint-dependent effects on recognition.

3.4.2 Viewpoint-dependent theories of object recognition

Early evidence of viewpoint dependence is due to studies such as that of Bartram (1974 1976), who found that when subjects learned a set of novel polygonal shapes at a single rotation, reaction times for "familiar–unfamiliar" judgments on the shapes rotated in the picture plane depended on the degree of rotation from the original orientation. Bartram (1974) found that subjects' reaction times in a naming task decreased more rapidly across practice trials in which each of the eight blocks presented the object from the same view as opposed to blocks in which pictures of objects were seen in different views. Bartram (1976) investigated recognition performance across changes in viewpoint in a sequential matching paradigm. Subjects made same–different judgments on pairs of line drawings of objects, members of which were presented sequentially. Reaction times were faster for identical pictures of the same object than for pictures of the same object appearing in differing viewpoints.

Jolicoeur (1985) found that naming times for line drawings of naturally occurring objects increased as the drawings were further from the canonical upright views of the objects. Palmer et al. (1981) studied the recognition of familiar objects rotated in depth around their vertical axes. The researchers established independently each object's canonical view via subjects' ratings of preferred view. In subsequent tests, they found that the subjects' naming times decreased as the rotation of the objects away from their canonical views increased. Evidence of viewpoint-dependent effects in recognition has led researchers to hypothesize that recognition involves the alignment of the perceptual representation to either a single canonical view (Palmer et al. 1981), or to multiple views (Tarr and Bülthoff 1995; Tarr and Pinker 1989). Both single and multiple view theories posit normalization mechanisms underlying object recognition. One early suggestion of what such normalization might consist in comes from the mental imagery literature. See the box on mental rotation.

Tarr and Pinker (1989) used novel two-dimensional stimuli to test the effects of rotation in the picture plane on recognition. Subjects studied the objects in a single orientation (upright) and then practiced naming the objects in unfamiliar orientations in the picture plane. When subjects recognized objects at unfamiliar viewpoints, performance was related monotonically to the degree of rotation away from the training viewpoint. Further, these effects were comparable to a control experiment Tarr and Pinker ran with the same objects used in handedness discriminations similar to those tested by mental rotation researchers (e.g., Shepard and Cooper 1982). Tarr and Pinker (1989) and Tarr and Bülthoff (1995) argued that this comparability provided evidence that the normalization mechanisms employed in recognition are similar to those used in mental rotation. While the Tarr and Pinker (1989, 1991) studies support the normalization hypothesis for rotations in the picture plane (see also Gauthier and Tarr 1997), other studies support normalization for recognition in rotations in depth. A typical example is Tarr and Bülthoff (1995), who conducted experiments intended as three-dimensional analogs to the experiments on two-dimensional stimuli in Tarr and Pinker (1989). Tarr's subjects were trained to perform a naming task on novel three-dimensional objects.

MENTAL ROTATION AND MENTAL IMAGERY

The following example from R.N. Shepard and his colleagues (e.g., Shepard and Cooper 1982) had subjects look at simultaneously presented pairs of objects. The second member of each pair was either the same as the first or a mirror image. Further, pair members could differ from each other in their rotations in depth and in the picture plane. The researchers found that the time it took for subjects to make "same–different" judgments increased monotonically with increases of rotational displacement between pair members. Shepard and colleagues took this reaction time data as evidence that subjects were rotating mental images to see if they would match the stimulus. Analogously, then, recognition may involve the rotation of a percept to match it against one or more canonical views stored in memory.

During probe phases the objects were rotated in depth around the horizontal or vertical axes. Rotations along vertical and horizontal axes were in increments of 10 degrees. It was found that recognition times and error rates increased with the distance from familiar viewpoint. Response times varied monotonically, so, for instance, in experiment 2, the rate of normalization for rotations around the vertical axis was calculated to be 119 degree per second. In similar naming tasks and rotations around the vertical axis, Tarr et al. (1994) reported rates ranging from 731 degrees per second to 895/sec and Tarr et al. (1994) reported ranges from 257/sec to 893/sec (see also Tarr and Pinker 1991; Gauthier et al. 1999).

3.5 FILLING IN THE EYE'S BLIND SPOT

Each of your eyes has a blind spot, because there is a spot on each retina where the optic nerve exits the back of the eyeball. You can demonstrate this to yourself by covering your left eye and focusing your right eye on the plus sign in Figure 3.10.

The figure should be about six inches from your face, but slowly move it nearer or further until the spot on the right disappears in your blind spot. One of the amazing things about the blind spot is how big it is. Why don't you perceive a hole in your visual field where the blind spot is? If you were to look at a uniformly blue painted wall, the entirety of your visual field would be blue: you wouldn't notice two blank spots, spots that have no color at all in your visual field. But, as a matter of fact, the information you receive through your retina does have a blank spot in it. How is it that we are not aware of it in everyday life – did you even know you had a blind spot until you learned about it? How does the brain go about producing a visual percept that is "non-gappy" even though the incoming information is incomplete?

In trying to explain how it is that we are typically unaware of our blind spots, there are two kinds of mistake that we must be very careful to avoid making: the homunculus fallacy (see box) and confusion of representational contents and vehicles.

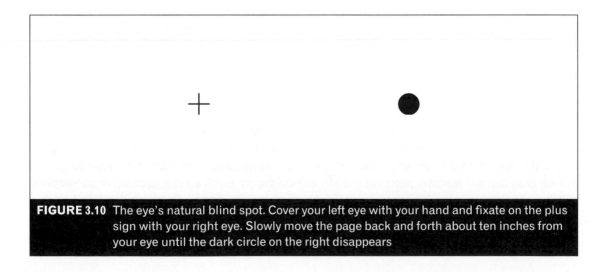

FIGURE 3.10 The eye's natural blind spot. Cover your left eye with your hand and fixate on the plus sign with your right eye. Slowly move the page back and forth about ten inches from your eye until the dark circle on the right disappears

HOMUNCULUS FALLACIES

In its most general, explicit, and obviously fallacious form, the homunculus fallacy involves attempting to explain how a person accomplishes some mental task by positing a homunculus – a little man – living inside that person's head performing the task for that person. Consider some examples of homunculus fallacies.

- How does a person understand a language? Well, words go in the person's ear, where the little man in the head hears them. The little man understands the language, and tells the person what the words mean.

How does a person visually perceive objects? Well, light goes in the eye and creates images on the retina. A little man in the head looks at these images . . .

This sort of explanation may strike the reader as so obviously absurd as not to need mentioning. *Of course*, there are no little men living in our heads. How silly! But note what is really wrong with the homuncular explanations: they are fundamentally circular, and thus do not really explain what they are supposed to explain. Explaining the way a person understands language in terms of a little man in the head is bad because it just begs the question of how the little man understands language. No explanation of understanding has been given. Likewise with explaining vision in terms of a little man examining images. The way people perceive has not been explained because it begs the question of how the little man perceives the images.

Explanations that do not literally posit the existence of little men in the head may nonetheless be guilty of committing homunculus fallacies if the explanations harbor a fundamental circularity. So, for example, to explain how it is that we can recognize shapes by sense of touch by doing nothing more that positing a touched-shape–recognition module in the brain is similarly an instance of a homuncular fallacy, since the question of how the *module* recognizes tactile shape information is begged.

When I look at a cloudless blue sky, blue light is shining on my retinas, but no light is transduced in the regions of my blind spots. How come I don't see gaps in my visual field then? Why don't I perceive regions without any blue in them in my visual field? One sort of explanation that invites the charge of homuncular fallacy is to suppose that the brain literally creates a painting with the areas corresponding to the blind spots painted in with blue paint. Such a painting would be inspected by the mind's eye, and since the painting has no gaps – the relevant gaps being filled in with blue paint – we thus perceive the sky as non-gappy. Such an explanation is an instance of a homuncular fallacy since the question of how we perceive the painting in our head gives a circular explanation of how we perceive the sky: perception itself remains unexplained.

Perhaps there is a way to defend the painting theory against the charge of homunculus fallacy, however. It posits a brain process which fills in a visual representation, and another process which is the "consumer" of that representation, that is, the process in the cognitive system which the visual representation is designed to interact with in the course of devising and executing actions on the basis of perceptions. Now, nothing at all says that this consumer process has to have all the abilities of a full-blown human being – who would ever think such a thing? The popularizer of the homunculus fallacy charge, Daniel Dennett, is clear that it is often useful to decompose complex systems into functional units. Some of these functions might have names such as "read the tape," as when one describes the operations of a computer. But there is no need to accuse computer theorists of hiding a person in their computer. What they call "reading" can be cashed out in terms of some rather basic causal interactions between basic physical objects; for example, holes in the computer tape allow light through which is transduced by a light-sensitive head into electrical signals. The process in the brain which consumes the filled-in representation is not a person, the painting theorist should insist. Rather, it is merely a brain process which causally interacts with the visual representation.

Another problem with the blue-paint explanation is that it leads to the second of the problems we said must be avoided: the confusion of a representation's content and a representational vehicle. Consider the written words "big" and "little." The word "little" is bigger than the word "big." The representational content of the word "big" is the property of bigness, a property that need not be instantiated by the word itself. That the word "big" is small – it has only three letters – is a property of the representational vehicle. That the word "big" is about bigness, not smallness, is a property of the representational content. One way to confuse contents and vehicles in cognitive science is to assume that since a certain property is being represented, the representation itself must instantiate that property. To assume that the way we perceive the sky as being blue is by having blue things in our brain, and the way we perceive ripe bananas is by having long yellow things in our brains is to commit a confusion of content and vehicle. Our neural representations of blueness need no more themselves be blue than the word "blue" needs to be printed in blue ink, or the word "big" needs to be bigger than the word "minuscule."

Again, though, the painting theorist has a possible response to the charge of confusing the representation with the things or properties it represents; that is, confusing vehicle with content. The painting theorist may quite literally mean that the representation itself is blue, that the representations in our brains are in some sense colored. Who would hold such a view, you ask? A color internalist would. This is a theory about the ontology of color properties which posits that colors exist not in the world, but rather are created by the visual systems of certain organisms in order to allow those organisms to better perceive and respond to the world. We treat this intriguing theory, as well as its more conventional competitors later in this chapter in section 3.7 on color perception. In constructing an explanation of why our blind spots don't give rise to a perception of gaps in our visual field, being careful about the distinction between content and vehicle will be very helpful. In brief, the distinction of content and vehicle allows us to see that the perception of the sky as non-gappy does not require a non-gappy representation. Because of the arrangements of nerves in the retina, there are gaps in the representations. But we would be unjustified in concluding that the perceptions should likewise be gappy and that the failure to perceive gaps requires the creation of non-gappy representational vehicles.

This point is put by Dennett in his discussion of blind spots. Dennett invites us to imagine that we walk into a room in which the wallpaper was designed by Andy Warhol and is covered with hundreds of images of the face of Marilyn Monroe. Your perception would be that there are hundreds of Marilyns. This perception would arise after only a brief moment – a period of time too short for you to focus on each and every Marilyn, and create a distinct mental representation for each one. According to Dennett, a likely way that the brain creates your perceptual representation is that the brain focuses on just a few Marilyns and "labels the whole region 'more Marilyns'" (Dennett 1991, p. 355). In the spirit of Dennett's hypothesis, being careful not to confuse content and vehicle means that the representation of hundreds of Marilyns does not require the existence in the brain of hundreds of representations of Marilyn: just one representation with the content "lots of Marilyns" will do the trick. The brain does not need a hundred representations for a hundred Marilyns any more than the word "hundred" needs a hundred letters in it.

How does this tie into the issue of blind spots? Well, if Dennett is right about the way the brain represents the Marilyn Monroe wallpaper, then whether one of the Marilyns falls into your blind spot poses no special problem: the brain is just saying "more Marilyns." Further, according to Dennett, the brain is effectively ignoring the regions in the area of the blind spot. Why don't we notice gaps? According to Dennett, it is crucial to note the distinction between the representation of an absence and the absence of a representation – a special instance of the distinction between content and vehicle. In order to notice gaps, the brain must represent gaps. But if the brain simply lacks the representations of gaps, then no gaps will be noticed. And if the content of the representation of the wallpaper is just something along the lines of "more Marilyns" then what we have is the absence of a representation of gaps: there need not be a representation of the absence of gaps. The same general point holds for the visual perception of the blue sky as continuous and non-gappy. According to Dennett, after focusing on a few regions of the sky, the brain leaps to the conclusion "more of the same" (1991, p. 355) and this is sufficient for our perception to lack gaps, and thus we do not notice our retinal blind spots.

Dennett's explanation has given rise to some controversy, and it is worth going into it here. One thing that has caused trouble is Dennett's denial that the brain creates a representation that "fills in" the gaps. Dennett has denied that the brain has to "fill in" or "provide something" and favors an explanation whereby the brain is instead ignoring something.

V.S. Ramachandran (1992) and Patricia Churchland (1993) have taken an apparently opposing view, and maintain instead that the brain does engage in filling in. Ramachandran and Churchland's case is independently interesting, although it does not refute, but instead is compatible with, Dennett's core insights.

Ramachandran (1992) replies to Dennett's case first by means of ingeniously devised figures which seem to show the filling-in process at work. Focus your eye on the little square in Figure 3.11 and adjust the drawing until the center of the ring directly to the left of the square disappears, so that it looks like a solid dot instead of a ring. Since it looks different from all the others, it "pops out" perceptually. On Ramachandran and Churchland's interpretation of Dennett, if Dennett is correct, this pop-out should not happen, since we wouldn't really see the ring as a solid dot. On Dennett's view, the ring in the blind spot cannot look different from the other rings because we are ignoring the area where the difference is supposed to be. But it certainly seems as if we see a solid dot.

Ramachandran's work has received support from the work of Fiorini et al. (1992), who showed that the parts of the visual cortex which topographically (see section 2.6.3 on topographic maps)

FIGURE 3.11 Salience of filled-in objects. Cover your right eye and fixate your left eye on the small white square. Move the figure back and forth until your blind spot encompasses the center of the ring directly to the left of the square. That ring will appear as a solid disc because of filling in, and will perceptually "pop out" from the other rings

correspond to the part of the visual field where the blind spot does seem to be mimicking the activity of adjoining areas which are mapping genuine information. Could this be the neural basis of genuine filling in?

Dennett has responded to the challenge put forth by data like the above. With regard to the bagels figure, Dennett writes:

> If they had asked me in advance of the experiment whether the subject would see "just more bagels" or rather a solid disk, I would not have known what to say; I would have recognized an ambiguity in my claim that the brain assumes "more of the same," for it all depends on whether the brain draws this conclusion locally or globally. [Churchland and Ramachandran 1994] assume that my view would have to predict that the bagel would be seen *as* a bagel (globally more of the same), but this does not follow.
>
> (Dahlbom 1993, p. 207)

Churchland and Ramachandran might respond, however, that this is not their assumption; their assumption was that the crucial bagel would *fail to pop out* on Dennett's view (since the brain ignores the center of the bagel). But the experiment seems to show the opposite: the crucial bagel is seen as a solid dot.

Perhaps it concerns how *abstract* the contents of the relevant brain representations are. It is a mistake to describe Dennett's view of the visual system as not providing anything at all. Consider another experiment concerning the blind spots and the question of filling in. Subjects were shown a figure that consisted of a vertical bar that passes through the blind spot. The top half is red and the bottom half is green. Churchland and Ramachandran (1994) write:

> Subjects still see the bar as complete, with extensions of both the red and green bar, but they do not see a border where the red and green meet, and hence they cannot say just where one color begins and the other leaves off.
>
> (Churchland and Ramachandran 1994, p. 31)

Dennett responds:

> Now this way of putting it blurs the distinction I am trying to make. Is it that the brain itself never "says" where one color begins and the other leaves off? If there is any sort of filling in worthy of the name, then each sub-area of the bar-as-represented must be filled in either red or green . . . or "reddish green" . . . Or I suppose areas could flicker back and forth between red and green, but one way or another, filling in requires explicit representation of the color at each "pixel" within the outline of the bar – that is what I mean by filling in . . . But if there isn't filling in, if the brain just concludes that it is a single solid bar with a red top and a green bottom and *does not go into the matter* of where and how the color changes, then there would be no fact of the matter about where "the boundary" was, just as there is no fact of the matter about whether Falstaff had a sister . . . It is not clear, from Churchland and Ramachandran's formulation, whether they suppose that there must be a boundary in the brain's representation, a boundary that is simply inaccessible to the subjects. I am claiming that while there *might* be – it is an empirical question – there *need not* be.
>
> (Dahlbom 1993, pp. 207–208, italics in original)

Whatever the final resolution of the blind spot controversy, it illustrates the keen interest that philosophers have in the nature of mental representation and the crucial role it plays in sensory perception. The history of philosophical approaches to perception is very telling when compared to contemporary cognitive science. To this history we now turn.

3.6 CLASSICAL PHILOSOPHICAL THEORIES OF PERCEPTION

Philosophical thought on the nature of perception occupies some of the most significant concerns in the history of philosophy. At first, perception may seem quite simple. Right now I am perceiving my coffee mug. I open my eyes, look at the mug and see it. What could be simpler? The mug is there, I am here, there's no obstruction between us in this clean, well-lit room, thus, I have no difficulty seeing the mug: I perceive it visually. And I may reach out and grasp it, thus perceiving it through sense of touch. Just as there is nothing between me and the mug to prevent me from seeing it, there is no obstruction between me and the mug to prevent me from reaching out and feeling it. Likewise, I may smell and taste the coffee contained therein, and if I drop the mug, there may be plenty for me to hear as well. Philosophical reflection renders things much more complicated, however. While common sense may say that there is nothing between me and the mug to prevent me from seeing it, much philosophical thought on the matter has led to the view that my mind itself gets in between me and the mug and that I *never* actually perceive the mug itself, but only states of my mind that, at best, represent the presence of a mug. But the mug itself, a thing that exists independently of my mind, is necessarily and permanently beyond the grasp of my mind.

Such a view goes far beyond common sense and may strike the untutored reader as absolutely absurd. Indeed, many professional philosophers have sought to defend common sense in this regard. Philosophical controversy on the matter rages on even today, and the core issue may be summed up thus: do we perceive anything besides the states of our own minds? If so, how? If not, why not?

In the history of these philosophical debates, we may discern three main kinds of philosophical theories of perception: direct realism, indirect realism, and idealism. Before going on to describe these three kinds of theories, it will be helpful to first describe the contrasts between directness and indirectness and between realism and idealism.

3.6.1 Directness and indirectness

The issue at stake regarding the question of whether perception is direct or indirect is difficult to pin down precisely, but at a minimum it involves the question of whether the objects we typically take ourselves to be aware of – for instance, when through vision we become aware of a chair – are objects that we are aware of only in virtue of being aware of something else. For an indirect theorist, I am not directly aware of the chair – I do not directly perceive the chair. I am aware of the chair only in virtue of being directly aware of some state of my mind. So, on one standard way of being an indirect theorist, one might say that I have a perceptual idea or perceptual mental representation in my mind that I am directly aware of, and I use that representation as the evidential basis for an inference that there is some object external to me – a chair – that is the cause of this representation, and I am thereby indirectly aware of the chair. Whatever indirectness ultimately amounts to for a particular indirect theory of perception, at a minimum it involves the idea that one is perceptually aware of external objects only in virtue of being aware of some internal object.

In contrast, direct theories of perception allow that one may be directly aware of external objects, that is, for instance, one may be aware of chairs without necessarily being aware of some state of one's own mind. This is not to deny that perceivers have internal states. Nor is it to deny that perceivers are aware of the external world in virtue of having internal states. What the direct theorists deny is that a person needs to be aware of his or her internal states in order to be aware of the objects and properties in the external world.

One way to get a grip on the notion of indirectness at play is by analogy with the things we see when we watch television. If I am watching David Letterman on TV, there is a relatively clear sense in which I am perceiving David Letterman. There is also a relatively clear sense in which I am perceiving David Letterman only indirectly in virtue of perceiving the images on the screen of the television: my perception of David Letterman is less direct than my perception of the images on the screen in virtue of which I perceive Letterman. For the indirect theorist, normal visual perception is like watching a TV in your head with the mind's eye: we "see" images in the mind more directly than the objects in front of our face.

It is crucial to keep in mind the prima facie compatibility of direct theories of perception with contemporary cognitive science. Recall that one of the crucial tenets of cognitive science is that the mind works in virtue of mental representations and computations that manipulate mental representations. One must caution against inferring that perception is indirect from the mere fact that perception involves mental representations of the objects perceived. Direct theories need not deny that perception involves mental representation: what they deny is that perceiving an external object involves first perceiving one's own mental representations. Thus it is important to realize that even in the context of cognitive science the question of whether perception is direct or indirect remains open. Representational theories of perception are not necessarily indirect theories of perception. Much confusion to the contrary is due to the historical practice of calling indirect realism "representational realism." In other words, directness in the theory of perception should not simply be equated, without argument, with the involvement of represen-tations in perception.

3.6.2 Realism and idealism

We turn now to realism and idealism. In general, to be a realist (in the philosophical sense of the term) about some thing is to hold that the thing exists and further, that it exists independently of your mind. Thus one is a realist about electrons insofar as one affirms that there are indeed electrons, and that there would be electrons even if no one held the opinion that there were electrons. Likewise, one may be a realist about properties as well as objects. So, one is a realist about the property of being purple if one affirms that there really are things that are purple and whether things are purple does not depend on anyone perceiving things as being purple. (There is a further wrinkle that we will not go into here, but briefly mention: property realism is sometimes identified with the view that properties exist over and above the things that have them, so, the property of being purple would exist even if nothing were actually purple at some particular time.) Now, to be an idealist about some thing is not to deny the existence of that thing, but instead to assert that the thing's existence is mind dependent. Likewise for idealism about properties. So, the common maxim that beauty is in the eye of the beholder is an expression of idealism about beauty. It does not deny that any one or any thing is beautiful, but instead asserts that whether something is beautiful depends on someone's mind. More specifically, whether something is beautiful depends on whether someone perceives it as beautiful.

The role that the notions of realism and idealism play in theories of perception concerns the objects we take ourselves to perceive and the properties we take those objects to have. To illustrate this in terms of an example, consider your visual perception of some piece of denim, or more specifically, your perception of the denim as being blue. A realist about color would say that the blueness of the denim is a property that does not depend on our minds: it does not depend on our perceptions of blueness. An idealist about color, in contrast, asserts that blueness is in the eye of the beholder. According to such an idealist, a world without perceivers would be a world without colors. Many readers may be familiar with the way of poking fun at philosophical debates that ask "If a tree falls in the woods and no one is around to hear it, does it make a sound?" The idealist about sounds answers "no": sounds do not exist if there is no one around to hear them. The realist answers "yes": sounds exist mind independently, and don't depend on anyone to hear them for their existence.

Perhaps the most crucial aspect of the debate between realists and idealists concerns the ontological status of the properties that we perceive objects as having: do the objects retain these properties even when unperceived? In a clean well-lighted room I perceive my coffee mug to be blue. When no one is around or the room is pitch black, is the mug still blue? For perceptual realists, the properties we perceive objects as having persist unperceived. For idealists, they do not.

3.6.3 Direct realism

For direct realists, the objects external to us that we typically take ourselves to perceive – tables and chairs, rocks and trees – are both directly perceived and retain their perceived properties even when unperceived. I am not aware of what a dog looks like only by first being aware of some mental representation of a dog. This is not to deny that we may sometimes become aware of our own mental representations. Right now I am thinking about the Eiffel Tower, and am quite self-consciously aware that I am mentally representing the Eiffel Tower. And if I were standing in front of the Eiffel Tower and visually perceiving it, I may perhaps pause to reflect on the act of perception itself, and thereby become aware of my own mental representation of it. But what the direct realist is denying is that this self-awareness is a necessary component of perception.

Direct realism is perhaps the closest to the common-sense view of perception. The world is there for us to see directly and we are capable of seeing it for what it really is. And the way we see it is the way it is even when we are not looking. We turn our backs on objects and they do not vanish. We pack our clothes into a suitcase and they retain their colors and textures even though we take a break from perceiving them. For various reasons philosophers have called this version of direct realism "naïve realism." Primary among these reasons is the belief that science has shown that many of the properties we perceive objects to have are not really instantiated by objects independently of our perceptions. One example might be the perceived solidity of a table. I knock on it with my knuckles and it feels quite solid. I set books on the table and they do not pass through it. But science tells us that the table is mostly empty space: the microscopic particles that constitute the mass of the table occupy only a tiny fraction of the volume that the table occupies.

A traditional way of spelling out scientific realism is in terms of a distinction between primary properties and secondary properties. According to philosophers who believe that there is such a distinction to draw, primary properties – typically shape and size – persist unperceived and do not depend on perceivers for their existence. Secondary properties – typically colors, tastes, and odors – do not persist unperceived, or if they do, are regarded as not having an existence independent of perceivers. One way of regarding colors as secondary properties is to regard them as powers to elicit certain responses in perceivers. According to some philosophers, just as we do not regard pain as residing in the pin that pricks us, nor should we regard yellowness as residing in the flower that looks yellow. Pins and flowers have certain powers to cause certain responses in us, and we erroneously think of perceived yellowness as a property of the flower as opposed to a property of our mind.

The traditional way of dividing properties into the primary and the secondary owes much to the fact that the science of the time (the science of Newton and Galileo) was enormously successful in explaining natural phenomena in terms of the so-called primary properties but fumbled badly in attempts to say much about the so-called secondary qualities. Shapes and motions of objects figured heavily in the mathematical physics of the day and the properties discussed in physical theory seemed easy to define without reference to the capabilities of human perceptual systems. Colors and odors, on the other hand, were resistant to these early mathematical descriptions of the natural world. In a move of intellectual sour grapes, it was concluded that what wasn't understood well was probably not really there: it was all in our minds. Thus the form of realism that we are calling "scientific" realism is really a mixture of idealism and realism. Unlike the naïve realist, the scientific realist is not a realist about all of the properties we take ourselves to perceive, but only some of them. It is important to note that the contrast between the naïve and scientific forms of direct realism here have to do with the realism, not with the directness. Thus, indirect forms of realism admit of both naïve and scientific forms (Dancy 1985). We postpone further discussion of realism and idealism until later in this section.

Turning to the directness of direct realism, we may ask what arguments there are to favor direct realism over indirect realism. The main argument for direct realism has to do with its closeness to common sense. Without reflecting much on the situation this is just how things seem to work: I perceive the table in front of me without necessarily perceiving anything else first. Further and more sophisticated arguments for direct realism hinge on criticisms of alternatives: indirect realism, for instance, runs into problems or has unpalatable consequences. For example, indirect realism may be incompatible with our belief that we know anything about things external to our own minds. Indirect realism has been charged with leading to the (to some) reprehensible view that you can't know if anything or anyone besides yourself exists. For further discussion of such topics, see the discussion of skepticism in section 4.4.1.3 of Chapter 4. Before delving deeper into these alleged problems with indirect realism, it will be helpful to say some more about what it is and what arguments favor it.

3.6.4 Indirect realism

Perhaps the single most popular and powerful consideration supporting the view that the external world is perceived only indirectly arises when we reflect on the nature of perceptual error. Examples of error abound: I misperceive a carpet sample to be purple when it is really brown; I mistakenly see a stick in the water to be bent or broken when it is really straight; I see a patch of water ahead on the road that turns out to be only a mirage. Most significant is the possibility of flat-out hallucination: when drunk or drugged one might see a pink elephant. Readers with healthy lifestyles may better relate to the massive perceptual deception involved in dreams: one may dream that there is a pink elephant in the room when there is no such thing. Now, from the point of view of the perceiver, there may be no difference in hallucinating that there is a coffee mug in front of you and having the accurate perception that there is a coffee mug in front to you. In both cases the contents of your mind are the same. What makes one accurate and the other hallucinatory is the state of the external world. In the accurate case, your perceptual state is caused by there actually being a coffee mug there. In the hallucinatory case there is no mug and it is your state of mind that tells you otherwise. Your percept is caused perhaps by LSD. Now come the crucial steps in the argument for indirectness. First, note that even in the hallucinatory case, it's very compelling to say that you are aware of *something*. Further, since the hallucinatory case is indistinguishable *by you* from the accurate case, in both cases what you are aware of first and foremost is the very *same thing*. And since what is similar in the two cases is the state of your mind, not the external world, what you are aware of first and foremost is the state of your own mind. Thus, even in the case of so-called accurate perception, you are aware of external objects like the coffee mug only indirectly, you are first and foremost aware of a state of your own mind, a state that could obtain without there actually being a coffee mug there, as In the cases of dreaming and hallucinating. Indirect realism, then, offers a very powerful and intuitive explanation of the very possibility of perceptual error.

Another argument for an indirect theory hinges on the time-lag between the events we perceive and the events of our perceiving. This is most easy to see in the case of looking at stars. Stars are very far away and light takes many years before it reaches our eyes on earth. In many cases, when you are looking up at a star, the light reaching your eye was first emitted by that star thousands of years ago. For all you know, the star exploded last year and no longer exists. But the light carrying the information about the explosion won't be here for a very long time. You look up at the sky and see a single shining unexploding star. But that star, the one whose light is entering your eye, no longer exists, let us suppose. The argument from time-lag to indirectness goes something as follows. In the case of the star, it no longer exists, but you are nonetheless aware of something. Since there is no longer a star around for you to be aware of, what you must be aware of is something else, and what better candidate than a state of your own mind? The time-lag argument, if it works at all, works equally well for objects not so distant: even the light bouncing off the furniture across the room takes some time to reach your eye. And even after it hits your eye, there is still a time-lag between that event and the occurrence of your state of perceptual awareness: the light must be processed by neurons in your retina, information is relayed from the retina through the optic nerve and on to various other parts of your brain until the moment of awareness that there is a chair in front of you. But you are aware right now.

The distal stimulus was an event that happened in the past. So what you are aware of right now is something closer to you than the distal stimulus. What, then, is it that you are aware of? Again, the indirect theorist asks: what better candidate than a state of your own mind (and/or brain)?

We might sum up these arguments for indirectness as follows. Whenever you perceive something you are in some mental state: a state of awareness. You are aware of something. If you were aware of nothing you would be unaware, unconscious. But you are not unaware or unconscious. Whatever state you are in when you perceive something, say when you perceive a mug to be blue, could be replicated under conditions in which the mug isn't blue or there is no mug at all. The external object is uneccessary for you to be in that state: the mug may have ceased to exist prior to the onset of that state as per the time-lag argument, or never existed at all as per the hallucination argument. Thus, what you are aware of is whatever it is that is necessary for you to be in that mental state. The external object is unnecessary. The internal state is necessary. Thus, what you are aware of is a state internal to you, a state of your own mind. The only way in which you are aware of a thing external to your mind is indirectly.

3.6.5 Direct realism revisited

Now that the arguments for indirect realism are in place, we can appreciate further considerations in favor of direct realism, since these considerations involve pointing out weaknesses in indirect theories and the arguments for indirectness.

Recall our discussion of homunculus fallacies from section 3.5. Very simple versions of indirect theories themselves invite the charge of homuncular fallacy, for they attempt to explain the perception of external objects in terms of the perception of internal ones. Until the perception of internal objects is explained, the question of how perception works remains begged.

A more powerful and important criticism that might be made involves the indirect theorists' explanation of error. In brief, the criticism is that while the indirect theorist has a nice explanation of error, the crucial components of the explanation can be had by even a direct theorist: the postulation of indirectness goes beyond what is needed to explain error. To spell this out a bit more, consider the following. The crucial component of the indirect theorists' explanation of error is that there is a mismatch between an internal state and the external world. When I misperceive a straight stick to be bent, there is a mental representation internal to me that represents the stick as being bent. But the stick external to me is actually straight, so there is a mismatch between appearance and reality, between my internal mental state and the external mind-independent world. Similarly for flat-out hallucination. When I hallucinate that there is a pink elephant in what in reality is an otherwise empty room, my internal state fails to match external reality. My internal state says that there is a pink elephant in the room, but in external reality, the room's contents are neither pink nor an elephant. Now, the direct realist need not deny this kind of extremely powerful explanation of perceptual error. What the direct realist denies is the part of the indirect realist's argument that moves from the fact that error involves a mismatch to the claim that what one is aware of is the perceptual representation itself. Recall that the indirect theorist argues from the premises

(1) you have to be aware of *something* even in the case of hallucination, and
(2) in the case of hallucination that something cannot be an external thing, because there may very well be no external thing (you may be hallucinating that you are talking to a unicorn even though there are no unicorns)

to the conclusion that the thing you are aware of (stated in the first premise) must be an internal thing. Another way of describing the argument is as a disjunctive syllogism: either you are aware of something internal or something external, there is nothing external to do the trick, so, what you are aware of is something internal. Now a typical way of finding fault with disjunctive syllogisms is by attempting to show that their disjunctive premise constitutes a false dichotomy. Thus, it is open for the direct theorist to say that even though there is no actual external thing for the hallucinator to be aware of, being aware of some actual internal thing is not the only option.

The way the direct theorist can explain perceptual error is largely the same way in which the indirect theorist does it. The explanation at hand is a representational explanation, and the direct theorist need not deny that both hallucinating and accurately perceiving the presence of a pink elephant involve having mental representations of a pink elephant. What the direct realist denies is that what one is aware of in either case is necessarily the representation itself. One way of being a direct realist would be to identify the objects of perceptual awareness with the representational contents involved. Thus, in the accurate case, one mentally represents there being a pink elephant in front of one, and there actually is a pink elephant. In the illusory or hallucinatory case one mentally represents there being a pink elephant in front of one but there is no pink elephant. In both cases the answer to the question "What are you aware of?" is the same as the question "What are you mentally representing?" – the presence of a pink elephant. Thus the objects of awareness are representational contents, and contents need not exist. That is, a representation can be about something that doesn't exist, as in the case of a representation of a unicorn. There is, to be sure, the unsolved mystery of how a physical thing like a brain state can come to be about, that is, have as a representational content something that doesn't exist. But that doesn't pose any special problem for direct realist: it's as much a problem for the indirect theorist.

What implications does cognitive science have for the debate between indirect and direct realists? As already mentioned, one of the core insights of cognitive science is the representational theory of mind, that mental processes involve mental representations. In keeping with this insight, the most obvious way of thinking of the perceptual awareness of some thing is as involving the mental representation of that thing. So if I am aware of some thing x, I have a mental representation y that represents x. Along these lines then, the indirect theory that says I am aware of an external thing x only in virtue of being aware of an internal thing y would be spelled out in accordance with the representational theory of mind by saying that in order to be aware of thing x I must not only represent it with mental representation y, I must necessarily be aware of y. Thus, there is some third item z that represents y that is involved in my direct awareness of y. For the direct realist, however, there need only be x and y, z is superfluous. The conflict between the direct and indirect theorist may then be seen as at least partially amenable to empirical investigation. It is open to empirical investigations whether there is anything in the nervous system that seems up to the task of playing the roles of *y* and *z* (thus supporting indirect theories), or if *y* is the only thing to be found.

Regardless of whether direct or indirect theories are true of perception, the nature of this philosophical debate has a close tie to cognitive science. One of the key insights that emerges from the debate, especially in wrestling with the problem of error, is the insight that perception involves representation. Further topics discussed in this chapter concern the nature of perceptual representation, and the relation between representations and the external world.

3.6.6 Idealism

The most global form of idealism says that nothing exists independently of our minds. Berkeley famously argued that to be is to be perceived. Idealism admits of more local forms as well; thus, one may be a realist about some objects and their properties and an idealist about others. The versions of idealism that figure in contemporary discussions most frequently are local.

Why would someone be an idealist? What arguments can be martialed in favor of idealism? One of the clearest modern idealist arguments is due to George Berkeley (1710, 1713). Of Berkeley's arguments for idealism, the one that he regarded as central to his system, and the one that has come to be called his master argument is the following. If one can "conceive it possible" that the objects one thinks about "may exist without the mind," then "it is necessary that [one] conceive them existing unconceived of or unthought of, which is a manifest repugnancy" (Berkeley 1710, §23).

The kinds of considerations just mentioned lead to a kind of tautological form of idealism. It is tautological insofar as it has as its basis the fact that everything that we think about is thereby thought about. Who could deny that? Everything that exists is thought about. Thinking the thought expressed by the previous sentence makes it the case that everything that exists is thereby thought about. Are these remarks sufficient to establish anything *interesting*? The claim that such and such depends for its existence on mind seems like a pretty bold and interesting claim.

Slightly different considerations in favor of idealism arise when we consider more local versions. Of particular relevance to the theory of perception is the question of the nature of the colors that we perceive objects as having. One kind of consideration in favor of idealism with regards to color asserts that we cannot conceive of color-as-we see-it existing unperceived. The philosopher Gareth Evans (1985) argues that there is a theoretical difficulty in imagining them instantiated unperceived. According to Evans the closest that we can come to imagining sensory properties instantiated unperceived is by imagining their non-sensory causal ground unperceived. Evans argues that it is quite difficult to see how an object "as we see it" can be the same as when we do not see it (Evans 1985, pp. 272–274). Suppose that I am seeing an apple as red. How can it be red when no one is seeing it, when, say, it is locked in a dark cellar? Evans contends that this is inconceivable. Evans writes that "All it can amount to for something to be red is that it be such that, if looked at in the normal conditions, it will appear red." Evans contrasts this view with one that tries "to make sense of the idea of a property of redness which is both an abiding property of the object, both perceived and unperceived, and yet 'exactly as we experience redness to be'." Evans objects to this latter view, maintaining that "it would be quite obscure how a 'colour-as-we-see-it' can exist when we cannot see it, and how our experiences of colour would enable us to form a conception of such a state of affairs" (Evans 1985, pp. 272–273).

One way to defend this latter view is by suggesting that the obscurity alleged by Evans arises due to a concealed ambiguity in sentences employing phrases like "as I see it." Once such phrases are properly disambiguated, it becomes quite clear how a color as we see it may be the same when it is not seen. Consider sentences employing phrases with the form "x as I am F-ing it." Consider the sentence "The chair as I am standing next to it is the same as when I am not standing next to it." There is a reading of this sentence whereby it is quite clearly contradictory. On such a reading the sentence expresses the claim that a chair stood next to is a chair not stood next to. This is contradictory on the supposition that a chair cannot be both stood next to and not stood next to at the same time. Suppose, then, that we were to read the following sentences along similar lines: "The chair as I see it is the same as when I do not see it." On such a reading, Evans would be correct that it is quite obscure how the chair as I see it can be the same as when I do not see it. There *is* a difference between the chair as I see it and the chair when it is not seen by me, namely, in the first case I am seeing it and in the second I am not. And on the supposition that the chair cannot be both seen and unseen at the same time, the sentence under consideration expresses a contradiction.

However, some sentences employing phrases with the form "x as I am F-ing it" may be read in different way than that considered so far. The sentences in question are those in which the verb phrase describes a representational act. Consider a sentence like "The chair as I am describing it is the same as when I am not describing it." This sentence admits of a reading whereby it expresses a contradiction. On such a reading the above sentence is equivalent to "The chair described is not described." But on the alternative reading – the representational reading – a chair can be as I describe it even when I am not describing it. Suppose that I am describing the chair as having been manufactured in Switzerland. I am uttering the sentence "This chair was manufactured in Switzerland." My describing the chair is just my uttering a sentence. The chair being as I describe it, however, is not its being a chair in the proximity of someone uttering a sentence. The chair being as I describe, in this case, is its having been manufactured in Switzerland. Clearly a chair may have been manufactured in Switzerland regardless of whether I am now describing it as such. With this last point in mind, then, we may read "The chair as I am describing it is the same as when I am not describing it" as non-contradictory on the grounds that a Swiss chair doesn't stop being Swiss when I stop talking. Thus, the sentence "The chair as I am describing it is the same as when I am not describing it" admits of a representational reading which reveals the sentence to be non-contradictory. Similarly, if we view color vision as a largely representational affair, "The chair as I see it is the same as when I am not seeing it" does not express a contradiction. My visual system may be representing the chair as being red, and the chair may be red even when I am not seeing it as such, just as the chair may be Swiss even when I am not describing it as such.

This argument does not definitively settle matters, however. Representational realists about color perception are still engaged in battle with color idealists or subjectivists, as we describe in the next section.

3.7 COLOR PERCEPTION

One popular theory in sensory neuroscience of how the brain codes for sensory qualities (like color) is the *opponent process account* (Hardin 1988). Churchland (1993) describes a three-dimensional activation vector state-space in which every color perceivable by humans is represented as a point (or subvolume). Each dimension corresponds to activity rates in one of three classes of photoreceptors present in the human retina and their efferent paths: the red–green opponent pathway, yellow–blue opponent pathway, and black–white (contrast) opponent pathway. Photons striking the retina are transduced by the receptors, producing an activity rate in each of the segregated pathways. A represented color is hence a triplet of activation frequency rates. The varieties of perceived colors may be represented as points in a three-dimensional space. Each dimension in that three-dimensional space will represent average frequency of action potentials in the axons of one class of ganglion cells projecting out of the retina. Each color perceivable by humans will be a region of that space. For example, an orange stimulus produces a relatively low level of activity in both the red–green and yellow–blue opponent pathways (x-axis and y-axis, respectively), and middle-range activity in the black–white (contrast) opponent pathway (z-axis). Pink stimuli, on the other hand, produce low activity in the red–green opponent pathway, middle-range activity in the yellow–blue opponent pathway, and high activity in the black–white (contrast) opponent pathway. The three-dimensional color-space not only represents the average frequency of action potentials in neurons, but also represents the structure of the way colors appear to us. Locations in this space and geometrical proximity between regions reflect similarities between the perceived colors. Colors that seem more similar will be closer in this space.

A longstanding philosophical dispute is whether colors are objective properties existing external to perceivers or rather identifiable as or dependent upon minds or nervous systems. Are objects in the world literally colored, or is color added by the brain's visual system?

One consideration in favor of color subjectivism or color internalism has to do with the "hue circle": color similarity judgments produce color orderings that align on a circle (Clark 1993). Red is similar to orange which is similar to yellow which is similar to green which is similar to blue which is similar to purple which is similar to red, leading us back to where we started. The question arises of what accounts for the hue circle: features of the external stimulus or features of the neurophysiology of the visual system? Identifying colors with particular frequencies of electromagnetic radiation does not preserve the structure of the hue circle, whereas identifying colors with activity in opponent-processing neurons does. Such a tidbit is not decisive for the color objectivist–subjectivist debate, but it does convey the type of questions under consideration

Another consideration in favor of color subjectivism is the phenomenon of Benham's top. Benham's top is a simple spinning top that has only black and white arcs on it, but when spun, the arcs change into rings of color. Perhaps the top tricks the brain into adding colors to the visual percept. Some philosophers argue that what we think of as colors in the world are actually similar to the "false colors" that are added to infrared photographs in order to make certain contours and edges in infrared intensity stand out to humans viewing the photographs. This is all rather shocking, you say, didn't we learn in grade school that colors are just light having certain wavelengths, bouncing off of objects and into our eyes? Saying that an object is red just means that the object reflects light predominantly in the range 600 to 650 nanometers (a nanometer is a billionth of a meter). This in itself is a bit shocking when you think about it, since it also implies that objects themselves are not colored. Some philosophers have attempted to square the intuition that objects are colored with the alleged scientific fact that colors are electromagnetic frequency ranges by arguing that colors are not properties of light, but rather dispositions which objects have to reflect light in those ranges, and hence colors really are properties of objects. But there is one large problem with this position, the disjunction problem: there is no one property of objects which can make them reflect light at this frequency. All kinds of materials, with all kinds of different molecular structures, can emit light at these frequencies. So really, it is the light frequency itself which is the essential thing, and this again makes it the better candidate for color.

Even the theory that color corresponds to light frequency is subject to a more general type of disjunction problem, however. There are a large number of ways to produce sensations of, say, red, which do not involve light traveling at the wavelength between 600 and 650 nanometers. Such as the following:

(1)   When I push rather firmly on my closed eyelid, I get an impression of redness. It seems right to say that there is no light at the appropriate frequency under my eyelid. And yet there is a sensation of redness, or, something is red, we want to say. One sort of tack to take to defend the traditional view would be to argue that this is in some way not a legitimate instance of red. But surely something is red there, and we need a good reason, in the form of a working theory, to deny this.
(2)   Stare at a green square on a white background for a few minutes, then look at a clear white piece of paper. Again, you will have an impression of redness, an afterimage. But once again, there is no light involved traveling at the supposed right frequency for red.
(3)   Form a mental image of a red square. This certainly seems to be an instance of redness, yet there is surely no actual light of any frequency bouncing around inside your brain.

One sort of objection to the above cases is that none of them involves the impression that the redness is actually out there in the world. They are all instances of a sort of phantom, hazy "mental red," some distant echo of the real red that is in light (or on objects) out there. Benham's disk is the answer to this though. It is a top with a flat, circular surface containing only black arcs of certain lengths printed on a white background. But spin the top and watch it from above, and colors appear (usually red, green, blue, and yellow) which seem quite obviously to be features of the top. Yet when the top stops spinning they are gone again. It can be shown that there is no light of the predicted frequency entering the eye. What has apparently happened in the Benham's disk case is that the mechanisms which add color to visual representations have been tricked into painting the visual representation a certain color by a deviant causal process, one other than light of the right frequency entering the eye.

The above cases, however, do not definitively settle the debate in favor of idealism or internalism about color. Just because there are many divergent ways to get the perceptual system to represent an object as being colored does not mean that color is not an objective property in the external world. As the philosopher Fred Dretske (1995) has pointed out, there are similarly divergent ways of fooling a person into thinking that they are looking at a woman – convincing wax statues, holograms, and even a life-sized cardboard cut-out in the right lighting may fool you into thinking that you are seeing a woman when you really are not. But from this mere fact we would not be warranted in asserting that whether something is a woman is in the eye of the beholder. Again, a reliance on the representational theory of the mind may be invoked to solve the problems involved. Color externalists such as Dretske (1995) and Michael Tye (1995, 2000) say that there is indeed a relatively non-disjunctive objective physical property of the surfaces of objects that colors may be identified with. Cases like the Benham top are thus treated as an instance of illusion: the top is not really red or green, but has fooled the visual system into representing it as red or green just as a cardboard cutout may fool the visual system into representing it as a human female.

3.8 THE THEORY-LADENNESS OF PERCEPTION

Most of the words we use for perception have many different meanings. Consider the word "see" for instance. There is an initial distinction between visual and non-visual senses, the non-visual sense being roughly equivalent to "understand." The visual sense of "see" contains different senses of its own, however. One might distinguish between a cognitive and a non-cognitive sense of "see." One might express this distinction with the truism that sometimes I do not see something because I do not know what I am seeing, while other times I see something, even though I do not know what I am seeing.

Take a person from a Stone-Age culture deep in the jungles of Borneo and a car mechanic from New Jersey and have them look under the hood of a car. In one sense of "see" the two will see the same thing; in another sense, though, the mechanic will see a great deal more than the Bornean. One way to objectively evaluate the claim that the mechanic sees more would simply be to have the two give a verbal description of what they saw. The mechanic's description would contain more information, and would be far more likely to contain useful information about the functional state of the engine, for instance the fact that there is an oil leak at a certain location.

Something quite similar happens when we look at "ambiguous" figures, such as the duck/rabbit (Figure 3.12).

When we switch from seeing the duck to seeing the rabbit, we are seeing something new in the cognitive sense of "see," but if we use the non-cognitive sense, what we see has not changed. In the cognitive sense of "see," what you know conditions how you see things. In other words, observation is theory laden: how one perceives the world depends on the theory with which one conceives the world. For instance, a newborn baby, if shown a cathode-ray tube, would not see it *as* a cathode-ray tube because the baby would understand an insufficient amount

FIGURE 3.12 The duck/rabbit

of theory to know what cathode ray tubes are. There is much controversy in cognitive science, however, about just how theory laden perception actually is. Fodor (1983), for example, argues against the view that perception is theory laden. He argues that many perceptual processes are modular in the sense of being "informationally encapsulated" or "cognitively impenetrable" so that their outputs are immune to influence by theoretical and other acquired beliefs. Fodor sees such a view as supporting realism about the relation between the mind and world. Fodor contends that observational reports can be treated as univocal even when theorists hold different theories. But if observation is extremely theory laden, then observation cannot be called upon as an objective arbiter between competing theories, thus seeming to leave us powerless to determine how the world really is independently of our changing opinions about it.

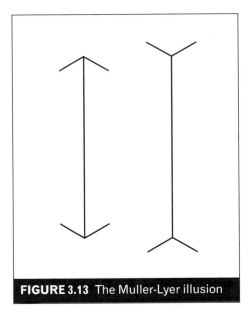

FIGURE 3.13 The Muller-Lyer illusion

To illustrate the case in favor of the view that perception is informationally encapsulated, consider certain illusory figures such as the Muller-Lyer illusion (see Figure 3.13).

In the Muller-Lyer illusion, one of the line segments looks longer than the other. You may measure them and confirm that they are indeed the same length. But this acquired belief, the belief that they are the same length, does not change the way you perceive the figures. Even after learning that they are the same length, you still perceive one as being longer than the other. Likewise for the world's largest human-made optical illusion, the gateway arch in St. Louis, Missouri. The arch seems taller than it is wide, as is evident from Figure 3.14, but measurement confirms that the height equals the width.

The largest non-human-made illusion is the moon illusion. The moon looks larger when it nears the horizon than when it is high in the sky, but the image that is hitting your retina is the same in both cases. The earth's atmosphere is not acting as a lens to magnify the image. Were you to observe the moon through a glass window and trace an outline around the moon with a grease pencil at different times in the evening as it moves from near the horizon toward the zenith, the penciled outlines would all be the same diameter. All of these illusions are resistant to change by the acquisition of theoretical knowledge. Even though you come to learn that the height of the St. Louis Arch is equal to its width, this doesn't change the visual appearance. These considerations in favor of informational encapsulation are not intended to deny that perception is "smart" in that it embodies certain "theoretical" assumptions about the world or deny that perception involves inferential processes. Such theoretical and inferential processes may be hardwired into the perceptual modules. What Fodor (1983) intends to argue against is the view that the acquisition of new knowledge by central cognitive systems can alter the outputs of perceptual modules.

The philosopher offers a contrary view on the question of informational encapsulation. Consider the Kaniza figure in Figure 3.15. Patricia Churchland (1993) writes of such figures:

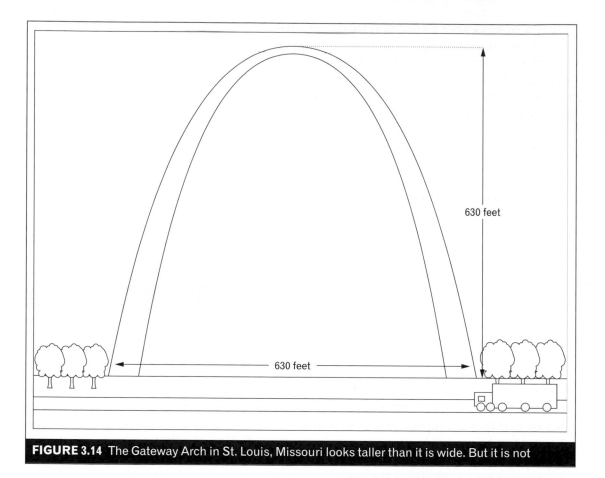

FIGURE 3.14 The Gateway Arch in St. Louis, Missouri looks taller than it is wide. But it is not

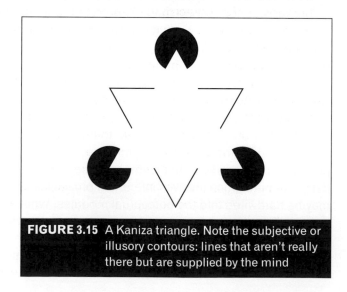

FIGURE 3.15 A Kaniza triangle. Note the subjective or illusory contours: lines that aren't really there but are supplied by the mind

The white background . . . is, of course, entirely uniform. But most of us can see a slightly brighter triangular figure interposed between us and the three black circles, a figure with distinct rectilinear contours marked by a sharp change in luminance, even in the gap between the black circles. Here the eye-brain conjures up luminance differences where in reality there are none. And again, the illusion is penetrable and reversible. Tell yourself that the circles have wedges cut out of them; see the elements of the diagram as six independent objects artfully arranged against a uniform background; center your attention on the two prongs of any V; and the illusory contours disappear.

(Churchland 1993: 261)

This is one of several examples that Churchland gives of illusions that do not persist in the face of a change in belief and knowledge. Churchland also argues that even if perception is encapsulated, it does not provide an assurance of objectivity. Even if everyone has hardwired non-penetrable perceptual modules to turn to as arbiters in theoretical disputes, there is no guarantee that the modules would be hardwired to provide evidence about the way things really are. There is no guarantee that our modules are not wired-up to be systematically deceptive.

3.9 PERCEPTUAL PLASTICITY

A feature of perception closely related to cognitive penetrability is perceptual plasticity. Perception is plastic: it is pliable and amenable to change. Here we describe two main types of perceptual plasticity. The first kind of perceptual plasticity is due to the acquisition and application of concepts. The second kind is perceptual–motor adaptation.

The cases cited above in favor of the existence of cognitive penetrability are all instances of concept-based perceptual plasticity. Perhaps one of the most exquisite examples of perception changing because of the acquisition and application of concepts is due to the philosopher Paul Churchland (1979). Churchland's example has to do with the way in which we perceive the night sky. When you look at the night sky it is very easy to see it as the ancients saw it: as a large dome peppered with lights or pinpricks through which light shines. It is very easy to see the stars and planets as being equally far away from you, even though you may know that the distances of the heavenly bodies vary greatly. Some of the stars are thousands of light years away, some merely hundreds of light years away, and the planets are mere light minutes away. Churchland describes a procedure by which one can come to see the night sky in a very different way. The procedure is easy to employ and the results can be quite striking. Assuming that you are in the northern hemisphere, the procedure is as follows. The next clear evening, make a note of the location on the horizon where the sun set. Note too the locations in the night sky of the planets Jupiter and Mars. Now imagine a straight line drawn in the night sky that connects Jupiter, Mars, and the point on the horizon where the sun set. This line is pretty much parallel to the solar disc: the region in which all of the orbits of the planets in the solar system and the asteroid belt are contained. Tilt your head so that it is perpendicular to the line drawn: the vertical axis of your head will be perpendicular to the plane of the solar disc. Contemplate the picture while you do this and you will get a very clear sense of the three-dimensional arrangement of the sun, earth, and other planets in the solar system. You will have a sense of where Mars and Jupiter are on this disc, and further, you will have a sense of the stars not being on this disc. The stars are scattered throughout the universe and quite far away from the solar system. These various facts about the arrangements of the heavenly bodies become perceptually apparent if the above procedure is followed.

We turn now to discuss instances of perceptual plasticity that involve perceptual–motor adaptation. The first instance concerns glass with special lenses that can drastically alter the visual appearance of the world. Glasses with prism lenses can be fashioned that will shift the visual scene several degrees to the right or left, and some will turn the whole scene upside-down. At first the experience is disorienting and your visually guided movements will be awkward. With lenses that shift the scene to the left, however, you will still have enough hand–eye coordination to throw some small bean-bags at a target on a wall about ten feet away from you. At first, you will miss the target in a systematic way, all of the bean-bags end up missing it to the same side. After only a minute or so of practice, you will find that you are able to hit the target about as reliably as before you put the glasses on. Perceptual–motor adaptation has taken place. Now if you remove the glasses and attempt to hit the target with the bean-bags, you will miss the target again, but this time the bean-bags will be thrown to the other side. The perceptual–motor system is over-compensating, but again, only about a minute needs to pass before you will be back to normal.

Such perceptual–motor adaptation is able to compensate for changes even more drastic, as in the case of lenses that completely invert the visual scene. Some researchers, experimenting on themselves, have found that they could eventually get along relatively well with the glasses on, even to the point where they could ski. The interesting question that arises is how things seemed to the subject after the adaptation had taken place. Did the world look right-side-up after a while or were they simply used to the world looking upside-down? Here the matter is not clear cut. Subjects report that frequently they didn't notice the difference, but that, upon reflection, they could tell that something wasn't quite right. One possibility is that there really isn't a distinction that makes a difference between the world looking right-side-up and having a certain level of perceptual–motor coordination with respect to the world. What matters for getting around is knowing, for instance, where your head is with respect to an obstacle so that you do not injure yourself. Perceptual–motor adaptation allows the brain an enormous amount of flexibility in how it achieves accurate representations of the world and the body's position within it. The representations in the brain need not themselves be "right-side-up" in order to represent things in the world as being right-side-up any more than things in the brain need to be bright orange in order to represent things in the world as being bright orange. We know that in normal cases the image on the retina projected by the lens in our eye is "upside-down" with respect to the visible world. Why do things nonetheless look "right-side-up"? Because one way or the other the brain comes to represent things as being right-side-up regardless of whether the brain's representations are themselves right-side-up.

Some of the most dramatic cases of perceptual–motor adaptation are due to experiments Paul Bach-y-Rita (1972) performed in developing prosthetic vision devices for blind people. The devices typically consist of a camera worn on the subject's head that sends low-resolution video signals to a 16-by-16 or 20-by-20 array of tactile stimulators worn on the subject's back (see Figures 3.16 and 3.17).

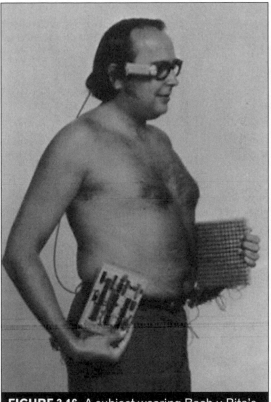

FIGURE 3.16 A subject wearing Bach-y-Rita's prosthetic vision device. The subject is strapping the stimulator array across his belly

After only a few hours of training with the device, subjects could utilize the tactile stimulation fed to the surface of their skin by the camera to recognize distal faces and objects and read printed words that the camera was focused on.

Arguably, the trained subjects' experiences manifested many of the features of normal vision. Just as a person's tactile point of view can extend to the tip of a walking cane, the point of view of the trained subjects shifted from the sites of stimulation on their back to the point of view of the camera. Bach-y-Rita reports an occasion in which the zoom control of a subject's camera was activated without warning by an experimenter, causing the image in the camera to loom suddenly. The subject reacted by raising his arms to his head and lurching backwards (Bach-y-Rita 1972, pp. 98–99). Although the tactile stimulus array was located *low* on the subject's *back*, the subject's behavior indicates that he located the percept *high* and *in front of* him. And in looming, the objects seen through the camera were seen by the subject as rapidly approaching him.

A necessary condition on being able to "see through" the camera-driven tactile array is that the subject be allowed to exert control over the inputs to the camera (Bach-y-Rita 1972). Bach-y-Rita notes that the major portion of the first few hours of the subjects' training is occupied by learning the techniques of camera manipulation, including controlling the operation of the zoom lens, the aperture and focus, and also the direction of the camera towards regions of the subjects' immediate environment (1972, pp. 3–4). Bach-y-Rita further notes that subjects with a high degree of manual dexterity acquire the ability to see through the prosthetic vision devices more quickly than those with a low degree of manual dexterity (1972, p. 7).

In discussing the case of the subject who raised his hands to protect his head in response to an unanticipated activation of the camera's zoom control, Bach-y-Rita writes: "The startle response described above was obtained by a well-trained subject who was accustomed to have camera movement, zoom, and aperture under his control" (1972, p. 99).

Further, Bach-y-Rita writes, when subjects receive tactile array inputs from a *static* camera, they "report experiences in terms of feelings on the skin, but when they move the camera their reports are in terms of externally localized objects" (1972, p. 99).

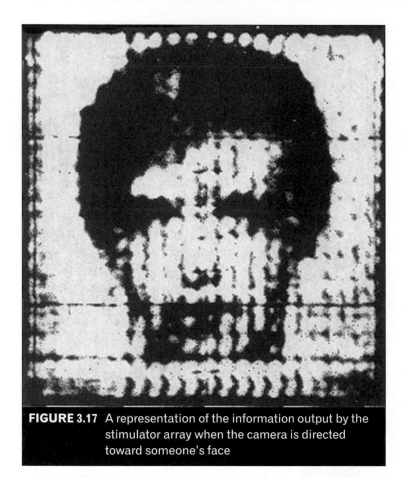

FIGURE 3.17 A representation of the information output by the stimulator array when the camera is directed toward someone's face

Although the exercise of motor control over the inputs is necessary for the projection phenomena, it is not sufficient. Consider, in this regard, a datum presented by Bach-y-Rita: when a subject trained to see through the tactile array of the prosthetic vision device later scratches his back, he does not "see" the scratches (1972, p. 32). But, nonetheless, in scratching his back, he is in control of the tactile input. Thus, while necessary for instantiating the sensory projection essential to functioning as a distance sense, exerting motor control over one's sensory inputs seems not to be sufficient.

3.10 THE CONCEPT OF FEEDBACK

The phenomenon of perceptual–motor adaptation is one of many illustrations of the foundational concept of feedback systems. This is a crucial concept, since one of the essential characteristics of all biological systems is that they self-regulating. Understanding how a machine can achieve some measure of this at the most elementary level is the first step in understanding the sort of feedback between system and environment required for various degrees not only of perception but also of all computational models of stimulus–response functioning. As one investigator put it, "If you truly understand X, you must be able to build a machine that does X."

The reason feedback is such an important concept is that investigating perception in our own case quickly reveals that the notion that we simply receive input from the surrounding environment and thereby "see" it is grossly antiquated. Consider, for instance, what happens when you spot a coin on the ground and reach to pick it up. You perceive a smooth motion in which your hand reaches for the coin and picks it up. But what appears phenomenally as a smooth legato motion is, in reality, a staccato: the body makes a rapid-fire series of muscular adjustments, aiming at the target, overshooting, undershooting, back and forth in a complex feedback between the perceptual representational system in the brain and the motor controls that move and adjust the muscles accordingly to fit both the input data and the phenomenal events being observed in the representational manifold inside the brain. This complex neuroanatomical process involves the eyes, the optic nerves, and many different parts of the brain, all of which must be coordinated to achieve the simple result of picking up a coin. One of the biggest and most difficult questions to answer about human perception is how these separate functions get coordinated. Studying machine perception allows us to try to understand this piecemeal, one component at a time, in a way that we could never do simply by studying our own brains. Second, no amount of a priori conceptual analysis or purely mathematical modeling of perception can generate what we have now come to understand as the single most important factor to perception, namely, that the perceiving system is situated in an environment. Third, the perceiving system must be able to regulate itself not just in relation to that environment but also in relation to itself: for fully fledged perception to take place it must be able to regulate within itself both a representation of its surrounding environment and of itself in that environment. This too requires a complex array of constant internal adjustments, allowing the perceptual system to thereby track its external relations to the surrounding environment through changes in its internal relations.

3.11 COMPUTATIONAL VISION

One important area of study within cognitive science that tries to understand the information processing necessary for any such perceptual system to operate involves generating computational models of vision. How is information about an environment extracted, say, from light signals by a mechanical device? The cognitive scientist then integrates this knowledge with studies of vision systems in biology, psychology, and neuroscience in order to determine what would be required for a neural mechanism to be able to carry out such information processing at the highly sophisticated level of a human being.

Obviously, a key question has to do with the physical measurement of information encoded in light reflected from the surfaces of objects and that enters some receptor such as the eye. What we have learned about the process from computational studies is that there is not just one but three primary levels of vision representation necessary to extract sufficient information from a light-saturated environment to make perception possible, which we shall refer to as primary, secondary, and tertiary representation (these levels correspond, for instance, in the visual representational system, to what has generally come to be known as lower-level, mid-level, and higher-level vision). Primary visual representation encodes information about an object such as its location, contrast, sharpness of edges, etc. In computer-rendering programs you can see these as boundaries between object and surrounding space or other objects, surface textures and texture contours, shadows, highlights, and so on. If the object is in motion, this too will be captured by the primary representation information-processing subsystem.

Secondary visual representation manages to encode the three-dimensional shape of objects from the observer's perspective, thereby achieving at the same time the representation of location of the perceiving system in relation to its surrounding environment. But the most complex representational system is that of tertiary visual representation, which encodes information that may at first glance be similar to and difficult to distinguish from secondary visual representation, but is immensely more difficult and complicated to achieve: the location, shape, and three-dimensional structure of the perceived object in relation to a fixed frame of reference conceived from a standpoint coordinated to some particular location in the world conceived as an observer-neutral "public space." It has been discovered through computer vision modeling and mechanical robots that tertiary-level computational abilities of object recognition, motion, and object manipulation are impossible without the secondary and primary representations operating in consort with a three-dimensional map of the environment within which the observer is situated, along with a surprisingly rich store of laws, or principles, about the nature, structure, and behavior of physical objects in a physical environment – how they move (continuously unless interrupted by some force, for instance), that they persist, that they are conjoint units whose parts remain in the same relation to each other, laws of mechanics, of fluidity and rigidity, and so on. In other words, the perceiving system must in some sense and to some degree have the laws of physics encoded into itself to enable a representational system to generate visual perceptions.

Our knowledge of the anatomy and physiology of the human perceptual apparatus can be greatly increased by thinking of these processes as computational. The primary benefit we derive from this is that it allows us to bring to bear all of the highly developed theories computer scientists have about their creations: computers. Ensembles of neurons, as different as they seem from your laptop, can be understood using many of the same principles involved in the design and construction of your computer. Thinking of neural nets as performing computations typically comes with certain claims about what certain sets of neurons are representing. Our current thinking about the nature of the neural representations is that they are not local to a single cell – the infamous grandmother cell which fires when (and only when) you perceive or think about your grandmother. Rather, they seem to be distributed among several neurons. In short, thinking about neurons as computational units gives us a framework to understand the myriad of mind-numbingly complex circuits we see in the brain. Understanding neurons this way also allows us new insights into what computations our brains are capable of, but not currently performing.

According to the classical way of thinking, however, by mating an a posteriori science such as biology with an a priori discipline such as the study of computation, we are trying to mix oil and water. Biology is a hands-on, formaldehyde-smelling, real science, while the study of computation can be conducted strictly in the mind of the investigator, making it more akin to mathematics or philosophy than to science. However, without a study of the actual computational properties of physical computation systems such as your laptop, the science of computation has no application to the real world. The argument cuts the other way too. Biology has always kept and used the robust notion of form it inherited from Aristotle. If we examine the history of computational work on vision, we find a trend toward interest in computational systems which are increasingly human-like in their structure and capacities. The interesting thing about the sciences of computation and robotics is that, because of the general nature of science, once they arrive at creations which are the equal of human perception and other abilities, they will soon begin to produce systems which exceed human abilities. Of course in a sense this was always the case: scientists do computer analyses on their data to uncover patterns not visible with the naked eye.

Neural networks and connectionism both share the idea that sets of neurons store information in the connection strengths between units. However, one difference of opinion in the two theories concerns whether something called non-local learning can happen. That is, for instance, can the strength of the connection between two units be adjusted by something other than one of those two units – by some connections feeding back from further down the line of processing? Instead, more biologically minded modelers prefer to use a local learning rule, such as Hebb's rule, which specifies that connection strength between two units (or cells) is altered depending on the level of activity of the two cells. Typically, the connection is strengthened when both cells are active at the same time (or within the same time interval).

A neuron receives several inputs, which are either excitatory, making it more likely that the neuron will fire, or inhibitory, making it less likely that the neuron will fire. Drawings do little justice to the complexity of this procedure, since neurons often have from 5000 to 20,000 inputs. The neuron sums these inputs, roughly by adding all the excitatory inputs and subtracting from this all the inhibitory inputs. If this result exceeds a certain threshold, the neuron fires an electrical signal down the axon, toward the next synapse.

One of the most remarkable aspects of this sort of approach to the study of perception is that it allows us to explain how perception can occur without the need of a homunculus. This is accomplished through theories of self-organizing systems that over time learn to actualize a proper response to some given situation. Slight variations in the surrounding environment must activate swift changes in the system, which is achieved through adaptation, learning, and evolutionary processes.

3.12 NEUROPSYCHOLOGY AND PERCEPTUAL DISORDERS

Much light can be shed on how perception works by studying cases in which it does not. The systematic ways in which things can go wrong help us to understand how it accomplishes its tasks when things are going right. Neuropsychology offers many examples of telling perceptual disorders.

3.12.1 Prosopagnosia

Prosopagnosia is a neurological syndrome in which patients are unable to recognize the faces of people they are familiar with, such as family members, in spite of having otherwise normal vision. A prosopagnosic may have to wait until people speak before being able to identify them. But curiously, he or she is able to identify ordinary objects just fine, something which indicates that the brain uses different resources for recognizing people and for recognizing objects. Typically the site of damage in prosopagnosia is the inferior temporal cortex, bilaterally (although recently patients have been found who seem to have damage on only one side).

In the mid-1980s, however, first Bauer (1984), then Tranel and Damasio (1985, 1988) discovered that prosopagnosics register a larger skin conductance response to photos of familiar people, just as normal subjects do. Skin conductance response (formerly known as galvanic skin response) is a measure of sweat gland activity produced by the sympathetic branch of the autonomic nervous system (see Chapter 5 for more on the autonomic nervous system). If a normal person is seated in front of a computer monitor and shown several pictures of familiar and unfamiliar faces, as his or her skin conductance responses are recorded, the SCRs to the familiar faces will be larger than those to the unfamiliar faces. Tranel and Damasio did this with several prosopagnosics and found that some of them also registered this "unconscious familiarity response."

This work shows that there are (at least) two visual face recognition routes in the human brain, a conscious one that is disrupted in prosopagnosia, and an unconscious one, which remains intact in some prosopagnosics. (It is an open question as to whether the "conscious route" is itself conscious, or whether it sends input to some other area specific to conscious mental activity; for purposes of simplification, we shall simply call such routes and functions "conscious," that is, when they have a conscious state as an output.) While it seems clear that the area is important for the conscious recognition route, little is known about which areas of the brain are involved in the unconscious recognition route. These findings also suggest that there is far more to mentality than consciousness, and again raises the problem – to be discussed in Chapter 7 – of what consciousness itself is and what role it plays.

3.12.2 Phantom limbs

Patients with phantom limbs experience an amputated extremity as still present, and in some cases also experience pain or cramping in the missing limb (see Ramachandran and Hirstein 1998). Patients recognize that the sensations are not veridical: what they experience is an illusion, not a delusion. Patients also frequently complain that the phantom is painful. The incidence of severity of pain is such that it poses a major clinical problem; as many as 70 percent of phantoms remain painful even twenty years after the loss of the limb. Almost immediately after the loss of a limb, between 90 percent and 98 percent of all patients experience a vivid phantom. There are hints that the incidence may be higher following a traumatic loss or if there has been a pre-existing painful condition in the limb than after a planned surgical amputation of a non-painful limb. Phantoms are seen far less often in early childhood. Perhaps in young children, there has not yet been enough time for the body image to "consolidate."

Now, what is the body image? We'll use the example of dreams to illustrate because it is very clear to you right now, as you are reading this, that in the dream the body you are situated in is not your actual physical body but only a representation. What is not so obvious to you right now as you are reading this is that the body you seem to be situated in at present is also a representation of your body. In other words, typically in a dream you seem to be located – just as in waking states – in a body. You have limbs, arms and legs, a torso, and seem to be situated where you take your head to be. Suppose you dream that you are at a doctor's office for a migraine headache, and she asks you where it hurts. You lift your hand and put it on the top of your head. But of course, neither the head nor the hand holding the head are your actual head and hand, any more than the body that seems to be yours in the doctor's office is really your body. For what you are situated in inside your dream is a body image, along with an imaginary head from whose perspective the dream is being experienced by you. Now, the limbs that move in a dream – your arm and hand, for instance – are parts of your body image. Your actual arm and hand are in reality at your side for you are lying in bed asleep. The virtual world of your dream contains images of objects, up to and including your body image; however, these objects do not correspond as they do in waking states to things in the surrounding physical environment (in reality you're home in bed and not at the doctor's office) and, most importantly, your body image is, in a sense, "off line." That is, the willed movement of your body image does not affect the movement of your physical limbs. In this limited sense, all your limbs in a dream are phantom limbs: they do not correspond to the actual movements of your physical limbs. When you wake up, your body image is still your body image; the difference is that now it is "on line" and corresponds to some sufficiently veridical degree to your physical body and, most importantly, the willed movement of your body image moves your physical limbs. Of course it may be quite shocking to realize that the body you are situated in – regardless of whether you are asleep or awake – is but a body image, and the environment you perceive – regardless of whether you are asleep or awake – is a virtual reality that, in waking states, corresponds to some sufficient degree to the surrounding physical environment. (Again, keep in mind that there are two different but related questions that we are exploring in this chapter: how such events come about in the brain and, second, how they can correspond to an external environment.) The early Indian philosopher Shankara (AD 788–820) is aware of the implication that the dream body image and the waking body image are both representations, but draws a skeptical conclusion from this:

> You never identify yourself with the shadow cast by your body,
> Or with its reflection, or with the body you see in a dream, or in your imagination.
> Therefore you should not identify
> yourself with this living body either.
>
> (Shankara, *Vivela Chudamani*, Vedic scriptures, quoted in Cronk 2003)

Now, in the case of the phantom limb patients who have had a limb amputated, the problem seems to be that the brain has still some key aspect of the original full body image in place, so that even though they do not see the missing limb they still feel it. In many cases the phantom is present initially for a few days or weeks, then gradually fades from consciousness. In other cases, it may persist for years, even decades. Some patients are able to recall a phantom limb at will after its disappearance with intense concentration or sometimes merely by rubbing the stump.

The vividness of phantoms appears to depend on the extent of cortex devoted to representing that body part (hence the vividness of perception of the hand) as well as the subjective vividness of that part in one's body image prior to amputation (which would explain why they occur more often following a traumatic loss or after a painful appendage has been removed). This might imply that factors such as pre-amputation attention to a body part can modulate the subsequent vividness of the phantom – an observation that may have important clinical implications. Patients often comment that the phantom occupies a "habitual" posture (e.g., partially flexed at the elbow, forearm pronated). Spontaneous changes in posture are also common, however. For instance, soon after waking up in the morning it may assume an unusual and sometimes uncomfortable posture, only to return to the habitual posture a few minutes later. Sometimes the phantom may also temporarily assume, or even become more permanently fixed in, an awkward and painful posture (e.g., the arm twisted back behind the head). It is not unusual for patients to complain that their phantom hand goes into involuntary clenching spasms, complete with a feeling of nails digging into the palm. The patient is then typically unable to unclench the phantom voluntarily and may actually start sweating from the excruciating pain. Mercifully, such episodes usually occur only during the first few weeks after amputation, and eventually stop altogether.

Intriguingly, memories of the limb's posture and form prior to amputation often survive in the phantom. There is even an anecdotal report of a soldier who had a grenade explode in his hand, leaving behind a phantom hand stuck in a permanently clenched and painful posture. In addition, after a deformed limb is amputated, the deformity is often carried over into the phantom, and patients also often complain that the pains that had existed in their limbs prior to amputation continue to persist in the phantom.

If indirect or idealist theories of perception are correct, the phenomenon of phantom limbs seems to show that when we are aware of the body image, this is not awareness of the body itself but rather awareness of a representation of the body, in the brain. In other words, the virtual reality that we inhabit and, ordinarily, call "reality," is one to which we are conjoined through a virtual body situated inside that mental space through the brain's representational system. Phantom limbs are possible because the representation of the body part remains even after the body part is gone.

4 Thought: Memory, Reasoning, and Knowledge

4.1 INTRODUCTION

So much of what we do depends upon the harmonious interaction of diverse cognitive processes. Consider, for instance, what kind of cognitive activities might figure in the construction of a piece of furniture. The kind of furniture that you build will probably be determined by your needs. Thus, before you can settle on a design, you will have to access your knowledge of what kinds of things (e.g., chairs) fulfill particular needs (e.g., sitting down to dinner). After settling on a design, you will have to generate a plan – that is, an envisioned sequence of activities that will lead to the fulfillment of your goal. This plan, in turn, will be made up of various subgoals and thoughts about how to fulfill *them*. Having plotted out a course of action, you must then implement it. To do so, you might draw upon what you know about how to locate materials suppliers, your memory of the tricks your father used when doing carpentry, some basic skills at arithmetic and geometric reasoning, motor skills, and your ability to deal with such unforeseen contingencies as bent nails and fractured boards. Intuitively, at least, these seem to be cognitive processes that enable you to build your chair. Many of the same processes (perhaps a subset of the ones just described) may come into play when you think about such things as the possibility of life on other planets or the nature of electricity.

If the above description is correct, then it may be improper to view thinking as a single process. Instead, thinking should be viewed as involving the combined effort of several processes. Before we can truly claim to understand the nature of this collaboration, we first need to understand the collaborators themselves. The latter is, in fact, the goal of much research in cognitive science. That is, instead of one single cognitive scientific research program whose goal is to explain the nature of thought, there seem to be several distinct branches of ongoing research, each of which has a particular component process as its object of study. Moreover, the task of understanding a particular process is seldom relegated to one specific discipline. Rather, each discipline makes its own unique contribution to the overall goal of understanding of a particular cognitive process.

In this chapter, we'll explore the science of thought by examining, one by one, the findings of each of these interdisciplinary branches of research. As thought and knowledge are intimately related, we'll close out the chapter with an overview of past and current philosophical wisdom concerning what knowledge is and how one attains it – that is, we'll take a brisk jaunt through the field of epistemology.

4.2 THE SCIENCE OF MEMORY

Many of the branches of research alluded to above fall under the broad umbrella of memory research. Memory has traditionally been broken down into two main types, declarative and procedural.

To get a sense for the nature of this distinction, think about what you did last night. In so doing, you are retrieving, and somehow reawakening past experiences. It would seem that in order for these experiences to be reawakened, the relevant information will have had to be stored somewhere until something causes it to be brought on line, or acted out once again in the theatre of conscious awareness. Something similar seems to be taking place when you recall information of a less personal nature. For instance, you can recall the name of the famous individual defeated at the battle of Waterloo. Indeed, in order to understand the previous sentence, you need to recall other kinds of information related to word meanings – like the meanings of famous, individual, Waterloo, and so on. Memory for the kinds of information just described (i.e., facts of a personal or non-personal nature) is known as *declarative memory*. This kind of memory seems to play a central role in your thought processes as you figure out how to build a table. You rely on declarative memory, for instance, in order to remember where you keep your tools, how your father used to work with wood, or the proper procedure for buying things (e.g., lumber and tools).

There is another kind of memory as well. This kind of memory is implicated in your ability to hammer a nail, drive your car to the lumber yard, and perhaps even multiply and divide. These things depend less on *knowing that* as they do on *knowing how*. Philosopher Gilbert Ryle (1949) can be credited with drawing our attention to this important distinction and for realizing that knowing how is as essential for intelligent behavior as is knowing that (though he would surely balk at the non-behavioristic bent of cognitive science). Nowadays this distinction is widely viewed as being more than an intuitive or introspective distinction. Rather, to this intuitive distinction corresponds a real joint in the cognitive system – that is, there really are two different kinds of memory, called declarative and *procedural*, respectively. As we shall see, the latter sometimes takes over for the former, and so the dividing line between the two can become blurred (see box on memory below).

To list further characteristics of each form of memory, declarative memory is usually taken to be attention-demanding, and the kind of information handled by declarative memory systems is easy to verbalize. Procedural memory has the opposite properties. It seldom requires careful attention, and procedural knowledge is often difficult to put into words. Consider, for example, how difficult it is to describe how to keep a bicycle upright.

ENDEL TULVING (1995) ON MEMORY

Memory is many things, even if not everything that has been labeled memory corresponds to what cognitive neuroscientists think of as memory. Memory is a gift of nature, the ability of living organisms to retain and to utilize acquired information or knowledge. The term is closely related to *learning*, in that memory in biological systems always entails learning (the acquisition of information) and in that learning implies retention (memory) of such information.

Memory is a trick that evolution has invented to allow its creatures to compress physical time. Owners of biological memory systems are capable of behaving more appropriately at a later time because of their experiences at an earlier time, a feat not possible for organisms without memory.

Memory is a biological abstraction. There is no place in the brain that one could point at and say, Here is memory. There is no single activity, or class of activities, of that organism that could be identified with the concept that the term denotes. There is no known molecular change that corresponds to memory, no known cellular activity that represents memory, no behavioral response of a living organism that is memory. Yet the term *memory* encompasses all these changes and activities.

4.2.1 Declarative memory

Your ability to remember facts seems to involve the three component processes of encoding, storage, and retrieval. To see why, notice that in order for the information to be *re*awakened, it must have been awake to begin with. The process by which this takes place is known as *encoding*. Subsequent to encoding, the relevant information must be *stored* on either a short-term or long-term basis. If it were not stored, there would be no way in which it could later be *retrieved*, or reawakened. Contemporary research into declarative memory boils down, in large part, to the study of encoding, storage, and retrieval processes.

As suggested in Chapter 2, the length of the storage period will vary depending upon which of the two main declarative memory stores is being utilized. That is to say, there are two forms of declarative memory, short term and long term. This distinction is supported by a variety of findings, several of which have to do with the well-known serial position curve.

4.2.1.1 Short-term memory

If you will recall, short-term memory is the kind of memory implicated in your ability to remember an unfamiliar phone number in the time between looking it up and dialing. There are actually at least two different kinds of short-term memory. When you are remembering a phone number, you are probably relying on a mechanism known as the *phonological loop*. This is a short-term memory system that stores linguistically encoded information for short periods of time (often on the order of seconds). We also have a short-term memory system, the *visuospatial sketchpad*, that holds information about visuospatial relationships for short periods of time. These are usually viewed as the two most basic forms of short-term memory though, as we shall see, there are reasons for thinking that there are others.

4.2.1.1.1 The phonological loop subsystem

A variety of experimental manipulations, usually involving some variation on the error score methodology, have helped to shed light on precisely how the phonological loop subsystem operates. To start with, the kind of information represented by the phonological store concerns either motor commands involved in the production of speech sounds or the acoustic properties of speech sounds (the jury is still out on the matter). At any rate, the encoding of linguistic stimuli is effected on the basis of phonological (sound-based) rather than orthographic (vision-based) properties. One way this has been revealed is by testing how well certain items are stored. It seems that immediate recall of linguistic stimuli (e.g., items from a list) is impaired when, to quote Alan Baddeley (1990, p. 20), "items are similar in sound or articulatory characteristics." This is known as the *phonological similarity effect*. A related finding is that unattended speech stimuli also disrupt the immediate recall of linguistic stimuli. (Some of you may recall teasing a friend or sibling by yelling irrelevant words at them as they try to remember a set of words or numbers.) The magnitude of this *unattended speech effect* seems to be unrelated to the semantic properties of the stimuli (i.e., the meaning of the words) since both nonsense syllables and meaningful stimuli prove to be equally disruptive. The magnitude of the effect does, however, vary with phonological similarity.

Manipulations that affect the shape of the serial position curve have also shed light on the nature of the phonological loop subsystem. As was noted in Chapter 2, when a distracting activity like counting backwards is interposed between the time that the last list item is presented and the start of recall, many items are lost from memory. Indeed, the more time that elapses, the more items are lost (Glanzer and Cunitz 1966). It is thought that the distractor activity prevents the rehearsal of list items (you can get a good sense for what is meant by rehearsal if you try to remember an unfamiliar phone number for about a minute). In other words, a kind of replay loop keeps items from disappearing from short-term phonological storage – hence the name, "phonological loop."

The reason why items are lost from storage is not entirely clear, though there is some evidence to suggest that, rather than simply fading, items are overwritten by other incoming stimuli. One reason for thinking this is that the recency component of the serial position curve seems not to significantly diminish in size when the distraction task involves the repetition of a single, simple stimulus (see Longoni et al. 1993). One reasonable explanation for this finding is that repetition may prevent rehearsal but, given the dissimilarity between the repeated item and most list items, repetition fails to cause stored list items to be overwritten. Thus, instead of serving the function of refreshing fading memory traces, rehearsal may instead prevent other linguistic stimuli (perhaps even the sound of one's thoughts) from overwriting list items. It is also worth noting that a certain kind of Kohonen map (discussed in Chapter 2) exhibits some of these very same properties (Miikkulainen 1993).

There is no requirement that the stimuli encoded in short-term memory be meaningful (as Ebbinghaus [1885] discovered, the same can be said of long-term memory). When stimuli *are* meaningful, however, later recall will be facilitated. This may be due to the influence of long-term memory on short-term memory rather than reflecting a peculiarity of short-term memory. In other words, the best available evidence indicated that linguistic information is encoded in the short term on the basis of phonological or articulatory characteristics.

The system responsible for the recognition of speech sounds may, however, be distinct from the system responsible for short-term phonological storage. A number of patients have been identified who fail to exhibit the standard phonological similarity or recency effects (Martin and Breedin 1992). These patients do, however, show normal performance on phoneme discrimination tasks. Thus, these patients evidence a dissociation of short-term phonological memory and language recognition. In addition, patients have been identified who have impaired phoneme discrimination but normal recency and phonological similarity effects. This *double dissociation* of phoneme identification and phonological short-term memory presents a compelling case that there are two distinct mechanisms involved in carrying out these functions. Functional imaging research corroborates this proposal, as do studies of impairments to phoneme identification ability and immediate recall following direct cortical stimulation (see Chapter 2 for an overview of each of these techniques). Not surprisingly, phonological storage mechanisms have been localized to an area of the temporal lobe that overlaps with an area that has long been thought to be implicated in auditory processing. As you can see, as far as interdisciplinary collaboration goes, the study of the phonological loop subsystem is one of the success stories.

4.2.1.1.2 Short-term visuospatial memory

In Chapter 2, if you will recall, the use of reaction times in psychological investigation was illustrated by considering findings about the nature of mental imagery. Mental imagery is taken by many to depend upon short-term memory mechanisms that are distinct, in certain ways, from those comprising the phonological loop. The main component of short-term visuospatial memory is what Baddeley (1990) calls the *visuospatial sketchpad*.

One of the interesting findings about the visuospatial sketchpad is that when subjects are issued spoken instructions concerning a how to carry out a visuospatial reasoning task, they perform better than when they are issued written instructions. This is taken to indicate that some of the same mechanisms involved in the visual processing of linguistic information are tapped during mental imagery. This finding has been corroborated by functional neuroimaging research which suggests that the sketchpad might be localized to the occipital lobe (the known locus of early visual processing) and areas that are contiguous and anterior (Kosslyn 1994).

Also of interest are findings concerning the role of the frontal lobes in visuospatial short-term memory. Using what is known as a *delayed-response task*, Patricia Goldman-Rakic (1992) found that a certain portion of the prefrontal cortex may be implicated in keeping information on line – that is, active and available for use in behavior guidance. In a typical delayed-response task, a monkey is shown a small object at a certain position in its visual field. The object is then taken away, and after a delay of several seconds, the monkey must indicate where in its visual field the object appeared. This delay is important, because it means that the monkey's response must be guided by an internal representation of the object and its location, as opposed to behaviors which are based on objects present at the time. Lesion data supports Goldman-Rakic's hypothesis about the neural substrate of working memory: when the part of the prefrontal cortex thought to contain this memory system is temporarily deactivated by cooling it, the monkeys are unable to respond correctly.

While clearly relevant to the study of short-term memory, it may be that the role of this area of the frontal cortex is not specific to visuospatial memory. Rather, this region may comprise an important component of an executive network that regulates the activity of slave systems – including the phonological store, the visuospatial sketchpad, and other systems implicated in on-line processing.

4.2.1.2 *Long-term declarative memory*

On one view of the relationship between short-term and long-term memory (the origins of which can be traced back to Ebbinghaus), information is first entered into short-term storage and, following a period of repetition, the information is transferred into long-term storage. While this proposal seems to provide a reasonable account of many empirical findings (recall the discussion of the serial position curve in Chapter 2), it fails to do justice to many of our pre-theoretical intuitions about how long-term memory systems operate. Imagine being told, for instance, that George W. Bush has converted to Scientology. You would probably be able to retrieve this bit of trivia at some later date, and without ever having taken the time to repeat it to yourself. In fact, there aren't very many cases when repetition is required in order for information to be entered into long-term memory. Instead, the transfer of information into long-term memory seems, in many cases, to be carried out quite automatically (i.e., in a way that requires little or no attention or effort on our part). Cognitive psychologists have devised many ingenious experiments that corroborate this proposal and further refine our understanding of the interplay between long-term encoding, storage, and retrieval processes.

One important set of findings about long-term storage processes suggests that the manner in which information is initially encoded has a very strong influence on whether, and under what conditions, it will later be retrieved. This line of research began with a set of experiments carried out by Hyde and Jenkins (1973), who employed the traditional method of measuring recall for list items – in this case words. They divided their subjects into two groups, only one of which was informed that it would later be tested. Given that the former group expected to be tested, one would expect that they would put more effort into remembering list items. They might, for instance, repeat the words to themselves. Each of these groups was further subdivided (in the very same way) such that one subgroup was asked to perform a task that would require them to pay attention to the outward form of each word (namely, deciding whether or not the word contained a particular letter), while the other subgroup was asked to perform a task that would require them to pay attention to the meaning of each word (namely, rating the pleasantness of the word's referent). As it turns out, having prior knowledge that a test would follow list presentation had no significant effect on subsequent recall. Encoding the meaning rather than the form of the stimulus turned out, on the other hand, to have a profound (and statistically significant) facilitating affect. You might bear this in mind the next time you find yourself studying for an exam. That is, rather than simply repeating facts (e.g., "procedural memories are automatic and difficult to describe") over and over again, you might try instead to concentrate on what the various sentences mean.

The manner in which memory is affected by the depth to which linguistic information is processed (where shallow processing is that concerned with outward form and deeper processing concerns meaning) has since been studied quite extensively. Baddeley (1990), for one, thinks that the best explanation for the above effect might be related to the explanation for why information is lost from short-term memory. When material is processed only in terms of its overt linguistic form, it will have a good chance of being overwritten by stimuli that are overtly similar. This is because there is only so much variation in the realm of words. On the other hand, there is tremendous room for variability in the semantic realm. Thus, phonological or orthographic similarity effects will be much more common than semantic similarity effects – though the latter have been found to occur quite frequently under the right conditions.

One of the most important findings of neuropsychology has been that the seahorse-shaped *hippocampus* (which means "sea monster" in Greek), a structure buried beneath the surface of the temporal lobe, is a mechanism that plays an essential role in the long-term storage of information. Individuals who suffer damage to this area (for reasons ranging from accidental head trauma to Alzheimer's disease) can be stricken by a severe form of amnesia. This disorder has two components to it. On the one hand, these individuals can lose their ability to store new information on a long-term basis (this is the *anterograde* component of amnesia). Accordingly, their window onto the immediate past may extend only as far back as their short-term memory systems will permit – usually just a few moments. (It is worth taking a moment to imagine what that would be like.) On the other hand, these individuals may also lose memory for the events that preceded the time of injury. This *retrograde* component of amnesia can extend as far back as three years. The extent of retrograde amnesia can be determined by asking subjects to answer questions about public or personal events for which dates can be assigned (e.g., by questioning friends or consulting newspapers).

At present, the most popular way of accounting for these findings is to view the hippocampus as a device for organizing long-term memories and, so to speak, filing them away. Where they might be filed *to* is indicated by the extensive anatomical connections (both incoming and outgoing) between the hippocampus and the sensory areas of the cortex. In light of this connectivity, some have speculated that particular memories are ultimately stored (or *consolidated*) in or near the very areas of cortex that were active during their initial encoding. According to this model, the role of the hippocampus is to store memories for as long as it takes (i.e., up to three years) to effect this consolidation process. Thus, any memories that have not yet been filed away at the time of damage to the hippocampus will forever be lost. While quite compelling as an explanatory model, the details of the consolidation process themselves stand in need of explanation. Some have begun to speculate that this process takes place when we are asleep (and is, in fact, the very point of sleep). In addition, connectionist systems have been created that may give us a glimpse into the details of the consolidation process.

4.2.1.2.1 Episodic and semantic memory
There are those who feel that long-term memory mechanisms might be further subdivided on the basis of the kind of information being stored. The distinction at issue was alluded to above when it was pointed out that you can remember facts of a personal nature (e.g., what you did last night) as well those of a non-personal nature (e.g., that Napoleon was defeated at Waterloo,

or the meaning of "famous"). Memory for the former sort of information is called episodic memory while memory for the latter is called semantic memory. The driving question for those interested in this distinction is whether or not the two kinds of information at issue are handled by two distinct long-term memory mechanisms.

Some early support for the claim that there are distinct memory mechanisms was offered by informal (or *anecdotal*) evidence concerning individuals with hippocampal damage. Such individuals often have intact memory for non-personal facts and word meanings, but their memory of personal events is severely impaired. It is unclear what should be concluded on this basis, however, because it is very difficult to assess precisely when non-personal information was learned. Try to remember, for instance, when you first learned of Napoleon's defeat at Waterloo. Some recent studies suggest that the hippocampus plays a critical role in both episodic and semantic memory.

In one study, a comparison was made among amnesiacs between their memory for personal events and their memory for events of a more public nature, such as the Iran-Contra hearings (MacKinnon and Squire 1989). For each subject studied, it was found that the onset of retrograde amnesia was the same whether the events at issue were public or private. It is plausible, then, that memory for public events (namely, those that occur during one's lifetime) should be categorized under the heading of *episodic* rather than semantic memory.

There is at least one case study that may shed light on the matter of whether or not distinct mechanisms underwrite episodic and semantic memory and, if so, where, precisely, the boundary between the two should be drawn. De Renzi et al. (1987) describe an Italian woman (known to the scientific community as L.P.) who suffered encephalitis. L.P. was found to have severe semantic memory deficits without any impairment to episodic memory. Specifically, she had no memory for most of the facts that she had learned at school – facts about geography and history for instance (e.g., she had no knowledge of Hitler or of any facts at all concerning World War II). Her ability to remember personal events, on the other hand, was completely intact. In addition to supporting a dissociation between the two forms of memory, what is interesting about L.P.'s case is that her memory for public events that transpired during her lifetime was found to be restricted to facts that had a very *high* personal significance. For instance, though L.P. had no recollection of either the location or nature of the Chernobyl disaster, she did remember that it had caused her plants to suffer. Thus, insofar as there is a distinction between episodic and semantic memory mechanisms, L.P.'s case may indicate that episodic memory handles information only about the most personal aspects of public events while semantic memory mechanisms handle the rest. A single dissociation in one case study is, however, far from conclusive.

4.2.1.2.2 The cellular bases of information storage

Experience changes us, but how exactly does this happen? We are so accustomed to the fact that doing something slowly makes us better at it, or the fact that reading a book leaves us with memories of its contents, that we fail to notice the work which the brain does in making this miracle possible. Donald Hebb is generally credited with being the first to propose the cellular basis by which the brain is changed by experience. What has come to be known as Hebb's rule (discussed briefly in Chapter 1) is still a vital principle in the understanding and design of cognitive systems. Hebb's rule reads as follows:

When an axon of cell A is near enough to excite cell B and repeatedly or persistently takes part in firing it, some growth process or metabolic change takes place in one or both cells such that A's efficiency, as one of the cells firing B, is increased.

(Hebb 1949, p. 62)

In short, whenever two adjacent neurons tend to fire in synchrony, the connection between them is strengthened, so that firing of the first neuron makes it more likely that the second neuron will fire. A second quotation from Hebb makes this point more clearly: "Two cells or systems of cells that are repeatedly active at the same time will tend to become 'associated,' so that activity in one facilitates activity in the other" (Hebb 1949, p. 70).

The existence of such a mechanism was verified in the simple nervous system of the mollusk *Aplysia*. A process known as long-term potentiation (LTP) may constitute part of the biological basis for Hebb's rule. Researchers in the 1970s found that briefly applying electrical stimulation to the hippocampus of the rabbit made cells adjacent to the stimulated cells more likely to fire, at least for several hours. Later researchers have been able to verify that electrical stimulation can produce LTP lasting for days or even weeks.

It is worth noting, however, that long-term memories seem to be stored in the hippocampus for up to three years. Thus, unless LTP is shown to operate over such lengthy spans of time, scientists will have to begin searching for other cellular mechanisms that can account for long-term memory. One possibility is that LTP is an effect that lasts just long enough for the hormones associated with an emotional response to circulate through the blood to the site of LTP. When these hormones reach sites where LTP has taken place, they set in motion cellular changes that give rise to truly long-term strengthening of inter-neuron connections. According to this model, not just any paired neural firing is worthy of strengthening, and the measure (or one measure) of significance is the associated affective response.

4.2.1.3 *Confabulation about memory*

Certain types of brain lesion can produce a curious phenomenon known as *confabulation*. Specifically, when asked a question which touches on deficits caused by the injury, rather than simply acknowledging any problems, patients will give a false or irrelevant answer, as if they were attempting to cover up their deficit. Korsakoff's syndrome is a form of amnesia, most often caused by a lifetime of heavy drinking. The locus of lesion is not as clear in the case of Korsakoff's amnesia as in certain other cases, though the most frequent sites of damage seem to be in the lower, more "primitive" parts of the brain. Korsakoff's amnesia is severe enough that patients will typically have no memory at all of the events of the preceding day. But when asked what they did yesterday, Korsakoff's patients will often produce a detailed description of plausible (or not so plausible) events. These events are either entirely made up at the time of utterance, or traceable to some actual but much older memory.

The patients give no sign that they are aware of what they are doing; apparently they are not lying, and genuinely believe their confabulations. They do not give any outward signs of lying, and their demeanor while confabulating is that of any normal person talking about their actual recent experience.

4.2.1.4 Frames and other large knowledge structures

Up until now, we have mainly been concerned with the mechanisms responsible for storing particular pieces of information. Long-term memory mechanisms do more than encode, store, and retrieve a bunch of disconnected facts, however. To get a sense for the kind of global organization that some researchers have been investigating, consider for a moment what you know about the steps required in order to go from not being enrolled in a university to passing your first course. Your ability to envision the appropriate sequence of events suggests that your knowledge of how universities operate is not encoded in the form of a bunch of disconnected facts. Rather, the mechanisms of long-term memory somehow capture the relationships between the individual facts.

What we have been calling *traditional AI* has, for quite some time, taken the lead in investigating the global organization of knowledge. Marvin Minsky (1985) was an early pioneer in the effort to model large-scale knowledge structures. He modeled knowledge for everyday circumstances in terms of a set of schematic (i.e., detail-poor) knowledge structures centered around particular kinds of situations. If the information relevant to filling in the details of these *frames* is not explicitly provided, certain values are simply assumed by default. For instance, a system might be equipped with a frame associated with how to ride public transportation. It might assume, unless instructed otherwise, that public transportation always requires a fee. A further frame, with its own default assumptions, might be called upon in order to supply information about the kind of token-selling mechanism, and so on. Frames are thus said to be organized in a *recursive* manner (i.e., there can be frames within frames).

The ability to organize bits of knowledge into large-scale structures seems to play a prominent role in text comprehension. A given passage of prose will often leave out a great deal of information, the implicit assumption being that the reader will fill in the relevant details. Should, for instance, the main character in some story buy a hotdog from a street vendor, you might take for granted that the vendor has a cart with heated containers and condiments, that money is exchanged, and so on.

The task of modeling this kind of filling was one of the goals set for Schank and Abelson's (1977) SAM (see Chapter 1). SAM could read passages of text from a newspaper and generate sensible answers to questions about the text by filling in the information that was only implicit. Evidence that this kind of filling in actually does takes place has been gathered on the basis of behavioral research concerning the time it takes to recognize that a given stimulus is a word. There are certain conditions, for instance, under which the time it takes to recognize that an item is a word (as opposed to a meaningless collection of letters) is reduced. One such case is when the word to be recognized concerns the implicit details of a passage of text read prior to the word recognition task. For instance, after reading a sentence about the collapse of a building, it was found that subjects were faster at recognizing "earthquake" as a word than they were with other words (Kintsch 1998). This and other evidence suggests that we quite naturally draw upon our background knowledge of particular kinds of situations in order to fill in details that were never mentioned.

4.2.2 Procedural memory

Procedural memory, or *know-how*, has not always been viewed as a key player in the mental life of the individual. Procedural memory is often thought of as the kind of memory that underwrites particular motor skills, such as riding a bike. To see why it might play a more prominent role in our thought processes, the consideration of basic motor skills is actually a good place to start.

Can you recall your first clumsy attempts at driving a car? When you first sat behind the wheel of a car, it probably took all of your concentration to heed traffic signs and signals, work each of the pedals and the gearshift, and keep the car moving smoothly and in a straight direction. If you were anything like the rest of us, when you first started driving you were probably quite awful. Eventually, however, you got to the point you are now at. Now, when you drive home from work or school you are probably scarcely even aware of what you are doing. Many researchers now believe that you have your cerebellum to thank for this, though a set of nuclei buried underneath the cortex (the *basal ganglia*) also seem to play an important role. One of the interesting anatomical features of the cerebellum is that it is wired up to the rest of the brain in such a way that it has many incoming connections from the sensory areas of the cortex and many outgoing connections to the motor areas. Moreover, a look at the low-level anatomical details of the cerebellum reveals a structure that is configured in a manner remarkably reminiscent of a connectionist perceptron (see Chapter 1). In other words, every indication is that this structure is ideally suited to the task of learning how to pick up on input/output regularities. Many researchers thus view the cerebellum as a system that monitors the cortex for input/output patterns. For example, when the sensory system delivers information about sitting behind a wheel and seeing a red hexagon with the word STOP on it, the motor system responds with a characteristic motion of the right foot. When you first learned to drive, this characteristic motion may have only occurred after the most deliberate and attention-demanding effort. Eventually, however, your cerebellum (and basal ganglia) picked up on this input/output pattern and took over in such a way that you no longer had to think about it. It became automatic.

There are lots of sensory-motor input/output patterns for the cerebellum to pick up on. For instance, if you do a lot of pencil-and-paper arithmetic, you'll find that this process is also highly automated. The same can be said in the case of formal logic. Insofar as the cerebellum is responsible for automating these activities, it should be viewed as a crucial player in our everyday thought processes.

Some support for this proposal comes in the form of connectionist modeling research. Bechtel and Abrahamsen (1991), for instance, designed a pair of networks which learned to accomplish such tasks as assessing the validity of formal logic proofs and filling in missing information. On the basis of this and other data, they propose:

> logic problems, when viewed as pattern recognition tasks, can be solved by networks which, like humans, seem to be capable of learning from errors and tuning their performance . . . The ability to reason using logical principles may not need to be grounded on proposition-like rules, but rather reflect a kind of *knowing how*.
>
> (Bechtel and Abrahamsen 1991, p. 208)

Indeed, it may be that cognitive automation is not restricted to perceptuo-motor patterns. It may be that the patterns associated with everyday, deliberate reasoning may themselves become automated (see Thach et al. 1992). The attempt to determine what the precise role of procedural knowledge is in our everyday thought processes is thus one of the exciting new areas of interdisciplinary investigation.

4.3 REASONING

Assume, for a moment, that the moon is made of green cheese. Assume, furthermore, that all green cheese comes from Wisconsin. On the basis of these assumptions, what can you conclude about the origin of the moon? More importantly, what memory system do you utilize to reach this conclusion? The process of reasoning seems to be an active, on-line affair (see also section 1.2.1 in Chapter 1). Perhaps, as just suggested, the cerebellum plays an important role in this process as well. Of course, long-term declarative memory is also a key player. The study of reasoning is thus intimately related to the study of memory. Indeed, perhaps a full understanding of the memory systems and their interactions will exhaust what there is to know about reasoning. While this is a reasonable long-range plan for cognitive science, researchers have found ways to investigate reasoning in its own right.

Crudely put, reasoning is a process whereby one derives certain information (e.g., facts, knowledge, sentences, etc.) from other information, as in the following:

(1) Lulu is a cow.
(2) All cows chew cud.
(3) Therefore, Lulu chews cud.

There are two broad ways in which one might undertake the study of reasoning. On the one hand, there is the study of how one ought to reason, or the *norms* of reasoning. Philosophers have always been the experts in this area. Because logical argumentation is the philosophers' primary research tool, they have always been both cognizant and critical of the methods by which people are led to conclusions. Alternatively, though, one can investigate how we actually *do* reason under everyday circumstances. One characteristic method for investigating reasoning on an empirical basis is to determine the extent to which humans depart from the norms established by philosophers and other cognitive scientists. One thing (perhaps the only thing) that philosophers generally agree upon is the basic taxonomy of reasoning methods. The central division in this taxonomy is between monotonic and non-monotonic forms of inference.

4.3.1 Monotonic reasoning

There are many who feel that "monotonic inference" and "deduction" are co-extensive (i.e., the two labels pick out all and only the same things). Good (or *valid*) deductive inferences are such that *if* the premises (the reasons given) are true, then the conclusion *must* be true as well. The inference to (3) above has this property.

4.3.1.1 *Deduction*

Because deductive inferences supply this kind of certainty, and the philosopher lusts after absolute certainty, the study of deductive reasoning has been a mainstay of philosophical investigation. If you will recall from Chapter 1, it was the formalization of the rules for deduction by philosophers that eventually led to the creation of mechanical deduction devices (i.e., electronic computers) and, ultimately, to the advent of the field of artificial intelligence.

Introspectively and intuitively, it seems as though we do engage in deductive reasoning. As much as possible, however, cognitive scientists have aimed to do away with introspection in favor of replicable and objective empirical data. Much effort has accordingly been expended on the task of generating data that will help to clarify whether or not human reasoning actually accords with prescribed norms; if so, what the precise mental operations are by which these reasoning activities are carried out; and if not, what are the hidden causes of these observed shortcomings.

One of the most important research programs concerning the nature of deductive reasoning began in the very early days of cognitive science. In the 1960s, Allen Newell and Herbert Simon began an investigation into the procedures by which humans solve formal reasoning problems. They utilized and helped to pioneer the now-popular technique of protocol analysis – whereby subjects are presented with a task and are asked to verbalize their thought processes as they go about solving that task. Newell and Simon (1972) recorded and analyzed the reports issued by subjects who were asked to solve tasks that seem to have a substantial deductive reasoning component. Their ultimate goal was the creation of a computational system capable of implementing these very procedures. The pay-off was the creation of the production system approach to cognitive modeling described in Chapter 2.

This line of research continues, unabated, to the present day. Lance Rips, for instance, utilizes production systems in order to model the reasoning processes (revealed by protocol analysis) that subjects engage in when solving problems such as this one (Rips 1994):

Each of A, B, and C is either a knight or a knave.
Knights always tell the truth and knaves always lie.
A, B, and C make the following statements:

A: Both B and C are knaves.
B: C is a knave.
C: A is a knight.

Question: Is A a knight or a knave?

Not only do subjects seem to draw upon a competence at deduction (e.g., their ability to infer *q* from "If *p* then *q*" and *p*), they also use a number of *metalogical* strategies – that is, strategies for deploying their core deductive capacities. For instance, one strategy for solving problems like the one above is to make a provisional assumption about whether a particular character is a liar or truth-teller. Subjects follow through on these provisional assumptions by examining their implications in terms of the lying or truth-telling status of the other characters.

The above problem, for example, might be solved by first assuming that A is a knight and that what he says is therefore true. Based on this assumption, it can be concluded both that B is a knave and that B's statement is false. This implies that C is really a knight. Since this contradicts A's claim that C is a knave, either the initial assumption was mistaken or the problem is paradoxical. To see that it is not paradoxical, we can assume that A is a knave. Based on this assumption, we can conclude that either B or C, or both, is a knight. If B is the knight, then according to B's truthful assertion C is a knave. This implies that C is lying, and that A is a knave. This is consistent with our initial assumption. There is thus a consistent assignment of knight–knave status to the characters according to which A is a knave. There is no consistent assignment of knight–knave status to the characters in which A is a knight. A must therefore be a knave.

At the foundation of such research lies the assumption that humans are, in fact, competent deductive reasoners. This contention can be traced back to the theorizing of philosophers such as Kant and J.S. Mill, who held that the laws of thought and the norms of reasoning uncovered by philosophers are one and the same. Cognitive scientists are far from unanimous in their acceptance of this view, however.

THE LANGUAGE OF THOUGHT AND THE FRAME PROBLEM

Many philosophers and cognitive scientists believe that one of the most fundamental and distinctive human capacities is our power to plan by envisioning the consequences of our actions. This thesis has been in circulation for millennia. One finds it clearly stated in the works of Aristotle, reiterated in the works of Hobbes and Leibniz, revisited by Gestalt psychologist Wolfgang Köhler, and infused into many modern-day efforts to create intelligent computational systems.

The central assumption of the forethought thesis is that we humans harbor representations which we are able to manipulate in order to generate predictions. For instance, most of us can predict what would happen if a disposable paper cup full of water had a hole poked in its side. We can also predict what would happen if the cup were tipped over or if a golf ball were dropped directly into it. A model that enjoys widespread support has it that we mentally represent these items and their relationships, and we generate predictions by somehow altering these representations.

Assuming that we do represent the world and the way it changes under various circumstances, it seems eminently reasonable to investigate how our mental representations are structured. Also for millennia, philosophers and (later) psychologists have attempted to understand the nature of our mental representations by invoking metaphors rooted in other known forms of representation. Given the prominent role played by languages in human activity, it should come as no surprise that one of the most widely discussed metaphors for human mental representation has been the language metaphor.

Rather than comparing mental representations to natural languages, the most recent incarnation of the language metaphor compares mental representations to the artificial notations developed in formal logic. What is so nice about the logic metaphor for thought is that it not only provides a way to make sense of the structure of mental representations, but also explains the human capacity to predict the consequences of alterations to the world. This, in fact, is its biggest draw.

To see why the logic metaphor is so appealing, notice that the techniques of formal logic not only support the representation of countless distinct states of affairs, but also enable the manipulation of representations in a truth-preserving manner. Specifically, a properly devised set of representations and rules will be such that the consequences of alterations to the representations will track the consequences of the corresponding alterations to the world. Specifically, this can be accomplished by representing the consequences of alterations in terms of inference rules that take the basic form of an "if . . . then . . ." statement. For instance, if the logic metaphor is correct, then we humans might have in our heads some notational variant of the following rule:

If (both *there is a paper cup and the paper cup is full of water* and *the paper cup is punctured*), then *water will be released*.

There are many in philosophy, psychology, and artificial intelligence who view the logic metaphor as the only way to make sense of the human capacity to predict alterations to the world. Termed the *language of thought* (LOT) hypothesis by philosopher Jerry Fodor (Fodor and Lepore 2002) and the *mental logic* model by psychologist Lance Rips (1994), this model of human cognition has given rise to contemporary production systems (described in Chapter 2) and other traditional AI devices.

Despite its superficial promise, there are serious worries about the LOT hypothesis. For about as long as computer scientists have been attempting to model forethought on the basis of logic-like formalisms, they have also been aware that there is a heavy cost associated with the use of rules like the one above. The problem with using such rules is that one would need a truly massive number of them in order to predict the consequences of alterations to even a very simple setup like the paper cup, water, golf ball scenario. To see why, take a moment in order to consider all of the possible ways in which this exceedingly simple domain can be altered. Indeed, no matter how many alterations you envision, there are probably scores more that you failed to imagine. The problem of trying to envision each of these countless possible alterations is precisely the problem confronting researchers in AI. The problem just described is called the *prediction problem*, and it falls under the broader heading of the *frame problem*. McCarthy and Hayes (1969) are generally credited with being the first to recognize (and name) the frame problem, which has to do with the general difficulty of getting a logic mechanism to track what will change and what will stay the same following various alterations.

Another side to the frame problem is the *qualification problem*. This problem has to do with that fact that there will, for any given rule, be countless exceptions. For instance, dropping a golf ball over a cup full of water will result in water being spilled, provided that, among other things, the temperature is above freezing; there is nothing between the ball and the top of the cup; there isn't a string connecting the ball to the ceiling; and

continued

so on indefinitely. That is, in order to capture what we know about the consequences of this and other alterations, the rule we devise will have to be qualified in countless ways.

The frame problem becomes all the more troublesome once it is recognized that the prediction problem and the qualification problem are not separate. That is to say, in order to predict how even a simple setup would change in light of various alterations, one would need to build into a system a seemingly endless number of rules, and each rule would need to be qualified in a seemingly endless number of ways.

Though the frame problem was initially viewed as a practical obstacle that might be overcome by some clever modeling tricks, no clear-cut solution has yet been supplied. This may pose a problem for the LOT hypothesis itself. If you will recall from Chapter 1, one of the main reasons for creating computational models of cognitive processing is to determine the precise implications of a theory without having to rely upon intuition. In the present case, intuition dictates that the LOT hypothesis is a promising model. It seems to account for the human capacity to predict the consequences of alterations to the world. Considering that no one has successfully implemented the model computationally, however, the LOT hypothesis begins to look highly suspect. Of course, considering that no other model has been put forward that is able to account for human forethought, it comes as no surprise that the LOT hypothesis continues to enjoy such widespread support.

One piece of evidence often cited by those who think that humans are far from ideal reasoners is the Wason Selection Task experiment (Wason 1966). In the basic selection task, subjects are presented with four cards, each of which has one of four alphanumeric characters printed on it such as "A," "H," "4," and "7." Subjects are informed that each card has a number on one side and a letter on the other.

They are then presented with the following rule:

If a card has a vowel on one side, then it has an even number on the other side.

Subjects are asked to turn over just those cards that will bear on the veracity of this rule. Wason found that only 4 percent of subjects responded correctly by turning over the "A" and "7" cards. To most subjects, it seemed clear that an odd number on the other side of the "E" card would disprove the rule. On the other hand, most subjects failed to recognize that finding a vowel on the other side of the "7" card would have equal bearing on the veracity of the rule – and that neither of the other two cards will support such a clear-cut judgment.

In fact, most subjects chose the "4" card over the "7" card. This is because the "4" card, if it were to have a vowel on the other side, would seem to support the rule. This peculiarity of human reasoning is called *confirmation bias*. Simply put, confirmation bias is our natural tendency to seek out or pay attention to information that will confirm what we suspect or believe to be true while ignoring information that runs contrary to such beliefs. This bias is thought to exert a pervasive, and often insidious, influence on our reasoning. We seem, that is, to have a hard time being objective, and the norms of reasoning tend to be violated in the process.

An interesting twist to the selection task finding is that the effect varies with the content of the materials involved. In one follow-up, for instance, University of Florida undergraduates were presented with a social contract version of the cards (Griggs and Cox 1982), where instead of the "A," "H," "4," and "7" they saw "Drinking a beer," "Drinking a Coke," "21 years old," and "16 years old." Subjects were then asked to turn over just those cards that bear on the veracity of the following rule:

If a person is drinking beer, then the person must be over 19.

The basic finding, which seems to be quite reliable, is that when the chosen materials are familiar to subjects, performance on the selection task improves drastically (Adolphs et al. 1994). While the rate of correct response for abstract and unfamiliar versions of the selection task is often less than 10 percent, this rate increases to around 90 percent when familiar materials are used. It seems that we are much better deductive reasoners when we have some familiarity with what we are reasoning about.

4.3.1.2 *Imagistic inference*

Another type of inference that some consider monotonic is imagistic or visuospatial inference. As an illustration, notice that if you are told that Lucy was shorter than Napoleon and that Socrates was taller than Napoleon, you would be able to conclude that Socrates was taller than Lucy. It may be that inferences of this sort are carried out by constructing a mental image of some sort. Yet, like a deductive inference, it is hard to see how the premises of this inference could be true and the conclusion false.

Some of the empirical support for the idea that we reason on the basis of images comes from the research on mental rotation discussed in Chapter 2 and in section 4.2.1.1.2. There is, however, a lively debate concerning whether or not this form of inference even exists in contradistinction to deduction (see Pylyshyn 1984). Specifically, there are many who feel that imagistic inference is effected on the basis of the cognitive equivalent of formal logic. One possibility, for instance, is that most of us have encoded in our long-term memories a statement specifying that if an object x is taller than another object y, and y is taller than a third object z, then x is taller than z.

As noted above, there are considerable data suggesting that the same cognitive mechanisms used in visual perception are also used in visual imagination (again, see section 4.2.1.1.2). There are many, however, who feel that the human brain is nothing but a computational system. If it is, then a fortiori visual processing is a computational (and thus formal) process. In other words, it may turn out that vision is itself best explained in terms of formal processing (see Fodor and Pylyshyn 1981). There is, at any rate, no a priori reason to rule out this possibility. Thus, how this debate is ultimately resolved may depend on whether or not, at the end of the day, the brain is most fruitfully viewed as a computational system.

4.3.2 Non-monotonic reasoning

In the case of non-monotonic inference, the truth of the premises fails to guarantee the truth of the conclusion. Such inferences are also called *defeasible*, since the truth of the conclusion can be defeated without thereby calling into question the truth of the premises. As an illustration, consider the inference from (4) to (5).

(4) Every cow I've ever seen or heard of has chewed cud.
(5) All cows chew cud.

This is a pretty strong inference, but it differs from a deductive inference in that the truth of (4) fails to guarantee the truth of (5). For instance, it is within the realm of possibility that a mutation will occur (or be induced by some mad scientist), such that a cow is created that fails to chew cud as part of its normal digestive process. So, even if (4) happens to be true, (5) may turn out to be false.

4.3.2.1 Inductive inference

The inference from (4) to (5) happens to be an example of an inductive generalization – an inference wherein a property characteristic of a known subset of a particular category is extended to other members of that category.

One form of inductive inference that has been studied extensively is the manner in which we generalize from our past experience and knowledge in order to assess the probability of some event, or the likelihood that an individual is a member of a certain category. As it turns out, we sometimes depart from the ideals of reasoning when we engage in this form of inference as well.

When reasoning about probabilities, we often rely upon one or more rules of thumb called heuristics. Unlike the rules of logic, heuristics are applied quickly, easily, and quite automatically. Because they are merely rules of thumb, however, they also have the potential to produce errors. It is the pattern of errors exhibited by subjects under controlled conditions, in fact, that has tipped us off to their existence.

To take one example (a variation on Kahneman and Tversky 1973), have a look at the descriptions of each of four individuals as specified in the first column of the table. Now, for each individual, ask yourself which of the two columns to the right holds the name of the more likely profession for that person.

Individual	Profession	
Athletic, competitive, likes guns	Major (US Army)	Philosophy professor
Compassionate, fair, honest	Lawyer	Doctor
Short, slim, likes poetry	Professor of classics (Ivy League)	Truck driver
Male, drives sports car, reads *Fortune* magazine	Home-maker	Corporate ladder-climber

In assessing the likelihood of each individual's profession, you may have based your decision on how typical (or *representative*) of each profession the listed characteristics are. This strategy, called the *representativeness heuristic*, often makes for accurate judgments. Indeed, in the present case it delivers correct judgments in three out of four cases. In the case of the third individual, however, it fails to pass muster. This is because there are *far fewer* classics professors at Ivy League schools than there are truck drivers. If one takes into account this *base-rate* information, it will appear far more likely that the individual described is a truck driver. In the other cases, the number of individuals in each profession was approximately equal, so the representativeness heuristic delivers an accurate judgment.

Here is another experiment devised by Kahneman and Tversky (1973). You may wish to try replicating their results in class. To do so, start by dividing your class into two equally sized groups. Have every member of one of the groups work, individually, on the following problem for about a minute:

> *Given a group of ten people, estimate how many subcommittees of two people each can be formed.*

Have everyone in the other group work, individually, on this problem:

> *Given a group of ten people, estimate how many subcommittees of eight people each can be formed.*

Now compute the average of the estimates from each group (throwing out, of course, any ridiculous answers). Are the two sets of estimates very different?

Here's the kicker. Every *unique* subcommittee of two that is formed leaves a remainder of eight people who could themselves make up a *unique* subcommittee. Likewise, every subcommittee of eight that is formed leaves two that could make up a new subcommittee. In other words, the correct answer is the same for both groups.

If your results were anything like Kahneman and Tversky's, the average estimates were very different. Why might this be the case? The reason seems to be that generating unique eight-person subcommittees is more difficult than generating unique two person subcommittees. The number of subcommittees generated after a certain period of time is probably fewer in the eight-person task than in the two -person task. This inclines people to make a more conservative estimate.

This is an example of the *availability heuristic* – that is, when some event or characteristic comes to mind easily (when they are more cognitively available) we assume that it is more common than those which don't come to mind easily. There are a few factors that seem to contribute to an increase in availability.

One such factor is the extent of one's experience with the entities or events in question. For instance, if a group of students at your university were asked to estimate the percentage of undergraduates, nationwide, who live in dorms, their estimate would tend to be influenced by the percentage of undergraduates who live in the dorms at your university. Another factor is the degree to which the entities or events in question grab one's attention. In one experiment (Fischoff et al. 1977), subjects were asked to estimate which of certain causes of death are statistically more frequent in the United States. For instance, when presented with a choice between suicide and diabetes, subjects tended to choose suicide (which has a certain social stigma about it) as the more likely when, in fact, diabetes is a more common cause of death.

Each of the above factors reflects something about the way we store the relevant information, but availability is also influenced by how easily that information is retrieved from memory. In one revealing experiment, subjects were asked to estimate the proportion of words with *k* as the first letter to those with *k* as the third letter (Kahneman and Tversky 1973). While the actual ration is about 3:1 in favor of words with *k* as the *third letter*, subjects consistently mis-estimated in favor of words *beginning* with *k*. It seems that it is easier, due to some property of the retrieval mechanism, to pull the latter from memory.

4.3.2.2 *Abductive inference*

There are other non-monotonic forms of inference aside from induction. One of the most central to our everyday reasoning practices is abduction. Consider the inference from (6) and (7) to (8).

(6) The car will not start.
(7) The gas gauge reads "empty."
(8) The car won't start because there is no gas in the tank.

This is a pretty strong argument, but it is also another clear-cut case in which the truth of the premises fails to guarantee the truth of the conclusion. Also called *inference to the best explanation*, abduction is a process whereby the cause of some phenomenon is inferred from available evidence. As with inductive inference, abductive inference is *defeasible*.

Abduction not only plays an important role in our day-to-day lives, but also is one of the main forms of inference used in scientific investigation – including, that's right, cognitive scientific investigation. Inferences concerning, for instance, the causes of such phenomena as the ability of rats to find their way to food (Chapter 1), the primacy and recency effects (Chapter 2), and the inability of certain individuals to form grammatical sentences (Chapter 2) are abductive in nature.

The process of abduction has not yet been extensively studied on an experimental basis, but there have been attempts to model this form of inference computationally. In particular, research efforts have recently been directed toward the creation of non-monotonic formalisms that capture the rules governing this reasoning process. Abduction also seems to involve a process of creative insight, and some experimental and modeling work has been carried out concerning this process as well. Currently, one highly favored hypothesis is that the creative side of abduction depends upon mechanisms that pick up on similarities between a familiar domain and the domain that we are trying to understand – that is, the mechanisms responsible for our ability to form analogies. In fact, analogical *inference* is widely viewed as another of our fundamental modes of non-monotonic reasoning.

4.3.2.3 Analogical inference

Analogical inference is a form of inference whereby one reaches a conclusion about a certain domain (e.g., an entity or entities, an event, a process, etc.) in virtue of the similarities between it and some other domain. For instance, British philosopher Thomas Reid (1785) once advanced the following argument in support of the thesis that life exists on other planets in our solar system:

> We may observe a very great similitude between this earth which we inhabit, and the other planets, Saturn, Jupiter, Mars, Venus, and Mercury. They all revolve around the sun, as the earth does, although at different distances and different periods. They borrow all their light from the sun, as the earth does. Several of them are known to revolve round their axis like the earth, and by that means, must have a like succession of day and night. Some of them have moons, that serve to give them light in the absence of the sun, as our moon does to us. They are all, in their motions, subject to the same law of gravitation, as the earth is. From all this similitude, it is not unreasonable to think that those planets may, like our earth, be the habitation of various orders of living creatures. There is some probability in this conclusion from analogy.
>
> (Reid 1785, p. 228)

Reid's arguments nicely illustrate the three steps involved in making an analogical inference. First, a comparison has been constructed between two domains (namely, the earth and the rest of the planets). Second, it is noted that, besides those properties and relations mentioned in the comparison, one of the domains (i.e., the earth) has an additional property/relation (namely, it harbors various forms of life). Finally, it is concluded that the other domain (i.e., the rest of the planets) is also likely to possess such properties/relations. Like induction and abduction, analogical inference is defeasible.

In support of the proposal that humans engage in analogical inference, there is (in addition to the intuitive plausibility of the proposal) the fact that analogy is a frequently used linguistic device – that is, an analysis of natural language stimuli reveals a wealth of analogies (and metaphors, which are closely related). As Gentner (1983) points out, however, it is entirely possible that the profusion of analogies in natural language discourse is little more than a peculiarity of language itself. In other words, the frequent use of analogy in discourse may or may not have a deeper basis at the level of semantic representation.

Gentner (1983) devised a way to shed light on this question based upon the following insight: if inferences regarding some unfamiliar domain truly depend upon a comparison with a more familiar domain, then the inferences one draws about the latter should reflect the peculiarities of the former. In his experiments, electricity constituted the unfamiliar domain. On the basis of protocol-style interviews, it was revealed that subjects commonly invoke one of two analogies when relating their knowledge about batteries, resistors, voltage, and current. One analogy compares the properties of an electrical circuit to those of a system of pipes through which water flows. The other analogy compares the flow of electricity through a circuit to a large number of individuals traveling through a series of corridors and gates.

In order to test whether or not there is a deeper semantic basis for the frequency with which subjects invoke these analogies, Gentner (1983) capitalized on the fact that each base domain is useful for drawing certain inferences about electricity and poor for others. Subjects were thus asked to answer questions about the properties of electrical circuits. It was found that subjects who had used the water analogy in conversation made the pattern of correct and incorrect inferences that one would expect based upon the water analogy. The same thing was true in the case of the moving crowd analogy. In other words, this study suggests that analogy is not just a linguistic phenomenon, it is a kind of thought process.

4.4 THE PHILOSOPHY OF KNOWLEDGE

What is knowledge? Who has it and how did they get it? What do you know and how do you know it? These questions and the problems that arise in answering them have been central concerns of philosophers. The traditional philosophical study of knowledge is known as epistemology. More recently there has been an explosion of philosophical interest in the epistemic practices of scientists. In this section we examine both epistemology and the philosophy of science.

4.4.1 Epistemology

Epistemology is one of the major branches of philosophy. It concerns the forms, nature, and preconditions of knowledge. One of the traditional concerns has been the problem of skepticism: the possibility that we know nothing at all. Other problems concern supplying an analysis of the concept of knowledge: is knowledge the same as "justified" true belief? What more or less could it be? Before describing how these problems have been tackled we briefly describe the main kinds of knowledge.

4.4.1.1 *Kinds of knowledge*

4.4.1.1.1 The senses of "know"
There are several kinds of knowledge, and they may be classified in terms of the different senses of the word "know." Here we discuss three:

- Propositional knowledge (knowing that)
- Procedural knowledge (knowing how)
- Acquaintance knowledge (knowing who).

The first and of primary interest to philosophers is propositional knowledge – the knowledge you have when you know *that* something is the case. (Recall the discussion of propositional attitudes from Chapter 1.) Examples of ascriptions of propositional knowledge include

- Mary knows that grass is green.
- Shaquille knows that 420 + 80 = 500.
- Xavier knows that Wolverine is angry again.

We will return to the topic of propositional knowledge; indeed, most of our discussion of epistemology in the following sections concerns it.

Moving to the next item on our list we have procedural knowledge, the knowledge had in knowing *how* to do something. Examples of ascriptions of procedural knowledge include

- Mary knows how to mow the lawn.
- Shaquille knows how to do arithmetic.
- Xavier knows how to calm Wolverine down.

One point of interest is the ways in which procedural and propositional knowledge relate, or fail to. For instance, knowing how to ride a bike does not seem to entail having any *particular* bit of propositional knowledge. And a head full of propositional knowledge like "the hands go here, the pedals should be pumped in this fashion" seems insufficient to bestow know-how; you could know all of that stuff without thereby knowing how to ride a bike. The distinction between procedural and declarative knowledge corresponds roughly to the distinction between procedural and declarative memory discussed elsewhere in this chapter in section 4.2.

Last on our list is acquaintance knowledge. Examples of ascriptions of acquaintance knowledge include

- Mary knows Shaquille.
- Shaquille knows New York City.
- Xavier knows Wolverine.

Our first and third examples concern acquaintance with a person, the second, acquaintance with a geographic locale. Note the disconnect between acquaintance knowledge and other kinds. For instance, one may know innumerable bits of propositional knowledge about some person, but this will be insufficient to render it correct to say that one *knows* the person: it is necessary that one meets the person to be acquainted with them.

As already mentioned, propositional knowledge has been of primary interest to those studying knowledge. From here on out, unless otherwise noted, when we discuss knowledge we are discussing propositional knowledge

4.4.1.1.2 *Kinds of propositional knowledge: a priori and a posteriori*

Is it raining where you are right now? How would you know? Perhaps you are near a window and need only look outside. Upon looking out the window you come to have knowledge of the weather, you come to know whether it is raining. Suppose, for the sake of example, it is raining right now, and you come to know it. This bit of knowledge that you have acquired is a bit of a posteriori knowledge: you knew the truth of the proposition in question (the proposition that it is raining) only *after* (thus *posterior* to, and thus the Latin "a posteriori") having some relevant perceptual experience, in this case, the experience of looking out the window. Consider now a different proposition: "either it is raining or it is not." This is obviously true and you need not look out the window to verify it. The truth of "either it is raining or it is not" can be known by reason alone and thus can be known *before* (thus prior to, and thus the Latin "a priori") having the experience of looking out the window. Propositions of the form "either P or not P" as in "either it is raining or it is not raining" and "either elephants are invertebrates or they are not invertebrates" are logical truths. They are knowable a priori because their truth is determined by their logical form. Another alleged class of a priori knowledge constitutes the so-called analytic truths, such as "all bachelors are unmarried males." These are propositions that are true in virtue of the meanings of the terms employed: anyone who knows the meaning of "bachelor," "unmarried," "male," etc. thereby knows a priori that all bachelors are unmarried males. Yet another alleged class of a priori knowledge is constituted by mathematical truths such as "2 + 2 = 4" and "the interior angle sum of any triangle on the Euclidian plane is 180 degrees." Mathematical truths are thought to be known by reason alone, but the question of whether to assimilate them to the logical truths or the analytic truths remains open. In fact, it is a matter of some controversy whether mathematics is a priori or a posteriori, but we will not pursue this here. The traditional view is that the knowledge generated by mathematics and logic is a priori knowledge.

The knowledge generated by the pursuit of the natural sciences is a posteriori knowledge, otherwise known as empirical knowledge. Empirical knowledge is acquired ultimately through the involvement of sensory experience. The methods of experimentation so crucial to the empirical sciences are ultimately ways to regulate the sensory experiences one has and the perceptual beliefs one forms while interacting with the world. We discuss the empirical sciences at greater length below.

An interesting question that we do not have the answer to is what sort of knowledge – a priori or a posteriori – is generated by the pursuits of philosophy and linguistics. If analytic truths like "all bachelors are unmarried males" are examples of a priori knowledge, then how about the "observations" of grammaticality considered by linguists? We know that "Mary ate the cookie" is grammatical English and "the ate cookie Mary" is not. How do we know? A priori or a posteriori? Similarly, the sorts of statements that philosophers hold dear, like that it is a necessary condition of knowledge that it be true, seems a candidate for a priori knowledge. As discussed in Chapter 1, differing answers to this sort of question of whether philosophy is a priori help constitute the differing conceptions of what philosophy is and what relation it bears to the natural sciences.

4.4.1.2 *What is knowledge?*

Philosophers have traditionally analyzed the concept of knowledge as being *justified true belief*. Thus, on this traditional tripartite analysis, for something to count as a bit of knowledge it is necessary and sufficient that it be a belief, that it be justified, and that it be true. After a bit of reflection, the classical analysis may start to seem obvious to you. Consider Mary. She believes that she has a ten dollar bill in her pocket, but unfortunately, the money fell out of her pocket about half an hour ago. So she doesn't *know* that she has ten dollars, no matter how strongly she believes it, since her belief is false. Consider Larry. He is asked to guess how much money Mary has in her pocket. Suppose that for no reason whatsoever, just by random chance, he forms the belief that she has no money in her pocket. He never met Mary, he never looked in her pocket, but somehow he just happens to have this belief, and it just happens to be a true belief. This true belief without justification is not knowledge: Larry may have guessed correctly the contents of Mary's pocket but he doesn't really *know* what is in there.

Or does he? Is justification necessary for knowledge? Consider the chicken sexers. Chicken sexers are people who sort baby chicks into sets of males and females. How they do this, however, is something that they cannot explain: there is no list of easily identifiable cues that they can recite, no explicit criteria that they employ. Nonetheless, for any individual chick, the chicken sexer may come to know that the chick is, say, female. Do chicken sexers have knowledge without justification? If having a justification for a belief entails being able to say how one came to have that belief, then it seems the chicken sexers have no justification for their beliefs about the sexes for chickens. However, as we will discuss later, there is an alternate conception of justification whereby perhaps chicken sexers do have justification for their beliefs. On a *reliabilist* conception of justification, whereby a belief is justified if it is the product of processes that reliably produce true beliefs, it may turn out that chicken sexers have justification for their beliefs.

The above remarks concern the necessity of justification, truth, and belief for knowledge. We turn now to briefly consider the question of whether these necessary conditions are sufficient. In 1963, Edmund Gettier drew attention to a class of seeming counterexamples to the sufficiency of justified true belief for knowledge. For one such example, consider the following. You put a ten dollar bill in your pocket and leave your home. As you walk down the street, unbeknownst to you, the bill falls out of your pocket. Later, while on the subway, a crazy person, gently and without your noticing, slips a ten dollar bill into your pocket. You have justification for believing that there is a ten dollar bill in your pocket: you remember putting one there in the morning. And due to happy though odd circumstances, your justified belief just happens to be true. But, so the story goes, this justified true belief fails to be knowledge: you don't really know that there is a ten dollar bill in your pocket.

Another Gettier-style example is based on a true story involving friends of the authors. Whit Schonbein telephoned Tad Zawidzki. Tad said that he couldn't talk right at that moment, but would call Whit back in a few minutes. A few minutes went by and Whit's phone rang. Whit picked up the phone and said "Hi Tad," thus completely surprising the person on the other line who was not Tad Zawidzki, but an old friend of Whit's – also named Tad – who hadn't spoken to Whit in years. When the phone rang, Whit formed the justified true belief that someone named Tad was on the other end of the line, but was this knowledge? Many philosophers would say "no": these sorts of situations present genuine counterexamples to the tripartite analysis of knowledge as justified true belief. What else, then, needs to be done to define knowledge? Is knowledge justified true belief plus some fourth element? Or perhaps we need different account of justification? This latter option will be discussed in section 4.4.1.4 on theories of justification.

4.4.1.3 Skeptical challenges

Skepticism is the view that we lack knowledge. The global skeptic denies the existence of any knowledge. Local skeptics deny knowledge about some restricted domain, for instance one might deny that we can have knowledge of states of affairs external to our minds. Another local skeptic might deny that we can know anything about supernatural entities and thus is agnostic about the existence of God.

The major kinds of arguments for skeptical conclusions may be classified in terms of the necessary conditions of justification, truth, and belief for knowledge.

Berkeley was a skeptic about mind-independent objects because, he argued, we could not even coherently believe in their existence. He argued that any attempt to do so would automatically make them mind-dependent. According to Berkeley's famous Master Argument for idealism, the attempt to imagine an object existing while no minds exist is self-refuting, because the act of imagining requires the existence of a mind.

Another famous argument for skepticism is the Pessimistic Induction against empirical knowledge. This argument attacks the claims to truth of so-called empirical knowledge. The inductive premises of the argument enumerate the times that claims to empirical knowledge have turned out false. Scientists used to think that the world was flat, and it turned out they were wrong. Scientists used to think that combustion was the rapid release of phlogiston and it turned out they were wrong. And so on. Therefore, everything scientists think will turn out to be wrong. Whether this is a good argument or not, you can't deny that it's pessimistic!

A kind of skeptical argument that focuses on justification is exemplified in perhaps the most influential form of skepticism: Cartesian skepticism (see box). The gist of Cartesian-style skeptical arguments is that some empirical proposition (e.g. that there are trees) cannot be known because we might be deceived (e.g. we might be brains in vats hallucinating that there are trees). These arguments attack our justification for believing some empirical proposition on grounds of possible deception.

Right now you may believe that you are wearing shoes. But do you really *know* that you are wearing shoes? If you do, then you have a bit of empirical knowledge about the external world. Your knowledge would be based on your perceptual experience: you look down at your feet and see that you have shoes on and this provides you with the justified true belief that you have shoes on. However, Descartes would point out that your senses cannot be trusted since you have been deceived by them in the past. The stick has looked bent when it is really straight, and in dreams it may seem that there is an elephant in your room and that he is pink. (Recall our discussion of perceptual error in Chapters 1 and 3.) For all you know then, even though your senses are telling you that you have shoes on your feet, they may be deceiving you. If, for all you know, your senses are deceiving you, then you don't really know whether you have shoes. Another term for this kind of skepticism is error skepticism: according to this style of skepticism, if a putative source of knowledge, such as perception, has ever been in error, then it can never deliver knowledge because it can never supply justification to the associated beliefs (even if those beliefs just happen to be true). These Cartesian thoughts about knowledge have exerted a powerful force on those who have contemplated them, and many thus despair that we may ever actually have empirical knowledge.

4.4.1.4 *Justifying empirical knowledge: theories of justification*

One of the main areas of contemporary epistemological research involves theories of justification. Here we briefly describe three: foundationalism, coherentism, and reliabilism.

4.4.1.4.1 *Foundationalism*
You may believe that grass is green. What is your justification for this belief? You have seen grass and it looks green and you believe that things are the way they seem. The justification of the first

EVALUATING CARTESIAN SKEPTICISM

How powerful are the arguments for Cartesian skepticism? Do they stand up to scrutiny? As usual, it will be useful to consider a schematic version of the argument.

Here is a simple Cartesian-style skeptical argument:

(A) I know that there are trees only if I know that I am not deceived that there are trees.
(B) I do not know that I am not deceived that there are trees.
(C) Therefore, I do not know that there are trees.

It seems pretty clear that this is a valid argument. But is it sound? Are the premises true? Let us turn to inquire into the truth of the premises starting with premise A.

One possible argument in defense of premise A is the following:

(1a) I know that there are trees only if I am not deceived that there are trees.
(2a) If I know that p, and p entails q, then I know q.
(A) Therefore, I know that there trees only if I know that I am not deceived that there are trees.

Again, we have a valid argument. But is it sound? Premise 1a seems true enough: knowledge of p entails truth of p and deception about p entails the falsity of p. Thus, I know p only if I am not deceived that p. But 2a is questionable. It is just a statement of the principle of closure of knowledge under entailment. It is called principle of closure under entailment because moving from something known to something entailed does not take us outside the closed area of knowledge. However, the principle of closure under entailment seems to be false. For example, someone can know that x is a triangle without knowing that the interior angle sum of x is 180 degrees, even though as a matter of fact, being a triangle entails having an interior angle sum of 180 degrees. If the principle of closure under entailment were true, then we wouldn't need to construct and examine valid proofs! Therefore, the second premise of the argument for A is false, rendering that argument unsound.

Perhaps premise A may be defended in the following way: instead of employing the principle of closure under entailment, we can employ the principle of closure under known entailment (i.e. If I know that p and I know that p entails q, then I know that q). This is called principle of closure under known entailment because moving from something known to something known to be entailed does not take us outside the closed area of knowledge.

This principle seems less controversial. For example, if someone knows that x is a triangle and knows that being a triangle entails that the interior angle sum is 180 degrees, then it seems that they must know that the interior angle sum of x is 180 degrees.

continued

So now we can revise the defense of premise A, replacing 2a with 2a′ and adding 3a, yielding the following:

(1a)   I know that there are trees only if I am not deceived that there are trees.
(2a′) If (I know that p and I know that p entails q), then (I know q).
(3a)   I know that (I know that there are trees only if I am not deceived that there are trees).
(A)   Therefore, I know that there are trees only if I know that I am not deceived that there are trees.

Note that in the revised defense of A we had to add a third premise. This kind of premise can be problematic for Cartesian skeptics who want to question empirical knowledge in general, since it itself is a piece of empirical knowledge. The skeptic who claims there is no knowledge of the external world is thus left without a good argument.

Let us now turn to examine premise B of the Cartesian skeptical argument ("I do not know that I am not deceived that there are trees"). One defense of premise B is that I might be a brain in a vat. But maybe we can prove that I'm not a brain in a vat. Hilary Putnam (1981), in the famous first chapter of his book *Reason, Truth and History*, attempted to do just that. Putnam's anti-skeptical argument is as follows:

(1) If I am a brain in a vat then I cannot think that I am a brain in a vat.
(2) I can think that I am a brain in a vat.
(3) Therefore, I am not a brain in a vat.

The argument is valid. Is it sound? Well, it all seems to depend on premise 1. Putnam advocates a kind of externalism about representational content. According to Putnam's brand of externalism, if I can think about vats, then I must have had appropriate causal contact with them: there must be an appropriate causal chain leading from my thoughts about vats to vats themselves . But if I am a brain in a vat, then I've never had appropriate causal contact with vats. Thus there is a problem for premise 1: Putnam's argument works only for brain in vat cases in which I (my brain) never was unvatted.

Let us suppose instead that I've lived a relatively normal life as an embodied brain, enjoying all sorts of normal causal contact with vats, brains, etc., until yesterday, when I was kidnapped in my sleep and turned into a hallucinating brain in a vat. It seems then that I could be a brain in a vat and think "I am a brain in a vat." And, if at the same time as my "envatment," all the trees in the world were, unbeknown to me, utterly destroyed, then my current hallucination that there are trees in my backyard would be a deception. So, the brain in the vat defense of premise B seems to hold water (not to mention brains). But if we shift our attention from local skepticism to global skepticism, the skeptic may still be in trouble. One fantastical hypothesis entertained by Cartesian skeptics is that our senses deceive us about everything: perhaps the only things that exist are you and a deceitful demon feeding you false experiences. You think there are trees, but there are not. There is only a deceitful demon feeding you illusory experiences that make you think that there are trees. However, if externalism is true, we seem at an utter loss to explain how your thoughts can come to have the representational content that there are trees.

belief is the second belief. But what is your justification for the second belief? Is it yet a third belief? Perhaps you have one. And perhaps we can ask for the justification of *that* belief. Can this game continue indefinitely, like the phase some children go through of repeatedly asking "why"? Or must instead the buck stop somewhere with self-evident and self-justified beliefs in need of no further justification? According to foundationalism the buck does stop somewhere.

According to foundationalism beliefs are justified by being either self-justifying or logically derived from other justified beliefs. The self-justifying beliefs form the foundation upon which all other beliefs are justified. The process of showing that a belief is justified involves showing that the belief may be logically derived from other beliefs that themselves are justified. This process may continue until a belief or set of beliefs is reached that is in need of no further justification in virtue of being self-justified or, as some philosophers say, given.

Foundationalism runs into problems. What are the self-justifying beliefs? And are there enough of them? Descartes offered "I think, I exist" as self-evident, but is it? And even if it is, does it serve to justify much of anything, yet alone claims to empirical knowledge? Even Descartes recognized that proving his existence (in his "I think therefore I am") was an insufficient ground for claims to empirical knowledge, thus he attempted to prove further that God existed and that God would not let sensory experience be systematically deceptive. Few philosophers find this solution satisfactory.

4.4.1.4.2 Coherentism

According to coherentism, *no* beliefs in a person's belief set count as foundational beliefs. Instead it is sufficient for the justification of a belief that it be the member of a coherent set of your beliefs, that is, a logically consistent set of beliefs. But a big question that arises is how many of your beliefs must be in this set? If you are epistemically modest, then you will admit the probability that at least one of the things that you believe contradicts at least one of the other things that you believe. You are not sure which of your beliefs are inconsistent with the rest, but it is likely that at least a few of them are. But, does this thereby render all of your beliefs unjustified? Intuitively it does not: just because not all of your beliefs are consistent with every other belief does not seem to entail that none of them are justified. Consider an example. Suppose that Xavier believes that Wolverine ate the last cookie in the cookie jar. Suppose later that Xavier comes to hold the contradictory belief that Rogue ate the last cookie; thus Xavier's most recent belief does not cohere with all of the other beliefs in his belief set. It contradicts at least one of them. Thus the entirety of Xavier's beliefs form an inconsistent belief set. But consider some belief of Xavier's seemingly unrelated to questions of cookies, for instance his belief that the moon is closer to the earth than the sun. He may be entirely justified in this belief regardless of holding contradictory beliefs about the cookies and the cookie jar. Thus coherentism should not make the justifying belief set the totality of a person's beliefs, but some relevant subset. But what is the relevant subset?

A different problem for coherentism is the way is seems to make justification totally float free of truth. A completely delusional person may have a coherent belief set: he believes that he is Napoleon, that his bed is a horse, that his broom closet is a castle, and so on. Every one of his beliefs may be false even though they form a consistent set. How, then, can mere coherence form a justificatory grounding for genuine empirical knowledge? Genuine empirical knowledge, if there is such a thing, is about the external world: it reaches out beyond our belief set to make contact with the truth of the matter.

4.4.1.4.3 Reliabilism

Reliabilism is a theory of justification that attempts to make contact with truth in a way that coherentism cannot. Reliabilism also offers to solve the problems raised earlier in discussion of the chicken sexers and the Gettier counterexamples to the tripartite analysis. Foundationalism and coherentism are both internalist theories since they make factors relevant to the justification of a belief internal to the belief set of the believer. Reliabilism is in contrast an externalist theory. The justifying factors relate a belief to things external to the believer.

Note that the contrast between internalism and externalism in the theory of justification is different from the contrast between internalism and externalism in the theory of representational content discussed in Chapter 1. Whether one is an externalist about justification is independent of whether one is an externalist about representational content, and so on.

According to reliabilism, a belief is justified if it is the product of a belief-forming process that reliably produces true beliefs. Thus, the chicken sexers who know the sex of a chicken without being able to say how they know are justified in their beliefs because their beliefs result from a process that is reliable in forming true beliefs about the sex of chicks. Some versions of reliabilism have built in to the theory that there be appropriate causal relations between the knower and the thing known. Thus there has to be an appropriate causal chain between the truth maker and the belief for the belief to count as justified. With this minimal sketch of reliabilism in place we can see how it makes contact with the problems raised by the Gettier counterexamples. In the story about Whit and the two Tads, the phone rang, causing Whit to believe that a person named Tad was calling, but this belief was about Tad Zawidzki, and Whit's belief was caused by the other Tad, thus, if a certain version of reliabilism is correct, it turns out that the Gettier examples are not cases of *justified* belief. This is because the normal chains of causation between the belief and the truth makers have been severed; the beliefs do not count as justified.

But is reliabilism the superior theory of justification? Many philosophers find it unintuitive and have raised other problems for it. We will not pursue these issues further here. Instead we turn to a slightly different shift in focus on similar issues. Another arena in which philosophers wonder about knowledge and its justification is in the philosophy of science.

4.4.2 The philosophy of science

4.4.2.1 *The influence of logical positivism*

If we were to place our bets on who is most likely to have empirical knowledge, we would be wise to bet on scientists. In particular, the phenomenal successes of physics, chemistry, and biology in the twentieth century have attracted the attention of philosophers trying to explain knowledge.

What is scientific knowledge? It seems to involve the formulation of hypotheses and the testing of those hypotheses by carefully controlled observations. Well-tested hypotheses are those most likely to be regarded as true theories. The continued activity of hypothesis formation and hypothesis testing thus gives rise to knowledge of the world and theories that explain how the world works. Philosophers have been interested in explaining in more detail how the processes of hypothesis testing and theoretical explanations work. Many philosophers of science have tried to explain testing and explanation in terms of logic. Foremost among such philosophical explanations of scientific activity were the logical positivists of the early twentieth century. Here we describe the two main outgrowths of logical positivism: the hypothetico-deductive model of theory development and the deductive-nomological model of scientific explanation.

4.4.2.1.1 The *hypothetico-deductive* model of theory development

Scientific knowledge is codified in the form of scientific theories. Prominent theories include the oxygen theory of combustion, and Einstein's General and Special theories of relativity. Where do theories come from? The basic answer that we inherit from the logical positivists is that theories start as hypotheses – educated guesses. Then these hypotheses are subjected to tests, and if they pass the tests, they rise to the level of theory. The hypotheses are confirmed and the process of confirmation bestows justification, and thus, we start with hypothesis and wind up with knowledge. The logical positivists offered a view of the logical structure of theory development and hypothesis testing known as the hypothetico-deductive (H-D) model of theory development. According to the H-D model, after a scientist generates a hypothesis, he then deduces implications of the hypothesis: statements logically derivable from the hypothesis. Next he performs observations and experiments to see if any of these implications of the hypothesis are true. If the implications of the hypothesis are held to be true, the scientist regards the hypothesis itself to be shown true.

Carl Hempel (1965) illustrates H-D with the example of Ignaz Semmelweis' work during the 1840s on childbed fever. Semmelweis observed cases of childbed fever contracted by women who gave birth in his hospital. He noted that cases were especially frequent among women for whom deliveries were handled by physicians instead of midwives. Semmelweis' key insight into the cause of childbed fever came when he observed that a physician came down with similar symptoms upon injuring himself with an instrument during an autopsy. Semmelweis hypothesized that "cadaveric material" on the instrument caused the disease, and that, similarly, the physicians associated with outbreaks of childbed fever had cadaveric material on their hands prior to delivering babies. Semmelweis tested this hypothesis by examining its implications. One implication of the hypothesis that cadaveric material is the cause of childbed fever is that its removal from the hands of physicians would result in a decrease in cases of childbed fever. Semmelweis tested this implication by requiring that physicians wash their hands in chlorinated lime prior to examining patients (which he assumed would remove the cadaveric matter). He observed that groups of women examined by physicians who washed with chlorinated lime had lower incidence of childbed fever than groups of women examined by physicians who did not.

The example of Semmelweis' hypothesis and test conforms to the H-D model in the following way. His hypothesis took the form of a general statement: "Any woman in the hospital who comes down with childbed fever must have been exposed to cadaveric material." An implication of the hypothesis is the statement "If some woman is not exposed to cadaveric material she will not contract childbed fever." Semmelweis tried to set up conditions in which he could observe women not exposed to cadaveric material by having a group of women examined only by physicians who had washed with chlorinated lime. Such women turned out to have lower incidences of childbed fever, thus confirming the initial hypothesis.

Another way in which hypotheses are thought to be confirmed is by way of induction. Semmelweis' observations could be formulated as a series of observation statements, statements of particular states of affairs such as "Jane Doe was exposed to cadaveric material and contracted childbed fever," "Mary Smith was exposed to cadaveric material and contracted childbed fever," and so on. His hypothesis took the form of a law-like general statement: "Any woman exposed to cadaveric material will contract childbed fever," which is a general statement inductively supported by a collection of particular observations.

4.4.2.1.2 The D-N model of explanation

One of the main goals of science is to explain things. An idea that goes back as far as Aristotle is that events are explained by showing that they conform to general laws. This idea was developed by the logical positivists into the deductive-nomological (D-N) model of explanation. The gist of the D-N model is that a phenomenon is explained by showing that a description of that phenomenon is deducible from one or more statements of law: statements that take the form of universal generalizations. One example of a law is Newton's law that force equals mass times acceleration. This law may be expressed as a universal generalization of the form, for any quantity of force exerted by an object, that force is the product of that object's mass and that object's acceleration. The explanation of why some particular object exerts the force that it does will involve showing that the relations of its force, mass, and acceleration are derivable from Newton's law. (Note the similarity to foundationalist accounts of justification discussed above.)

Combining the H-D model with the D-N model yields the picture of science depicted in Figure 4.1. According to D-N, particular phenomena are explained by showing how they are deductively derivable from general statements of law. According to H-D, general statements of law are supported by inductive arguments, the premises of which are observation statements: descriptions of observed particular phenomena.

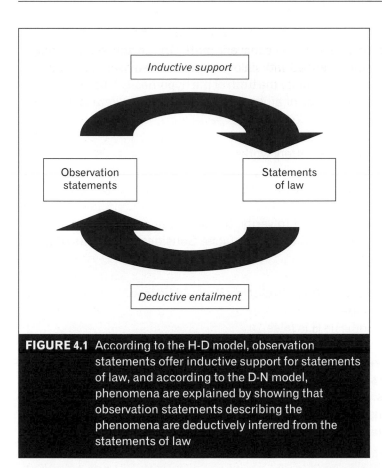

FIGURE 4.1 According to the H-D model, observation statements offer inductive support for statements of law, and according to the D-N model, phenomena are explained by showing that observation statements describing the phenomena are deductively inferred from the statements of law

POPPER'S CRITIQUE OF CONFIRMATION

Karl Popper (Popper 1958 [1935]) attacked the positivists' view that hypotheses could be confirmed. Popper argued that hypotheses could only be falsified.

According to the H-D model, the logic of the relation of hypotheses and tests had the following form:

Premise 1: Hypothesis H entails prediction P.
Premise 2: Prediction P is true.
Conclusion: Therefore hypothesis H is true.

Popper pointed out that any argument of this form embodies fallacious reasoning. The key to seeing this is to realize that statements of the form "If P then Q" are logically

continued

equivalent to "P is sufficient for Q" and "Q is necessary for P." In the above schematic argument, the second premise involves the truth of only one of the necessary conditions of the hypothesis, which is thus insufficient for the truth of the hypothesis. This fallacious form of reasoning is known as the fallacy of affirming the consequent. Here is a more obvious example of the fallacy:

Premise 1: If my car starts then the battery works.
Premise 2: My battery works.
Conclusion: My car will start.

Popper argued that instead of attempting to verify, the best that scientists could do to test for hypotheses was to try to see if they were false. Consider arguments of the following form:

Premise 1: If Hypothesis H is true, then Prediction P would be true.
Premise 2: Prediction P is false.
Conclusion: Therefore hypothesis H is false.

Here we have a valid form of reasoning known as modus tollens. This reasoning is valid because the second premise shows the failure of one of the necessary conditions on the truth of the hypothesis. Thus, Popper argued, scientists should try as hard as possible to devise tests that could falsify hypotheses. The hypothesis that has survived more attempted falsifications is the better hypothesis.

4.4.2.2 Kuhn: revolutions and paradigms

The logical positivists had a somewhat ahistorical view of science: they sought to uncover the timeless logical structure to which science should conform. Kuhn (1996), in contrast, saw science as a historically grounded phenomenon. Further, Kuhn saw science as something that changed radically over time. According to Kuhn, scientific theories vary so significantly over time that the findings and theories at one time cannot be meaningfully related to the findings and theories of other times: different theories are thus incommensurable. They constitute different languages that cannot be intertranslated. Instead of viewing the historical progression of science as the progressive accumulation of truths, Kuhn argued for a non-cumulative shift from one paradigm to the next. These changes over time conform to a cyclic pattern that can be broken down into five stages of

(1) immature science
(2) normal mature science
(3) crisis science

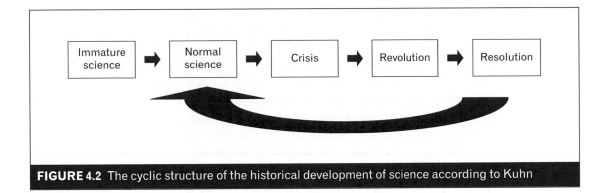

FIGURE 4.2 The cyclic structure of the historical development of science according to Kuhn

(4) revolutionary science
(5) resolutions, which is followed by a return to normal science (see Figure 4.2).

The key notion in understanding Kuhnian philosophy of science is the notion of a *paradigm*. The key stage is normal science and normal science is paradigm-based science. The remaining four of the stages are understood by way of contrast with normal science. What, precisely, a Kuhnian paradigm is supposed to be has been a matter of debate, but the following sketch will suffice.

For Kuhn (1996, p. 20), paradigms are "Universally recognized scientific achievements that for a time provide model problems and solutions to a community of practitioners." Further, paradigms define what problems and methods are to count as legitimate for succeeding generations of practitioners. Paradigms accomplish these feats in virtue of two essential characteristics (p. 10): first, "Their achievement was sufficiently unprecedented to attract an enduring group of adherents away from competing modes of scientific activity." Second, their achievement "was sufficiently open-ended to leave all sorts of problems for the redefined group of practitioners to resolve." Examples of paradigms include, according to Kuhn, Ptolemaic astronomy, Copernican astronomy, Aristotelian dynamics, Newtonian dynamics, corpuscular optics, and wave optics. Arguably, behaviorism constituted a paradigm in psychology that was superseded by cognitive psychology.

Normal science is science that takes place under the guidance of a paradigm: normal science is paradigm-based science. Prior to the arrival of a paradigm, science is immature, according to Kuhn. Immature science is science studying a domain recognizably the same as that studied by paradigm-based successors, but without the utilization of any paradigms. Examples include the cases of optics prior to Newton and electrical research in the first half of the eighteenth century (Kuhn 1996, pp. 12–14). Once a paradigm takes hold, its influence is not exerted forever. A paradigm exerts its influence only as long as a relative consensus as to its applicability exists. When the consensus begins to unravel, a stage of crisis emerges. After a period of crisis, novel approaches of problem solving emerge, thus constituting a scientific revolution. The fruits of revolution are a new paradigm, returning the cycle to a stage of normal science.

According to Kuhn different paradigms are incommensurable and thus choice of one over another cannot be subject to rational procedures. We can understand the incommensurability of paradigms by analogy to different languages, the terms of which cannot be translated into each other. For instance, the term "space" as used in Newtonian physics cannot be translated as the term "space" used in Einsteinian physics. Einsteinians mean different things by "space" than do Newtonians: they use the term in different ways. Unlike Newtonians, Einsteinians hold that space is curved by mass. Kuhn buys into an account of the meaning of theoretical terms whereby the meaning of a term depends on the theory it is embedded in. Where theories diverge, so do the meaning of their terms, regardless of superficial similarities like spelling and pronunciation.

Among Kuhn's arguments that paradigms are not open to rational choice are those that concern the theory-ladenness of perception and observation (recall our discussion from Chapter 3). According to Kuhn, observation statements cannot serve as neutral points of arbitration. There is no theory-neutral observation language because how one perceives the world depends on the theory with which one conceives the world.

Kuhn argues that since paradigms are incommensurable, the history of a scientific discipline is non-cumulative. None of the discoveries and theories of an earlier paradigm can be retained by later paradigms. Thus the progress of science is not the accumulation of scientific truths. Scientists are merely changing their minds over time, not adding to an ever-increasing store of knowledge. Non-cumulativity follows from incommensurability. Since the language of one paradigm cannot be translated into the language of another, the statements held to be true with one paradigm cannot be expressed, let alone judged to be true within another. Adding the theory-ladenness of perception to the equation means that just as theories are not accumulated, neither are observations, since observations depend on theories. Kuhn's thesis of non-cumulativity challenges the traditional view of science a source of progress. Instead, science seems more analogous to changes in clothing fashion: what is valued by one generation is no better or worse than any other. People are merely changing their minds about what they like. The history of science, as viewed through the Kuhnian lens, is of a series of paradigms and revolutions, none bearing any rational relation to any other.

Philosophers and scientists have reacted strongly against many of Kuhn's claims. For instance, Kuhn's hypothesis of incommensurability has been challenged. Some have argued against the view that the meanings of theoretical terms are determined wholly by factors internal to a paradigm, but instead may be determined, at least in part, by causal relations between the term and items in the external world. Putnam (1975) suggests that the meaning of certain scientific terms involves causal relations between the terms and things in the world that they denote. For instance, part of the meaning of water is the substance H_2O that was present when the term *water* was first brought into use to denote that substance. A causal chain leads from current uses of *water* to the initial dubbing of H_2O as water. These causal chains remain constant regardless of a scientist's theory. Thus, water discourse need not be incommensurable between adherents of divergent theories about water. The debate about meaning reflected here is a conflict between internalists and externalists about representational content as discussed in the box on Cartesian skepticism and in Chapter 1 in the discussion of theories of mental representation. We will discuss this further in Chapter 6 in the discussion of the philosophy of language.

Another challenge to Kuhnian incommensurability arises from theorists who propose that the mind is modular. Recall from Chapter 3 that Fodor (1983), for example, argues that many perceptual processes are modular in the sense of being "informationally encapsulated" so that their outputs are immune to influence by theoretical and other acquired beliefs. Fodor, therefore, contends that observational reports can be treated as univocal even when theorists hold different theories. Though, as discussed in Chapter 3, it is not clear that this solves the sorts of problems raised by Kuhn.

5 Action and Emotion

In this chapter we examine two closely related aspects of our cognitive lives, action and emotion – how we move and what moves us.

5.1 ACTION

The sensory systems provide internal representations of both our own bodies and the world outside. A major function of these representations is to extract the information necessary to guide the movements that make up our behavioral repertoire. These movements are controlled by a set of motor systems that allow us to maintain balance and posture, to move our body, limbs, and eyes, and to communicate through speech and gesture. In contrast to the sensory systems, which transform physical energy into neural information, the motor systems transform neural information into physical energy by issuing commands that are transmitted by the brainstem and spinal cord to skeletal muscles. The muscles translate this neural information into a contractile force that produces movements. As our perceptual skills are a reflection of the capabilities of the sensory systems to detect, analyze, and estimate the significance of physical stimuli, so our agility and dexterity are reflections of the capabilities of motor systems to plan, coordinate, and execute movements (Ghez 1991).

Actions complete the outgoing part of perception/action cycles. In order for action to be effective, the representations on which it is based must be faithful and robust, the effectors (humans' primary effectors are their hands and arms) need to be flexible enough to adapt to an infinite variety of objects, but strong and rigid enough to have real effects on the world. The human hand is a masterpiece of evolution; it is a combination sensor/effector, with amazing dexterity, sensitivity, selectivity, and adaptiveness. The arms and hands move in our natural workspace – the area directly in front of us – under the wary gaze of the visual system, working at its highest acuity. As Ghez (1991) notes, we must also not forget that speaking is a kind of action (although we still find it more convenient to treat the language abilities separately in Chapter 6). In spite of the large variety of motor areas, and the huge number of individual muscles whose force they carefully monitor and tune, all of this computational power needs to tend toward a single, unified course of action. This is of course not only because of the simple fact that we have only one body, but also because attempting more than one complex voluntary action at one time seems to be too much for our brains to manage; some of us can barely talk and drive at the same time. Yet by allocating attentional resources to the most important and complex actions and away from simple, well-rehearsed actions, we can learn to perform several complex actions at one time.

5.2 ACTION AND THE BRAIN

5.2.1 Motor areas of the cortex and their connections

Although we are treating action separately from perception, we need to remember that the brain runs the two tightly together. We are always perceiving in order to act, and acting in order to perceive. Seeing, for instance, is both perceiving and acting at the same time. Our eye movements are timed and coordinated in order to sample as much of the incoming light information as possible. (Recall our discussion of saccades in Chapter 3, section 3.3.) Aside from simple reflexes, we never really act blindly, that is, without perceiving at the same time. Even moving around in a dark room, we are acutely aware of our orientation in the room, using our vestibular system in the inner ear. To realize this is to realize how far we are from the classical computational picture in which the cognizer takes in input, computes, then acts. Feedback loops are constantly running at many levels. The brain is also constantly making predictions as to what our objects of interest will do, for instance consider the sorts of predictions we make about the path a bouncing grounder will take as it comes toward us on the softball diamond. Or consider: a bartender nudges a full mug of beer toward you. You reach to pick it up, and your arm jerks upward, almost spilling the precious contents. It is one of those plastic mugs, made to look like the much heavier glass versions. Your brain has made a prediction as to how heavy the glass is, and calculated the force required to lift it. Motor areas in the frontal cortex are organized into somatotopic maps, just as the somatosensory areas in the parietal lobes, insula, and prefrontal cortex are. There are three main motor areas of the cortex: the primary motor cortex, the premotor cortex, and the supplementary motor cortex (Figure 5.1).

Body movements can be elicited by stimulating these parts of the cortex with a tiny electrical current (which is how Penfield originally affirmed the idea that these areas were somatotopically organized, in the 1950s: see Figure 5.2), but stimulating different areas produces different sorts of movements.

Stimulation of the primary motor cortex produces simple movements, or muscle clenchings. Stimulation of the supplementary motor area or premotor areas produces more complex movements involving more muscle groups, and requires a more intense electrical current. These motor areas receive input from the thalamus, and from the somatosensory areas in the parietal lobes,

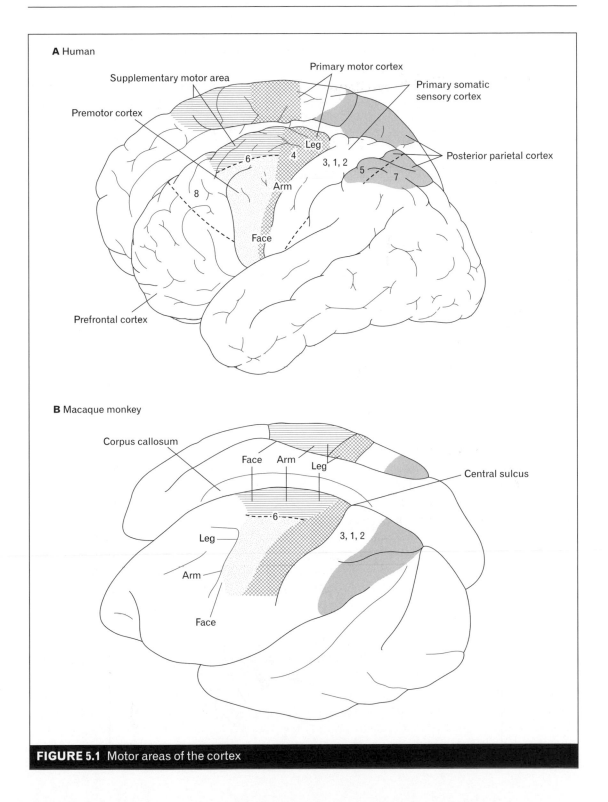

A Human

Supplementary motor area

Primary motor cortex

Primary somatic
sensory cortex

Premotor cortex

Posterior parietal cortex

Leg

6   4

3, 1, 2

5   7

8

Arm

Face

Prefrontal cortex

B Macaque monkey

Corpus callosum

Face   Arm

Leg

Central sulcus

6

Leg

3, 1, 2

Arm

Face

FIGURE 5.1 Motor areas of the cortex

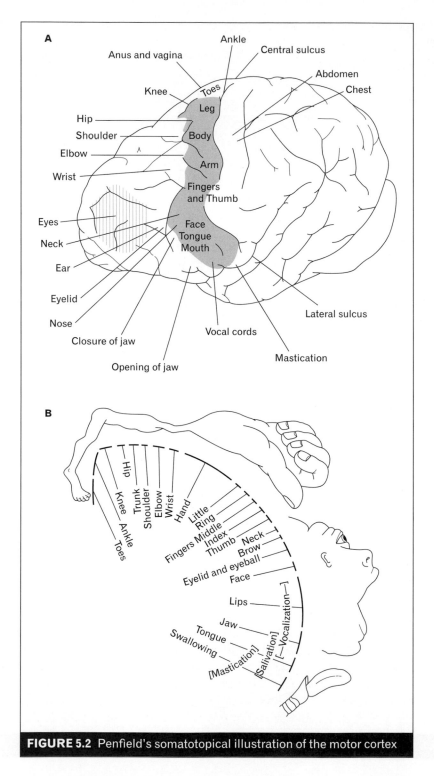

FIGURE 5.2 Penfield's somatotopical illustration of the motor cortex

as well as from the cerebellum and basal ganglia (see section 5.2.3). These motor cortical areas project directly to motor neurons in the spinal cord. Damage to them can reduce the strength of muscles, impair movement speed, and cause the patient to lose the ability to contract individual muscles.

5.2.2 Motor control

How does the central nervous system (CNS) coordinate intentional action? First, information from sensory inputs must be transferred into motor goals involving factors such as the direction, strength, and velocity of the intended action. Second, the intended action must be translated into information that controls muscles involved in limb trajectories, coordination of body parts, relay of new sensory inputs based on intended and actual movement, and so on. This means that information involving a few variables must be translated into many signals that are then transmitted to a large number of destinations, all of which must be synchronized into coordinated muscle activity, which involves a complex series of computations. How is this achieved?

A monkey sees a banana, the arm is raised, the fingers of the hand open, the monkey reaches for the banana and successfully retrieves it. How was that done? Well, the monkey's CNS first has to specify to itself not only where the banana is in relation to the monkey, but also where the monkey's arm is in relation to that banana, what positions the fingers of the hand are in, the balance of the body in its present position and how this will be altered by a sudden movement of the arm and what may need to be compensated by the arch of the back and position of the hind legs, how the curves of the balls of the feet lie against the floor and need to be adjusted so that the monkey doesn't fall, and so on. What makes all this possible is that retinotopic neurons in the monkey's parietal cortex and hippocampus are directly affected by and precisely tuned to signals from somatosensory inputs: the monkey's visual field is sensitive to inputs from the eyes, incoming information about head position, and so on, all of which involves spatial representation. This we know based on precise, single-neuron recordings of the parietal cortex and superior collicus which suggest that the representation of external, objective body-independent (allocentric) space within a subjective, perspectival, body-centered (egocentric) space occurs in the parietal area (see Andersen et al. 1993). Without the coordination of these two representational spaces – allocentric space and egocentric space – and the proprioception necessary to program the intended action and then execute it, the monkey's CNS could not implement even the simplest tasks such as are required to pick a banana.

The transformation of an intended action by the CNS into signals that control muscles involves a complex series of computations that must occur within a very short time frame. In robot arms, this is done either by computing the inverse dynamics of mechanical arm movements through sequences of algebraic operations that compute positions, velocities, accelerations, inertia, torque, and so on, or through a series of computations of equilibrium positions. In animal arms it has been suggested that equilibrium trajectories are tracked through the intrinsic elastic properties of muscles that are properly calibrated to the inputs and outputs of the CNS. The movement of the arm is achieved by shifting a neurally specified equilibrium point. Thus the physical (elastic) properties of muscles and other bodily materials involved in the movement themselves provide corrective information through feedback allowing the computation and control of the hand reaching for the banana. Stimulation of the spinal cords of frogs whose spinal cords were surgically separated from their brains reveals that activation of specific neural circuits of the spinal cord causes specific and precise contractions in the frog's muscles (see Bizzi et al. 1991). The brainstems of owls exhibit separate circuits for controlling horizontal and vertical head movements. And mathematical modeling of movement and posture has shown that control of different motor actions can be achieved through the superimposition of an elementary set of symbols (an "alphabet") operating as impulses across supraspinal pathways.

Clinical studies on humans with neurological disorders, brain imaging, and neurophysiological recordings of animal brains have shown that the cerebellum is in charge of adaptation and conditioning required for the learning and coordination of joint and muscle movements (see section 5.2.3). The basal ganglia (see section 5.2.3) are in charge of learning movement sequences that become habits. Actions performed repeatedly over time through motor learning cause changes in procedural memory, which is not accessible to consciousness (see the sections on memory), in the way that declarative or explicit memory of events or facts can be achieved through a single trial and then consciously recalled.

5.2.3 The cerebellum and basal ganglia

It was long thought that the cerebellum contributed only a sort of fine-tuning of movement, since people with cerebellar damage moved in a shaky fashion. More recently, however, we have come to realize that the cerebellum does much more than this. It has additional functions, both in action and cognition. In addition to the basal ganglia, the cerebellum regulates the timing and trajectories of arm movements, as well as eye movements, providing the accurate timing essential for real-world success. Neuroscientists divide the cerebellum into three functional regions: the vestibulocerebellum receives inputs from organs in the inner ear responsible for detecting changes in head position which it uses to control balance and eye movements; the spinocerebellum receives somatosensory information which it organizes into somatotopic maps and uses to adjust ongoing movements when deviations from the intended trajectory occur; the cerebrocerebellum receives input from both somatosensory and motor cortical areas which is uses to coordinate the precise timing and initiation of movements (see Figure 5.3).

The basal ganglia are five large, densely interconnected nuclei located below the cortex: the caudate nucleus, putamen, globus pallidus, subthalamic nucleus, and the substantia nigra (see Figure 5.4). They are primarily involved in the planning of motor activity. Their main input is from motor areas of the cerebral cortex, and their output runs to the thalamus back to the cortex to complete a circuit. The basal ganglia have at least three clearly separable functions in action: an oculomotor circuit running through the caudate nucleus is responsible for controlling eye movements to a target; a prefrontal circuit connecting portions of the upper part of the prefrontal cortex with the caudate nucleus may be involved with a type of memory required to orient the body in space; and an orbitofrontal circuit which connects more lateral areas of the orbitofrontal circuit with the caudate may be involved in the ability to change behavior based on changes in

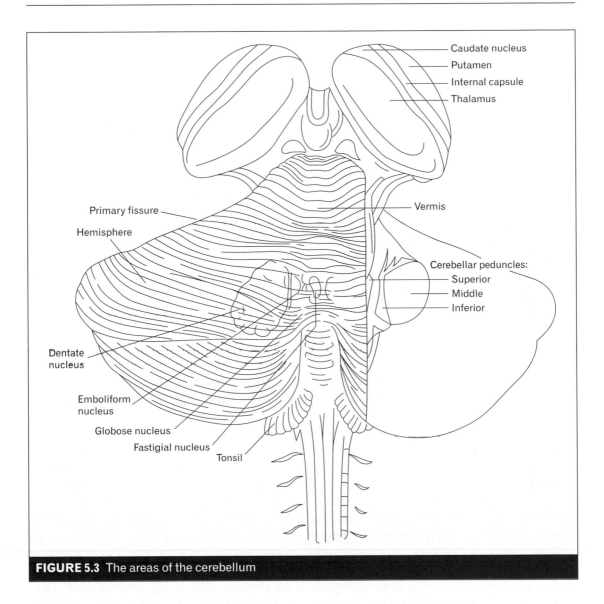

FIGURE 5.3 The areas of the cerebellum

incoming stimuli and their reward values. Lesions of the basal ganglia can also produce a loss of spontaneous movements, as well as abnormal involuntary movements.

5.2.4 Neuropsychological disorders of action

5.2.4.1 Parkinson's and Huntington's diseases

Both Parkinson's disease and Huntington's disease can be considered disorders of action. They affect the action system by producing involuntary movements, tremors, and changes in both

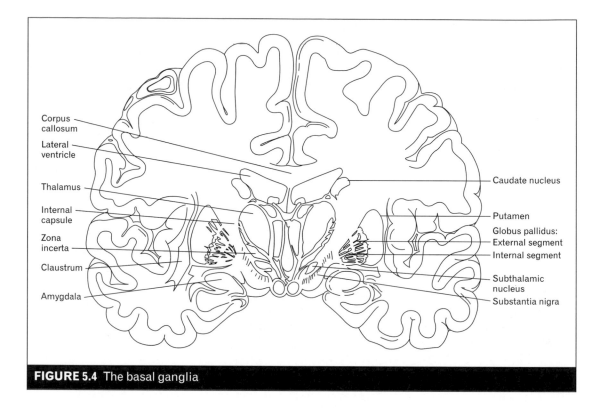

FIGURE 5.4 The basal ganglia

posture and muscle tone. Damage to the basal ganglia has been found in both of these diseases. The brains of Parkinson's disease patients have been found to have a dramatic reduction of dopamine, accompanied by a loss of nerve cells in one of the basal ganglia, the substantia nigra. (Recall our discussion of dopamine and associated disorders from Chapter 2 in section 2.6.4.) Supplementing the diet of Parkinson's patients with L-DOPA, a chemical precursor of dopamine, caused a short but nearly complete remission of their symptoms, a process which is still not well understood. In the early 1980s several drug users contracted Parkinson's from a form of synthetic heroin which was contaminated by a chemical called MPTP. It was found that this chemical is highly toxic to the dopaminergic neurons of the substantia nigra, which gave rise to as yet unconfirmed speculations that Parkinson's disease might be at least partially caused by some toxin found in the environment. Huntington's disease was originally called Huntington's chorea, from the Greek word for dance, because of the clumsy uncontrolled movements which Huntington's patients sometimes exhibit. These patients also gradually lose the ability to speak, and their facial expressions can become distorted. The disease is heritable: children who have a parent with Huntington's have a 50 percent chance of contracting it themselves.

5.2.4.2 Apraxia and other motor disorders

Apraxia is an inability to engage in purposeful action, which is tested clinically by asking the patient to perform a certain action. So for instance, a neurologist might ask a patient to pretend he is drinking a cup of coffee. When the patient's inability to do this is not due to his not understanding the command, or perceiving the doctor properly, and is genuinely a motor problem, we have a case of apraxia. The basal ganglia have been implicated in routine, frequently carried-out actions, such as opening doors, drinking, and so on, and some kinds of apraxia are traceable to their damage. Lesions of the cortical motor areas such as the supplementary motor area and the primary motor cortex cause disorders of more complex voluntary actions. Lesions of the primary cortex can cause weakness of the area mapped by the damaged part, while lesions of more premotor area disturb the ability to develop appropriate strategies for movement.

5.2.4.3 Alien hand syndrome

Alien hand syndrome occurs when a person's hand, usually the left hand interestingly enough, seems to "take on a mind of its own." One patient described his hand, to his horror, reaching out and grabbing people on a bus, without any intention to do so by him. A woman told of waking up in the middle of the night, her left hand with a death grip on her throat – she was able to peel the fingers off only with great effort. Phenomena such as these are no doubt a product of the brain's tendency to employ multiple independent loops of processing. Normally, conscious volition is tightly coupled to mechanisms at the next level down which coordinate complex actions – alien hand perhaps occurs when this coupling breaks. Often the lesion in alien hand syndrome is to the corpus callosum, suggesting that an inhibitory signal from the left hemisphere to the right is disrupted, leading to a sort of disinhibition of the left hand (which is controlled primarily by the right hemisphere).

5.3 ROBOTICS

Robots have been successfully implemented in a variety of areas, from agriculture and manufacturing to underwater and space exploration. These robots are able to perceive their environments and act accordingly. Understanding how we are able to achieve this at a machine level may give us important clues about ourselves and how we are able to do it. It is extremely interesting, for instance, to notice what sorts of evolutionary changes robotics has undergone over the past several decades, and how the solution to a variety of problems has required the implementation of less mechanistic and deterministic models to more probabilistic, computational, and complex structures that begin to resemble human structure and behavior. Thus early sensors and deterministic map-based navigation systems that used "dead reckoning" or "internal odometry," where the robot measured its positions with mechanical wheel rotations, have given way to stereo vision and probabilistic computational schemes that model the robot's state (its position, orientation, and internal states) using probability distributions both for its own states and the external environment using Bayes' rule. Obstacles can be treated as repulsive forces, goals as attractive forces, and the robot can calculate the vector sum or all such forces in order to determine where to go and what to do. Landmark-based navigation systems have been developed, where inputs are matched against topological graphs with nodes that represent major obstacles and landmarks, and with arcs that represent a variety of possible paths. Sometimes sonar and vision are used together, as well as laser-guided movement. Nowadays robots can take multiple data from various inputs to create a probability distribution for the likely placement of obstacles, match a variety of their own goals according to probability distributions of their own internal states, and thus use what begins to look more and more like internal belief states to decide what to do and where to go.

An important recent result in robotics is that a purely sequential perceive–decide–act cycle is insufficient for real-time operation in complex environments. Current work in execution architectures focuses on implementing perception, action, and planning into one feasible schema. Behavior-based systems implement parallel sets of operant behaviors to process external input from the environment and decide what course of action to take using, for instance, a variety of "voting mechanisms" to arbitrate among competing inputs and outputs. These behavior-based action robots are the most successful in terms of moving through and interacting with their environments but, perhaps not surprisingly, they are the most difficult to control! This is because at such complex levels of internal self-programming it is virtually impossible to preclude in advance a slew of unintended behaviors. In other words, the machines begin to at least seem more like autonomous agents, animals or humans, whose behavior is no longer perfectly predictable.

A related point of interest is that most often an executive sequencer is used to manage the complex flow of information inside the robot. The executive sequencer takes a current series of tasks, some of which may have just come about through changes in the environment, and breaks them down into subtasks that are then parsed to different subsystems. The executive monitors this work and in tiered or layered architectures integrates all the activities in a complex hierarchy that can exhibit incredibly complex behaviors, involving abstract feedback loops and various open parameters in which machines learn to make intelligent decisions. Intelligent agent architecture (see below) models such information-processing systems through an integration of subsystems with centralized and decentralized, self-programming control mechanisms. (An intelligent agent is an entity or device that can interact with its environment in appropriate, properly functional ways, using goal-directed behavior to achieve some purpose. See the discussion of the intentional stance below.)

5.3.1 Agent architectures

Architectures are templates, or generic models of shared structures, that allow us to model and develop intelligent systems in a variety of different applications. Two different sorts of engineering architectures have evolved in the attempt to build intelligent mechanical systems capable of action in an environment: top-down *deliberative* architectures and bottom-up *reactive* architectures.

Deliberative models are perhaps the most natural, insofar as they seem to take their cue directly from folk psychology, and model agents as symbolic reasoning systems. The first step is to represent the agent as a series of sub-agents each of which contains its own store of symbolic or propositional representations (which correspond to beliefs, desires, and intentions in humans), as well as modules that can process what would be the equivalent of perceptual information. Deliberating and reasoning can go on in each module separately, until there is some coordination, perhaps through an executive sequencer (see section 5.3), to enable the final result: action. Reasoning and abstract thinking, including memory, problem solving, and rationality, are all given computational interpretations and implementations. The computational complexity of such systems is immense, and has shown that the simplest sort of common-sense beliefs and intentions are extremely difficult to construct in a computer or robot to make it environmentally functional.

As a result, reactive models are used to supplement the deliberative approach with the idea that while symbolic reasoning may be appropriate for some cognitive processes, a slew of behaviors such as, most notably, driving a car or walking, involve completely different methods of information processing. These systems use feedback control methods, devised in mathematical engineering, in which the agent and the environment together form a dynamic system so that the inputs of one are the outputs of the other. Self-contained feedback "behavior modules" detect external states in the environment and create a sequence of subroutines in the system to generate an appropriate output culminating in some specific action.

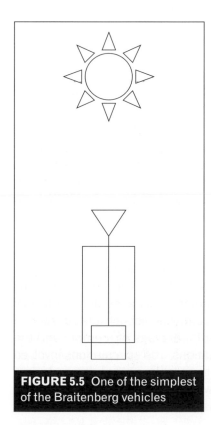

FIGURE 5.5 One of the simplest of the Braitenberg vehicles

5.3.2 Braitenberg vehicles

Some of the most interesting illustrations of the power of non-deliberative architectures in achieving agent control are due to a series of thought experiments conducted by Valentino Braitenberg in his book *Vehicles: Experiments in Synthetic Psychology* (1984). Braitenberg invites the reader to imagine the construction of simple artificial organisms out of a small collection of components: sensors, motors, and the connections between them. Figure 5.5 represents one of the simplest kinds of Braitenberg vehicles.

In Figure 5.5 we are looking down on a vehicle which inhabits a plane. At the top part of the figure is a stimulus source; we can imagine it, in this case, as a source of light. The bottom of the figure contains the vehicle itself. The triangular shape is the vehicle's single sensor, connected by a vertical line to a square shape at the back of the vehicle which is the vehicle's single motor. Light falling on the sensor activates the sensor to send a signal to the motor. If the connection is excitatory then increased activation in the sensor will yield increased activation in the motor. Thus the creature depicted in Figure 5.5 will accelerate toward the light. If instead the connection is inhibitory, then increased activation

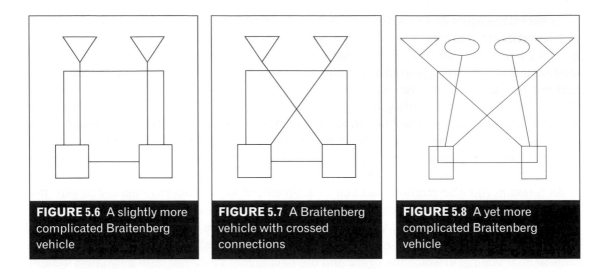

FIGURE 5.6 A slightly more complicated Braitenberg vehicle

FIGURE 5.7 A Braitenberg vehicle with crossed connections

FIGURE 5.8 A yet more complicated Braitenberg vehicle

in the sensor will yield decreased activation in the motor, thus moving the creature away from the light. A slightly more complicated creature is depicted in Figure 5.6.

This creature in Figure 5.6 has two sensors and two motors. Suppose that this creature's connections are excitatory and that it is in the proximity of a light source. If the light is closer to one of the sensors than the other, say, it is closer to the right sensor than the left sensor, then the right motor will be more active than the left motor and the vehicle will turn away from light. Suppose that we change the connections from excitatory to inhibitory. This will result in the right motor being less active than the left motor and the vehicle will turn toward the light. A similar effect can be achieved by keeping the connections excitatory but crossing them as depicted in Figure 5.7.

The vehicle with crossed excitatory connections will move toward the light, and a vehicle with crossed inhibitory connections will move away from the light. Braitenberg describes these vehicles as instantiating low-level analogs of fear and love. The vehicles attracted to the light behave as if they love it, those repulsed by it fear it. Were you to see computer simulations or robots built in accordance to these principles, you would see how compelling it can be to describe these vehicles in these anthropomorphic terms. Even more complicated vehicles can be created by multiplying the number of kinds of sensors, motors, and connections.

For example, we can imagine that the vehicle depicted in Figure 5.8 can detect concentrations of chemicals in addition to sources of light: the triangular receptors are photoreceptors and the oval sensors are chemoreceptors. Complexity of behavior can be further multiplied by increasing the kinds of components intervening between sensor and motor. Imagine adding the logical gates described in our box on Turing machines in Chapter 1 or connectionist networks described in section 1.2.6. Such alterations may endow the vehicles with analogs of memory and the capacity to reason about past experiences and future expectations. The speculations involved in imagining these vehicles are worthwhile for those who wish to understand the brain and mind, according to Braitenberg, because of what he calls the law of uphill analysis and downhill synthesis: it is easier to build something to accomplish a task than to figure out how mother nature contrived to do it. Then after the synthesis is performed, we have some better ideas how to conduct the analysis.

5.4 FREE WILL

The above discussions of brains and robots may strike the reader as having left out something crucial in the discussion of action: human actions are *free*. Don't we have free will? How can we if we are mere meat machines?

You may not have thought about it, but you probably hold two beliefs (or assumptions) about your freedom to do what you decide to which are contradictory. On the one hand, you believe that everything in the universe is made up of physical particles. These particles are moving in certain directions at certain speeds, and they are in fact inevitably going to interact in certain ways. Events in the world are in this sense completely determined; they could not have happened differently. If we had perfect knowledge of the position, speed, and direction of all these particles, we could actually predict what was going to happen in the future. Unfortunately, we probably never will have such knowledge, but this does not affect the fact that things are determined to act in certain ways (whether we know what those ways are or not).

One the other hand, you also probably believe that you have some variety of free will. You believe, right now for instance, that you are free to raise either your left or your right arm. There now seems to be a conflict, however. According to the first belief, which arm you raise is determined long prior to your apparent act of choosing now. Does this imply that our belief that we have free will is a kind of illusion?

It depends upon what is meant by "free will." If by free will you mean that your decision to raise, say, your right arm was uncaused, this cannot be right, for two reasons. First, it violates the first assumption, that events are determined, a claim which presumably eliminates any sort of uncaused event. Second, this cannot be what we mean by free will, since it really removes the person from the picture, and makes the decision to raise the right hand seem like a bizarre phenomenon appearing out of nothing, rather than a decision. What we mean by free will must mean not that certain of our actions are uncaused, but rather that they are caused by us. You decided to raise your right hand, you caused that decision to be made and the subsequent raising of your arm. As we say, "I decided to raise my right arm, and I raised it."

We will explain this view in further detail by describing some of the main positions held in philosophy regarding the relation of free will and determinism. The major factions in the philosophy of free will divide up in the following ways: first, there are the compatibilists, who think that freedom and determinism are compatible. In contrast are the incompatibilists. The incompatibilists divide into two main camps: the libertarians who believe in the existence of free will and not determinism, and the hard determinists who believe in determinism but not in the existence of free will. Compatibilists are also known as soft determinists, though the determinism believed by both hard and soft determinists is the same determinism: they disagree on whether free will is the sort of thing that can exist in a deterministic universe.

For the compatibilist, an act is the product of your free will if it is the causal consequence of your beliefs and desires. For instance, suppose you have a belief that there is beer in the fridge and a desire to drink beer. If as a causal consequence of this belief and this desire you get up, open the fridge, and drink the beer, then you have done so of your own free will. If, instead, contrary to your wishes, someone tied you up and forced you to drink milk, this would not be an act of your own free will.

Now, many people have a hard time shaking the incompatibilist intuition that free will cannot exist in a deterministic universe. But this is arguably mistaken. Instead, it may be argued that free will can exist *only* in a deterministic universe. Consider the following. What if determinism were false? Then events would not be caused by other events, but only by random chance. You are reading this book right now, but only because of random chance. Are you reading the note because you want to? Not in a world without determinism; in a world of pure chance, there is no "because": there is no causation. There is just as much chance that, regardless of your desires to keep reading this book, you will just jump up and throw yourself out the window, no matter how much you'd rather not. In a world of chance, you have no say-so in the matter.

Another way of seeing the necessity of causation for freedom: consider the relation of the notion of freedom and responsibility in connection with certain ethical and moral issues. When we want to hold someone responsible for a crime like murder, causation is a relevant factor. X is dead. Was X murdered by Y? Is Y responsible – guilty of murder? Only if the following factors obtain: (1) Y wanted X dead, (2) X is dead, and (3) the death of X is a causal consequence of Y's insidious motive. Without the third criterion, you would be guilty of murder if you wished someone were dead, and that person died!

It should be noted that the compatibilist position sketched here is not simply identifying an act's being free with its being the causal consequence of a subject's beliefs and desires. It is claimed only that these causal conditions are *necessary*. Many counterexamples can be given to the claim that they are sufficient. For instance, the following is adapted from Davidson's (1993) example of the mountain climbers. Climber X has climber Y in his grasp so that if X releases Y, Y will fall to his death. X has always hated Y and figures that this is as good a time as any to do away with him. Merely contemplating the murder of Y, however, makes X so excited that his hands sweat, thus unintentionally loosening his grip. Y falls to his death. The death of Y was a causal consequence of X's desire to cause Y's death, but the chain of causation was abnormal: it does not count as X's intentionally causing Y to die, thus Y's death was not the product of X's free will. Another sort of example showing the insufficiency of the mere identification of free acts with those that are caused by beliefs and desires is the following. Z is a mild-mannered citizen. He has no criminal record and has been kind to everyone he knows. Z is kidnapped and brainwashed by government agents, then he is hypnotized, drugged, and subjected to brain surgery. These extreme procedures make him into a programmable assassin. As a result of his government programming, whenever Z hears the national anthem, he forms a desire to assassinate the president. One day, at a public event, these terrible events unfold: Z hears the anthem, forms the desire to kill the president, and does so. It seems wrong, however, to say that Z was acting under his own free will. The murderous desires were forcibly installed by the government agents: they do not accord with the plans and goals that Z formed naturally. Even though the death of the president was a causal consequence of a desire Z had, this does not count as an act of Z's free will. This shows, like the case of the mountain climbers, that merely being caused by beliefs and desires is insufficient to make an act free. Nonetheless, the point still stands that causal relations between an act and a mental predecessor constitute necessary conditions for free will.

5.5 EMOTION

> On July 1, 2020, the centuries-old debate was settled by decree: There are no emotions. Thenceforward, no one was, or ever had been, in a state of "anger." The same fate befell fear, joy, embarrassment, grief and all the rest: Banished from discourse, in private thought policed by (dare we say it?) guilt, they became unmentionable and unthinkable. For all the furrowing of brows, the narrowing of eyes, the clenching of fists (sometimes precursors to nastier actions), anger and its kin were, in the words of decree, "Paleolithic fictions." The general terms "emotion" and "emotional" were, of course, outlawed as well – though these were hardly to be missed, save by a few philosophers and here and there an enlightened psychologist.
>
> Objectivity ruled.
>
> (Gordon 1987, p. 33)

In spite of the fears of some philosophers, no one has yet suggested that there is no such thing as anger, or fear, so at least those basic emotions seem safe from the threat of being eliminated by a future brain science, for the time being. What are emotions exactly, and why do we have them? Would we be better off if we were like Mr. Spock on *Star Trek*, or the android Commander Data on *Star Trek: The Next Generation*, and simply experienced no emotions at all? Why are emotions conscious, and how are they similar to or different from other types of conscious states such as visual perception?

Traditionally the role of providing the neural substrate for emotion has been assigned to a set of interconnected brain organs, including the cingulate gyrus, the amygdala, and the hippocampus, known as the limbic system (Figure 5.9). While the idea that this system, as it was classically described by James Papez (1937), or its more recent reformulation by Paul MacLean (1992), truly constituted a unified and significant functional unit in the brain has come under criticism, the notion of the limbic system retains its currency in most circles. The autonomic nervous system also plays a role in emotion, generating the bodily accompaniments of emotions we are all so familiar with: sweaty palms, pounding heart, dry mouth, dilated pupils, and so on. Indeed, William James (1890) suspected that these feelings are all there is to emotions:

> If we fancy some strong emotion and then try to abstract from our consciousness of it all the feelings of its bodily symptoms, we find that we have nothing left behind, no "mind-stuff" out of which the emotions can be constituted, and that a cold and neutral state of intellectual perception is all that remains . . . What kind of an emotion of fear would be left if the feeling neither of quickened heart-beats nor of shallow breathing, neither of trembling lips nor of weakened limbs, neither of goose flesh nor of visceral stirrings, were present, it is quite impossible for me to think. Can one fancy the state of rage and picture no ebullition in the chest, no flushing of the face, no dilatation of the nostrils, no clenching

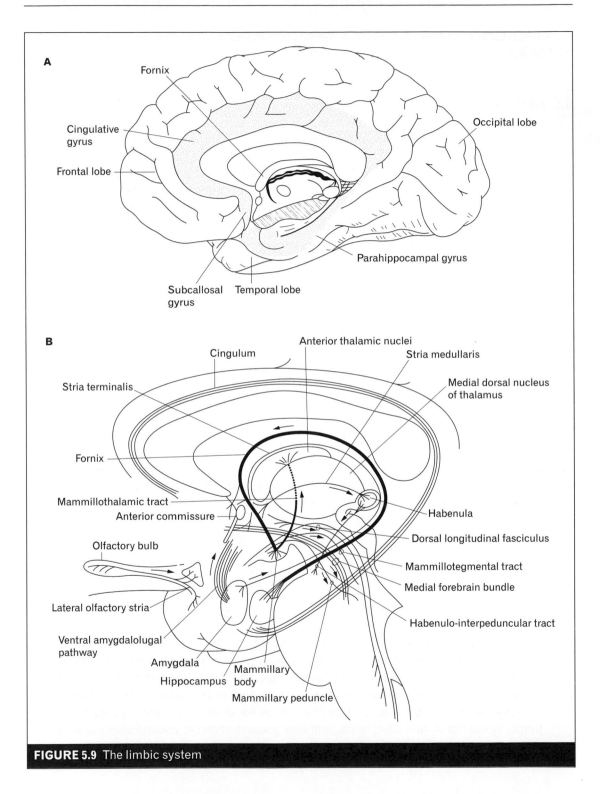

FIGURE 5.9 The limbic system

of the teeth, no impulse to vigorous action, but in their stead limp muscles, calm breathing, and a placid face?

(James 1890)

5.6 THE NEUROPHYSIOLOGY OF EMOTION

In 1937, Papez proposed that a set of brain structures including the hippocampus, cingulate gyrus, parts of the thalamus, and other structures are responsible for emotions, including their conscious sensation (which Papez believed was due specifically to the cingulate gyrus). MacLean expanded this system and for the first time referred to it as the limbic system. "Limbic" comes from the Latin word for border, and refers to the border formed around the brainstem by such parts of the cortex as the cingulate and the hippocampus (see Figure 5.9).

5.6.1 The autonomic nervous system

The autonomic nervous system is made up of three subsystems: the sympathetic, parasympathetic, and enteric nervous systems. The word "autonomic" means "self-governing"; the actions of the system are largely involuntary, although recently it had been discovered that certain aspects of it can be brought under voluntary control through techniques such as biofeedback and meditation. The sympathetic and parasympathetic nervous systems have roughly opposing functions: the function of the sympathetic system is to respond to emergency situations by adjusting the person's internal environment, something which has come to be known as the *fight or flight* reaction. The parasympathetic nervous system, on the other hand, maintains the internal environment in conditions of low stress, a function which is sometimes summarized with the phrase "rest and digest." The connection between the autonomic nervous system and the limbic system comes primarily by way of the hypothalamus, which is one of the main controllers of the autonomic system. Connections between the hypothalamus and the amygdala, and from there to the insular and cingulate cortices are thought to play a role in higher level activation and regulation of the autonomic nervous system (Figure 5.10).

The sympathetic nervous system is activated by the hypothalamus when an emergency is detected. Activation of the sympathetic system produces dilation of the pupils, dilation of the bronchi in the lungs, increase in heart rate, constriction of most of the body's blood vessels, and secretion of sweat from the sweat glands. The parasympathetic system typically produces opposing functions in the same organs: constriction of the pupils, reduction in heart rate, dilation of the blood vessels, among other effects. These effects often go unnoticed and, what is even more remarkable, they seem to process and compute a variety of semantic relations that often are associated with higher, conscious processes. For instance, in one classic experiment, a male subject is shown two photographs of a female face that look identical. He is asked to choose between them on the basis of which girl he would rather go out with on a date. Invariably the subjects insist that there is no way to choose, since they are being shown one photograph twice. When the investigator insists, the subjects choose, "randomly" in their view. However,

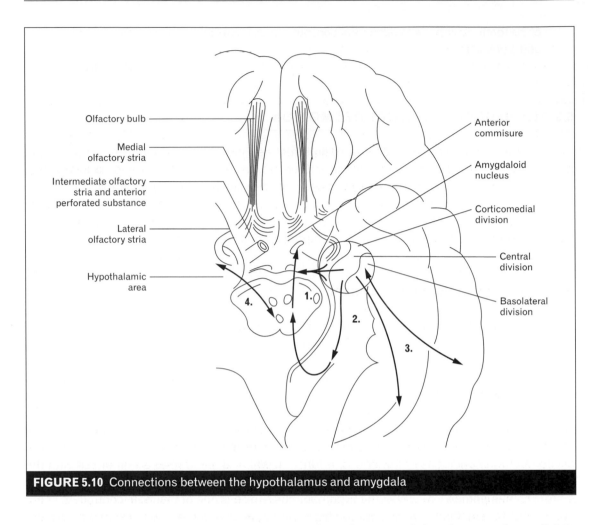

FIGURE 5.10 Connections between the hypothalamus and amygdala

unbeknownst to them, the pupil size has been altered on one of the photographs – slightly enlarged in the way that shows emotional engagement or interest. And, almost invariably, the subjects choose the face with the larger pupils. When asked why, they insist that they do not know. Only when it is pointed out to them that the pupils are larger do they notice the difference.

5.6.2 Measurement of autonomic activity

Skin conductance responses, or SCRs, are easy to measure yet allow a high-resolution measure of activity of the autonomic nervous system. They are produced by activity of the eccrine sweat glands, located on the palms and soles of the feet (as opposed to the body-wide apocrine sweat gland system, which functions primarily to regulate body temperature). Because of their connections to high-level brain systems, the eccrine sweat glands provide a window onto certain types of psychological activity. Along with dilation of the pupils and decreased motility of the gastrointestinal tract, the eccrine system is part of the sympathetic – or fight or flight – branch of the autonomic nervous system. The primary neurotransmitter of the palmar sweat system is norepinephrine, and its main receptor type is an alpha1 adrenergic receptor.

Several different cortical areas have been shown to be involved in the production of SCRs, or at least to possess the requisite neuroanatomical connections to do so. These may be subdivided into two types: those which produce SCRs related to bodily activity, such as hand clenching or deep breathing, and those which produce SCRs related to cognitive activity, such as the sight of a significant person, or the sight of a gruesome murder. One route by which a psychological SCR may be produced by visual perception begins in areas of the temporal lobes responsible for object analysis, then progresses to the lateral nucleus of the amygdala, where it then travels to the basal nucleus (Amaral et al. 1992). A circuit is completed when the amygdaloid basal nucleus returns projections to the same areas of the temporal lobes. Also though, the basal nucleus projects to the central nucleus, considered the output center of the amygdala. Via its connections to the hypothalamus and directly to the nucleus of the solitary tract, a part of the brain responsible for coordinating autonomic responses, the central nucleus can initiate sympathetic activity. The orbitofrontal cortex also sends projections to the lateral hypothalamic nucleus, one of several nuclei which makes up the hypothalamus, both via the amygdala, and directly.

5.7 DISORDERS OF EMOTION

The neurologist Norman Geschwind described a curious syndrome occurring in epilepsy patients which came to be known as Geschwind syndrome (Waxman and Geschwind 1975). Patients with this syndrome show various features, including excessive dependence on other people and paranoia, but the most interesting one is often described as a preoccupation with philosophical or abstract thought, coupled with a symptom known as hypergraphia, that is, a tendency to write huge amounts. Apparently what is happening in these patients is that their epilepsy is causing them to have strong emotional reactions to their thoughts. These emotional reactions cause the patients to attach deep significance to the thoughts; they feel the thoughts are so important that they must be written down, hence the hypergraphia. In some of these patients the thoughts are of a religious nature, or patients may feel they have discovered some great secret, such as the solution to the problem of perpetual motion, or the meaning of life itself. In his review of the literature on this syndrome, Trimble (1991) says:

> Such religiosity was the subject of a special study by Howden (1873). He thought it was not uncommon and recognized strong devotional feelings in patients which could manifest either as simple piety, or as religious delusions. He gave several case histories, emphasizing different shades of religiosity which could arise, and suggested that, "Many religious fanatics were epileptics." He included among these Mohammed, Ann-Lee (the mother of the Shakers) and [mystic Emanuel] Swedenborg.
>
> (Trimble 1991, p. 125)

The existence of such a disorder points out another important role of emotion: it helps us to determine the significance or importance of our thoughts. In these patients, exaggerated significance values are attached to their thoughts, causing them to realign their lives and their entire world views. Recall the times when you might have been thinking about something, and you formed a certain thought; before you arrive at a cognitive understanding of the importance of that thought, typically by connecting it to other thoughts, you will sometimes get a strong emotional reaction. We might call emotions such as these the intellectual emotions: they seem to provide a quick but correctable valuation on thoughts which allows us to determine whether they are worth pursuing or not. Another sort of intellectual emotion is a feeling of uneasiness we apprehend which seems to signal that there is something wrong with the current thought, perhaps that it contradicts some belief that we have. Paul MacLean, a pioneer of the modern limbic system concept, agreed that this system provides intellectual emotions and aptly expresses the significance of the idea that it plays such a huge role in our thought:

> It is of profound epistemic significance in regard to human belief that the symptomatology of . . . epilepsy suggests that the limbic cortex generates free-floating, affective feelings conveying a sense of what is real, true, and important. The same applies to feelings of discovery. Does this mean that this ancient part of the brain with an incapacity for verbal communication accounts for the feelings of conviction that we attach to our beliefs regardless of whether they are true or false? It is one thing to have this animalistic mind to assure us of the reality of food or mate, but what can we intellectually believe, if it is also requisite to assure the authenticity of our ideas, concepts, and theories?
>
> (MacLean 2002)

5.8 THE RELATION OF EMOTION AND REASON

On a classical understanding of the brain and nervous system, something such as the autonomic nervous system seems rather difficult to understand. In building a robot, for instance, we might simply leave out an autonomic nervous system. Approaching the same question from another direction, what sorts of problems would we encounter in building an intelligent robot which would lead us to put an autonomic nervous system into it?

When emotion and reason interact, reason is usually the worse for the encounter, according to the popular notion, one which spread into early science and philosophizing about the mind/brain. In the standard logic or critical reasoning course, students are taught that there are "emotive fallacies," such as appealing to pity or fear in the course of an argument. The teaching is always that emotion should be carefully extracted from the reasoning process, and kept at bay by constant vigilance, in short, we should strive to be robotic in our behavior, or Spock-like. In Stanley Kubrick's movie *2001: A Space Odyssey* (1968), the computer HAL has been programmed to "have" emotions, or at least to appear to have them, so that the crew will find it easier to interact with it. This addition turns out to be a fatal flaw, however, when HAL makes an error and seeks to cover it up, presumably out of something akin to pride. HAL systematically kills members of the crew until one of them can get his hands on the "off" switch. Once again, the message is that problems are solved more effectively without emotions. There are some voices on the other side: William James (1890) for instance claimed that every thought is accompanied by an emotion, and that these emotions play a guiding role in our thought process.

As usual, what is actually the case turns out to be a good deal more complicated than the ordinary conception. A new movement originating primarily in cognitive neuropsychology is based on the idea that, at certain strategic points, reason and emotion must interact, and that emotion plays a guiding function, without which reason is not only ineffective, but rendered useless. The effects of emotion seem to come at the input and output points of the "cognitive system," i.e., the system of concepts we possess, as well as the operations for manipulating them (see Chapter 4 for more on this). At the input point there may be occasions when certain emotional reactions are required in order for us to correctly conceptualize a thing or person.

A curious disorder known as Capgras syndrome may be a case where certain emotions are required for correct conceptualization. Patients with Capgras syndrome claim that people close to them, typically a parent, have been replaced by an impostor. The patient may say such things as, "He looks just like my father all right, but he's someone else." Recall in Chapter 3 our discussion of prosopagnosia, the inability to recognize familiar faces. In spite of this, some prosopagnosics register the normal larger skin conductance response to familiar faces. In the 1980s, Bauer (1984, 1986) and Ellis and Young (1990) hypothesized that Capgras syndrome is the "mirror image" of prosopagnosia, that is, Capgras patients recognize the face of, say, their father (albeit as an impostor), but fail to experience some emotional reaction to the person. We can imagine the situation from the point of view of the patient: "That man looks just like my father, but I feel nothing for him, so he must be an impostor." It was suggested that Capgras patients would lack the normal SCR to familiar faces, and several years later this was indeed verified (Ellis et al. 1997; see also Hirstein and Ramachandran 1997).

At the other end of the reasoning process, when the time comes for the conclusion of a piece of reasoning to have its appropriate effects on action, the human cognitive system is curiously weak – the cognitive apparatus seems to be rather rickety and prone to a number of characteristic problems. Probably the most widespread and serious problem at the reason–action junction is something classically known as *akrasia*, or weakness of the will. Imagine the following scenario attributed to the philosopher Donald Davidson. You just tucked yourself neatly into bed on a freezing cold night. As you slowly begin to drift off in the peaceful warmth under the covers, up pops the realization that you have forgotten to brush your teeth (of course, this example doesn't work on those people who have yet to grasp the importance of nightly brushing). You lie there torn right down the middle between the knowledge that you simply must brush your teeth every night, and the slothful desire to remain where you are. Perhaps only some sort of emotional reaction can get us up out of bed, and absent this, all the good reasons in the world cannot stir us.

In his fascinating book, *Descartes' Error*, neuropsychologist Antonio Damasio (1994) describes a patient he calls Elliot, who appeared to have fully recovered from an operation to remove a brain tumor which was pressing against his orbitofrontal cortex. Despite his normal appearance, bad things began to happen to Elliot after the operation: several businesses failed, he divorced his wife, remarried, and soon divorced again. Damasio gave Elliot all of the relevant tests of brain dysfunction but he scored well on them. Finally, it occurred to Damasio that Elliot's problem might be emotional rather than cognitive. He monitored SCRs of patients with brain damage similar to Elliot's while they played a gambling game in which the player must choose between selecting a card from a "safe" deck which allowed small but steady gains in winnings, or selecting a card from a "risky" deck, which offered large winnings, but even larger losses. Normal subjects got an SCR when they reached for the risky deck, and they soon learned to stay with the safe one. The brain-damaged patients, on the other hand, did not register this SCR and did not learn to avoid the risky deck. Damasio's conclusion is that Elliot's problem was that he often knew intellectually what the right course of action was, but this lack of an emotional reaction to certain situations caused him to continue engaging in dangerous or harmful activities.

5.9 EMOTION, COGNITIVE MODELING, AND COMPUTATION

A number of difficulties in both symbolic and connectionist cognitive modeling have prompted some researchers to try to develop a computational model of emotions in which their origin and function is explained in terms of cognitive aids to the processing of information. H.A. Simon, for instance, has argued, famously, that due to the paucity of cognitive resources in normal human functioning in relation to the complexity of the surrounding environment, emotions evolved as a means of helping the computational processes of the brain to function through a series of shortcuts and simplifications that can bypass or interrupt normal processing (Simon 1967). Emotions are crucial in allowing such interruptions. Simon argues that cognitive mental models that do not include such bypassing and interruptive emotive mechanisms will always be either incomplete or just simply wrong, because the cognitive system is so highly taxed in terms of both computational power and time. Moreover, rarely are human beings engaged in single-goal actions but, usually, multi-tasking is par for the course, so that we are at any particular time trying to satisfy more than one, often conflicting, goal. (This, of course, is a source of much tension and helps to explain Freud's psychoanalytic theory of emotions.) Finally, if we were limited to functioning as discrete individuals, independently of others, we could never achieve what we have been able to do collectively through organized groups, and the emotions work significantly to establish such connectivity not just within an otherwise fragmented and diverse psyche (the individual collective) but also between people (the group collective). Taken together, these constraints strongly imply that purely "rational" solutions to properly functioning cognitive systems in general and problem-solving tasks in particular will simply not work. And Simon's theory is that the way human beings have adapted to this problem is through the development of genetic heuristics encoded in the form of emotions, which are shortcuts to action and which function as simplified scripts, or schemas (mental models) for automated, evolutionarily ingrained behaviors, as well as for modifying old behaviors with new and improved ones. In this way emotional moods, such as anxiety and happiness, can impose strong, immediate effects on behavior by directing attention and action toward or away from certain behaviors (Mathews and MacLeod 1994).

5.10 THE PHILOSOPHY AND PSYCHOLOGY OF EMOTION

Emotions have played a central role in the systems of several leading philosophers, among them Aristotle, Descartes, Spinoza, Kant, and James. It was Aristotle who first proposed that emotions had a cognitive function in terms of evaluating and judging experiences, people, and events, and argued for a *rational* balance (from *ratio*) between reason and emotion, with emotion rarely, if ever, being given the upper hand. The Stoics agreed with the strong cognitive function and nature of the emotions but regarded them in purely negative terms, claiming that to be wise one must dispense completely with the psychological storms that emotions often bring about, impairing our rational judgments. Cognitive therapy, a twentieth-century psychoanalytically inspired theory, still holds to such a stoic view, in which emotional disorders are resolved through shifting the cognitive action to calm, cool-headed judgments of pure reason and rationality. Darwin's evolutionary theory did not help matters much, given that he equated the emotions with the "lower" functionings of primitive species, which gradually get superseded by the "higher" faculty of reason.

It was William James who first argued that emotions are simply effects of physiological or psychological processes but, rather, are apperceptions of the physiological states of the body by the conscious mind. In other words, emotions are like perceptions except not of the external world but of one's own physiological states; hence the extreme fear one feels when threatened, or is in an accident, or is alone in the dark in an unfamiliar environment, are but ways that the physical states of the body are being experienced, directly, by the mind. However, he claimed that emotions are merely bodily states and occur after the fact of whatever physiological and environmental factors caused them, and hence much of the subsequent research on the emotions was not cognitive but involved physiological studies of the body. Thus in his own way James, along with Freud and Darwin, helped precipitate a long stasis on cognitive studies of emotion.

It was the subsequent work in mental (cognitive) modeling (schemas) that, although it had its own limitations, provided the paradigm shift to cognition in which emotions were understood not only as enhancing, correcting, or even empowering rational processes, but as essential in learning theory and building shortcuts to a properly functional relation with one's natural and social environment.

6 Language

6.1 INTRODUCTION

Language is for representing the world, not only to others in communication, but also to ourselves in thought. For instance, the words "President of the United States" represent, or stand for, the elected official who lives in the White House. The folk conception of such naturally occurring languages as English (as opposed to the artificial languages devised by logicians and computer scientists) seems to be that the main function of linguistic representations is to enable the communication of thoughts, beliefs, suspicions, and other mental states. For instance, if your doctor states, "You have high blood pressure," he or she may be trying to convey a belief about your health. If this folk conception of language is correct, then cases like this one involve the translation of a mental representation, probably a sequence of neural events, into an external representation (whose vehicle is a set of pressure-waves) and back again into a mental representation (yours). There are, of course, many other vehicles of linguistic representation aside from pressure waves. Languages can be written, gestured, or encoded in the form of a texture, as in Braille.

Insofar as any given natural language constitutes a medium for the construction of representations, it makes sense to talk about the structure, or *format* of that medium. Talk of formats is, by and large, pitched at a higher level than is talk of the particular physical stuff out of which representations are constructed – whether it be air, ink, or flesh, because linguistic representations are multiply realizable with respect to their physical embodiments (see Chapter 1). For instance, your doctor could have produced the same sentence by writing it on a piece of paper or sending it as an email. Whatever their physical bases, natural languages have certain characteristic features. First, they are composed of a set of basic representational elements (i.e., words, prefixes, suffixes, and so on) and proper ways of combining these elements (called a *syntax*) into larger structures. To this extent, natural and artificial languages are indistinguishable.

In the case of natural languages, however, there is a further set of *morphological* constraints on well-formedness. Specifically, how words are formed will depend upon such contextual features as tense (e.g., "go" versus "went"), number (e.g., "a fly" versus "a swarm of *flies*"), and role (e.g., "*he* ate the shark" versus "the shark ate *him*"). One of the great wonders of human cognition is that humans, particularly young ones, quite naturally master the complexities of morphology and syntax. Moreover, once the complexities of natural language have been mastered, the processes of language production and comprehension usually proceed with about as much ease as driving a car. Thus, there seem to be grounds for viewing our mastery of language as inhering in some form of procedural knowledge (though, as we shall see, the cerebellum and basal ganglia may not be the best place in the brain to go looking for this kind of knowledge).

Another interesting property of natural languages is their *productivity*. That is to say, one can use natural language to generate a virtually unlimited number of distinct, well-formed representations. To get a sense for the tremendous representational potential of language, notice that, of the millions of sentences that you have heard and said over the course of your lifetime, you have probably never heard or said, "The trip to Jupiter is a real bore." The productivity of natural language parallels the apparent productivity of thought in such a manner that, for any of the unlimited number of things you might think, there is probably at least one natural language representation capable of expressing it.

Some form of communication may occur within, and perhaps even between, other animal species, but the grammatical richness and (perhaps as a result) the expressiveness of naturally occurring human languages seems to be a qualitative, rather than a quantitative step above the rudimentary forms of communication exhibited by non-humans. It should therefore come as no surprise that so many have speculated that the capacity to use language is what separates humans from beasts. Nor is it surprising that this capacity has, for as long as there have been sciences devoted to the study of the mind, constituted a major topic of investigation. Indeed, natural language has been studied from virtually all theoretical angles. In order to convey some of the richness of this ongoing interdisciplinary enterprise, in this chapter we highlight some of the key findings from cognitive neuroscience, psychology, and computer science. However, we begin this chapter with a discussion of philosophical insights about precisely how it is that words and sentences represent – how it is, in other words, they are able to pick out worldly entities, states, and properties.

6.2 THE PHILOSOPHY OF LANGUAGE

6.2.1 Truth, reference, and sense

There are many things that we use language for. For just a few examples, consider that we can use it to ask a question: "What is the weather like today?" or to give a command "Go clean your room." One of the uses of language that is of special interest to philosophers is the way in which it can be used to relay information – "I left the car on 54th Street" – and encode knowledge ("Columbus arrived in the Americas in 1492"). Truth is the main feature of language that distinguishes these latter uses – those concerning information and knowledge – from the former uses – those concerning questions and commands. While an answer to a question can be either true or false, the question itself is neither true nor false. Likewise, commands such as "Larry, take out the garbage" may be either obeyed or disobeyed, but are neither true nor false. In this section we describe some of the main philosophical ideas that arise in the struggle to understand the role of truth in language. Sentences that can be either true or false, like "I left the car on 54th" and "Columbus sailed the Atlantic in 1492" are *declarative sentences*. In contrast, questions are *interrogatives* and commands are *imperatives*. We focus here on declaratives.

One of the reasons for the philosophical interest in declarative sentences is the role that they play in logic and argumentation. For instance, consider the following famous syllogism:

> All men are mortal.
> Socrates is a man.
> Therefore Socrates is mortal.

Each of the premises and the conclusion is a declarative sentence. The logic of inference and truth functions upon which ideas of computation (discussed in Chapter 1) are thus based on declarative sentences.

Many of the philosophical questions that arise concerning the function of declaratives in language have to do with the problems in explaining how speakers can understand and produce such sentences. You hear the sentence: "Even purple rabbits love carrots" and, as long as you understand English, you understand the sentence. You understand under what conditions it would be true, and under what conditions it would be false. But this is a sentence that you probably have never heard before. Likewise you are able to produce sentences that neither you nor anyone else has produced before. The number of declarative sentences that can be produced and understood by users of a language is infinite. But our understanding is necessarily based on exposure to only a finite number of sentences. How is it that we are able to grasp the truth conditions of sentences that we have never heard before? What may and should strike the reader as a relatively obvious answer is that it has something to do with the fact that there are only a finite number of words in our language and sentences are created by the combinations of those words. So, even though you may have never encountered the sentence "Monkeys hate volleyball" before, you have encountered the words "monkey," "hate," and "volleyball" before, and have a general grasp of how words interact to create declarative sentences.

One way of putting the philosophical question that arises here concerns what the *semantic* properties of words are and how they contribute to the semantic properties of the sentences that they make up. The semantic properties instantiated by entire declarative sentences are *truth* and *falsity*. The sentence "The earth is round" is true. The sentence "Bill Clinton is ten feet tall" is false.

What then are the semantic properties of individual words, and how do they contribute to the truth and falsity of sentences? Individual words are seldom true or false – "red" alone is neither true nor false, neither is "Richard Nixon." The main semantic property that philosophers have attributed to individual words is *reference*. Suppose that the following sentence is true. "Rover barks." If so, this is in part due to the fact that there is something that the name "Rover" *refers* to. Some dog is the *referent* of the name "Rover." And further, what makes "Rover barks" true is that there is an action – barking – referred to by the verb phrase "barks" and Rover instantiates that property. We are simplifying the typical philosophical story a bit – some philosophers think that only noun phrases refer, for instance. But the basic story is to try to explain the semantic properties of sentences, truth and falsity, in terms of the semantic properties of words, namely, the reference of words.

The philosopher Gottlob Frege (1848–1925) famously argued that reference cannot be the only semantic property of words. Focusing here on names, Frege's (1950 [1884]) main points are as follows. A name has, in addition to its reference, a *sense*. When one understands a name, one not only knows what object or individual the name refers to, but also grasps the name's sense. What, more precisely, Frege thought the distinction between sense and reference amounts to will become more clear as we consider Frege's arguments for the distinction.

One of the key arguments for the thesis that understanding a name involves something more than knowing its reference hinges on *the informativeness of some identity statements*. Identity statements take the general form common to the following examples:

(1) a = a
(2) a = b
(3) Clark Kent is Superman
(4) Mark Twain is Samuel Clemens
(5) Mark Twain is Mark Twain

Note that of the examples 1–5 only 2–4 are informative identity statements: learning the truth of any one of them could count as learning something new, gaining a new piece of information. Part of the argument for sense involves pointing out that if knowing a name's reference was all there was to understanding a name, then we would have no explanation of why identity statements like (4) can be informative while identity statements like (5) cannot.

Frege thought that senses were "modes of presentation" of a referent. Frege gives as an example of different modes of presentation the following. Consider the point that lines a, b, and c all intersect at in Figure 6.1.

Thinking of one and the same point as either "point of interesection of a and b" or "point of intersection of b and c" would count as thinking of P under two different modes of presentation. For another example to see what modes of presentation might be, consider the fact that "the morning star" and "the evening star" both have the same referent, namely, the planet Venus. Part of what it means to say that the different phrases have different modes of presentation might be that one represents Venus as a heavenly body seen in the morning, whereas the other represents Venus as a heavenly body seen in the evening.

The phenomenon of the informativeness of identity statements gives us only one reason to think that words have semantic properties other than reference. Another is the problem of statements about things that don't exist, as in:

James Bond has a license to kill

Note that since James Bond doesn't exist, the noun phrase "James Bond" has no reference. If reference were the only semantic property of sub-sentential parts, then "James Bond" would be

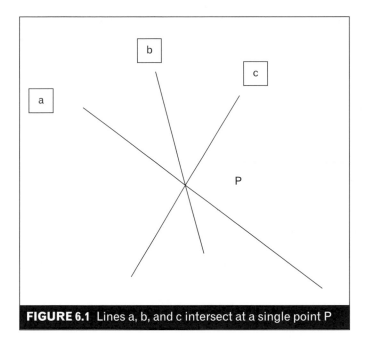

FIGURE 6.1 Lines a, b, and c intersect at a single point P

strictly meaningless (like "googoo-blahblah") and the sentence "James Bond has a license to kill" is neither true nor false (which seems odd) and also strictly meaningless (which seems ludicrous), or, at least, is no more meaningful than the bare predicate phrase "has a license to kill."

One way to solve this problem of non-existing referents is to postulate senses: "James Bond," while lacking a referent, nonetheless has a sense. Another way to solve this problem, one favored by the philosopher Alexius von Meinong (1972, 1983, 1993), is to enrich our ontology to include not only the things that exist, but also things which merely "subsist," which is the funny kind of existence shared by James Bond, Santa Claus, the Easter Bunny, and four-sided triangles. On this solution, the only semantic property of noun phrases is still reference, but the number of things that can genuinely be referred to includes not just the things that actually exist.

Many philosophers are bothered by the notion of subsistence. The philosopher Bertrand Russell (1910, 1914) showed how to solve the problem of inexistence that did not require postulating either senses or subsisting inexistent objects. Consider a definite description that doesn't have a referent, like "the present king of France" (this phrase has no referent because France, at present, has no king). If we were to say that its meaning was identical to its reference, we would have to say that it is meaningless, since it has no reference. But obviously it is a meaningful phrase. When you hear or read it, you understand it, unlike genuine meaninglessness like "ooggah booggah kazooey!!" Fregeans would want to say that these sorts of considerations point to the existence of sense. Russell has another way out. To understand Russell's analysis, consider putting the definite description together with a predicate (like "is bald") to create a sentence: "The present king of France is bald." If we were treating "the present king of France" as a name, then since it has no referent, the sentence itself would have to be regarded as meaningless (which seems bizarre) and thus as being neither true nor false. But Russell's innovation was to treat such a sentence as analyzable (decomposable) into several other sentences, each of which could be seen to be true or false. For example,

The present king of France is bald

Is analyzed as the conjunction of three sentences:

(1) There is at least one person who is king of France.
(2) There is no more than one person who is king of France.
(3) Any person who is the king of France is bald.

Since the first sentence is false (there is no king of France), the three-part conjunction is false, and thus the original sentence that is analyzed as the three-way conjunction is false. The Russellian analysis shows how the original sentence "The present king of France is bald" can be assigned a truth value without having to assign a sense or a referent to the phrase "the present king of France."

6.2.2 Indexicals

In the philosophy of language a distinction is traditionally made between "eternal" sentences, and sentences containing indexical terms, which we might call "contextual" sentences. An eternal sentence is one that expresses the same proposition whenever it is uttered, for instance "Richard Nixon was the thirty-fifth President of the United States." Other sentences, though, express different propositions in different *contexts* of utterance. "I am here now" is a sentence, utterances of which never express the same proposition, given a fine enough resolution of time measurement. A first attempt at listing the features that make up a context should include the agent of the context (for securing reference for "I," "me," etc.), the time (for "now," "today," etc.), and the "world" (for "actually") of the context. The context also contains items that allow demonstrative terms such as "this" and "that," or "he" and "she" to be interpreted. Richard (1990, p. 191) notes that contexts can also include standards of precision. For instance, in some suitably loose contexts it is acceptable to say that France is square, whereas in others – imagine a conversation among cartographers – it is an absurd generalization. There are, no doubt, other components of contexts.

6.2.3 Theories of reference

The great usefulness of language comes largely from the ability it gives those who have mastered it to speak about things which are not present before us. If everything we were interested in was in the nearby surroundings, we could presumably just make do with pointing. It seems transparent how pointing serves to pick out objects of interest, but how do names refer to people and things in the world? Reference is what ties language to the world, but what are these ties made of exactly? One possibility is that something in the mind of the speaker ties the name to its bearer. After all, the speaker knows what object he is referring to, he could go find it and point at it if he had to (let's ignore for the moment names whose bearers have disappeared, such as "Julius Caesar"). The description theory of reference begins with this insight. It might be summarized as follows: speakers are able to use a name to refer to an object because the speaker is aware of information about the object which is sufficient to pick out that object from among all others. Classical description theories typically cash this out by supplying a list of descriptions, known to the speaker, which together are true of only one object – the referent. For instance, Aristotle is the teacher of Alexander the Great, the most famous pupil of Plato, and so on. Some sort of condition like this does seem necessary in order for people to refer, since people who do not know anything about x cannot refer to x. We might teach a baby to say "Einstein" rather than "dada" as her first word, but we are reluctant to say that she is referring to Einstein, since she knows nothing about him. On further examination, however, the requirement that the speaker have knowledge which picks out the referent uniquely seems too strict. Consider a high-school student who has stayed up all night playing video games, walks into his history class the next morning and hears his teacher say, "Today we are going to learn about the famous Greek philosopher Aristotle." Unfortunately, this is all he hears of the lecture, since the lack of sleep catches up with him and he dozes off for the remainder of it. When he gets home, his dad, to test whether he went to school at all that day asks, "So, what did you learn about in history today?" "We learned about Aristotle," he replies sullenly, and bounds upstairs before further questioning reveals his complete lack of knowledge. Now, has our somnolent student succeeded in referring to Aristotle? Well, it certainly seems that he has, and unless we are in a picky philosophical mood, we would simply assume that he had. How then is this possible?

The causal theory of reference has an answer to this question. Roughly it goes like this: the student has referred to Aristotle because his use of the name traces back to Aristotle himself, by way of a long chain of causal connections. When Aristotle was born, his parents dubbed him "Aristotle" and they told their friends, who told their friends, and so on. Our use in the present day of the name "Aristotle" refers to that individual in virtue of there being a causal chain that leads from the initial dubbing to our current use. If there are aliens on the far side of the galaxy that make sounds that sound like "Aristotle" they are not referring to Aristotle because there are no causal chains leading from the dubbing of Aristotle to their use of that noise that sounds like "Aristotle."

The causal theory links words to objects by way of a causal connection, thus making reference a largely causal phenomenon. Note the resemblance between the causal theory of reference for language and the causal covariation theories of mental representation discussed in Chapter 1, section 1.4.2.3. These causal theories honor an intuition we have about reference and representation: we can refer to something we know little about because we have had a certain kind of contact, either directly with that thing, or with someone who has. Notice, though, that this seems to conflict with what we said above about the baby who says "Einstein." There is a difference between the baby and the sleepy student, however. Unlike the baby, the student knows that "Aristotle" is a name, that it refers to a historical figure, and that at least his teacher probably does have information which can pick out Aristotle from among all other objects. Also though, when the student says "Aristotle" to his father, he is intending to use the name in the same way that his teacher did. If he decided to name his pet ferret Aristotle, we would not say that his use of the word referred to the ancient philosopher in such a case because he is not intending to use the name in the same way his teacher did.

The bottom line here seems to be that both the speaker's knowledge about the referent and the causal connections between the use of a name and the referent seem to be important. What we really need is a theory that combines these two insights, and explains which features are more important on which occasions, and how the two elements, the internal knowledge of the speaker, and the external causal connection, interact to achieve successful reference. The result would be similar in kind to the two-factor theories of mental representation discussed in Chapter 1.

Admitting the importance of internal relations in determining meaning leads to semantic holism. Semantic holism (the opposite of semantic atomism) is the view that items have their semantic properties only in virtue of the relations that they bear to other similar items. So, for instance, the meaning of a statement like "snow is white" depends on its relations to other statements assented to by users of the language in which it is an item. Imagine another group of language speakers who speak something very similar sounding to English: call it Zinglish. Suppose we showed a Zinglish speaker and an English speaker some snow, and they both said, "That is snow." Suppose also that, unlike the English speaker, the Zinglish speaker would deny the truth of "snow is frozen water" and assent to the statement "all things below 50 degrees Fahrenheit are snow." Would you say, then, that Zinglish speakers *mean* something different from English speakers by "That is snow" in the presence of snow? If so, then you probably are a semantic holist.

KRIPKE AND RIGID DESIGNATORS

A rigid designator is a term that designates the same entity in any situation (or possible world) in which it designates at all. Non-rigid designators designate different things in different possible worlds. Kripke (1980, pp. 175–176) introduces the following "simple, intuitive test" for rigid designation. Some designator "D" designates rigidly if and only if we cannot say "D might have turned out to be a different thing than the thing it in fact (in this possible world) is." Let's try out the test for some different designators. Try, for example, "the square root of 81." Would it make sense to say that the square root of 81 might have turned out to be a different number than the number it in fact (in this possible world) is? Obviously not. Whatever number the phrase "square root of 81" refers to in this world is the number that the phrase refers to in all possible worlds in which it refers.

Try the test on a different phrase, like "the President of the United States." Now, in the actual world, "the President of the United States" picks out George W. Bush. Does it make sense to say, for instance, "The President of the United States might not have been George W. Bush"? It certainly does: had things gone slightly differently, Al Gore would have been president. Thus "the President of the United States" is a non-rigid designator. How about the proper name "George W. Bush," is that a rigid designator? It seems that it is: it makes little sense to say that George W. Bush might not have been George W. Bush. Kripke (1980) argues that proper names are rigid designators and that the causal theory of reference helps explain this. If the description theory of reference were true, then names would not be rigid designators. If the meaning of "George W. Bush" was some description like "the President of the United States," then it would make no sense to say that George W. Bush might not have been the President of the United States. But since it does make sense to say such a thing, we have some reason to reject the description theory of reference.

6.2.4 Quine and radical interpretation

According to Quine (1960), different languages are semantically and ontologically incommensurate with each other not because there is infinite room for error in translation between them but, even more radically, that there is no single correct truth about meaning. Suppose, for instance, that linguist A constructs a translation manual M that is supposed to translate any sentence in language X into language Y. Quine argues that linguist B could create a translation manual N that translates X into Y which was, however, so different from M that countless translations from M would not correspond with N. And yet, at the same time, M and N would both fit all the possible "objective facts," even though no M-translation of a particular sentence s would correspond to any N-translation of s!

To take the famous example of gavagai: suppose that an American linguist is visiting a faraway tribe where the native speaker uses the word "gavagai" in the presence of what the American would call a rabbit. Our linguist concludes that in the native language "gavagai" refers to rabbits. But does it? Or, asks Quine (1960), does it refer to attached rabbit-parts, phases of rabbit-appearances, rabbithood, or some particular appearance of a rabbit, and so on? No amount of pointing and noise-making can resolve this problem of what Quine calls the inscrutability of reference, which seems to show the indeterminacy of sentence translation. Quine concludes that meaning is not a genuinely explanatory concept. M and N could thus be incommensurate with each other even if they both fitted all the available facts about nature and human and animal behavior. This indeterminacy, as Davidson and Hintikka (1969, p. 22) point out, "withstands even . . . the whole truth about nature" (see also Kolak 2001). In other words, it's not only that linguists A and B cannot come up with the right interpretation of s or the language, S, within which s is a sentence, but there is no ultimate right or wrong about such interpretations. Even someone who is bilingual, Quine contends, and speaks both English and S, cannot avoid the problem since the indeterminacy thesis applies just as much to the translation of one sentence into another within the same language. Translation is simply not determinate.

Quine's thesis seriously undermines the notion that beliefs and desires, important ingredients of any standard psychology and philosophy of mind, are not matters of objective fact that can settle differences of meaning because there simply isn't any in the way we are led to believe by our surface psychologies.

6.3 THE NEUROPHYSIOLOGY OF LANGUAGE

One of the earliest and best-supported findings of neurology has been that our language abilities exist in the left hemisphere, primarily in Broca's area, Wernicke's area, and the arcuate fasciculus (Figure 6.2), the fiber bundles connecting them.

According to the Wernicke-Geschwind model (Figure 6.3), both the formulation and comprehension of language begin in Wernicke's area. From there, the information is transmitted over the arcuate fasciculus to Broca's area, the major site for articulation. Much empirical data from patients suffering from lesions supports this thesis. For instance, temporal lobe lesions typically leave articulated speech intact but disrupt spoken and written language comprehension, while frontal lesions leave comprehension intact while disrupting speech articulation. There are some difficulties with this model, mainly from patients that don't seem to fit the pattern. Likewise, the left cortex model of language production is true primarily of right-handed people; lefties, as usual, are a mixed bag. Most left-handed people have their language abilities on the left side, just as righties do. Smaller numbers of left-handed people have language on the right side; interestingly enough, some also have language abilities on both sides of the brain. Much of this knowledge about the *lateralization* of language comes from *Wada testing*, a procedure in which a drug is

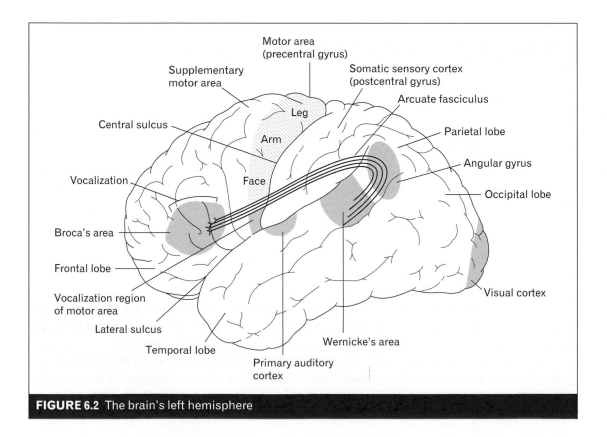

FIGURE 6.2 The brain's left hemisphere

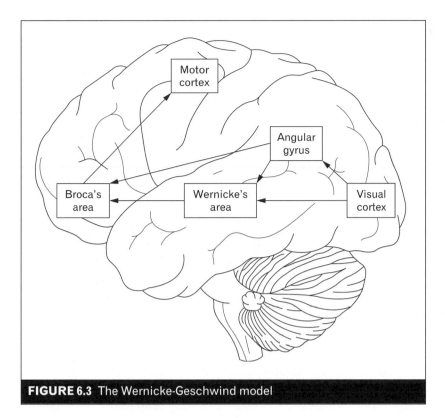

FIGURE 6.3 The Wernicke-Geschwind model

injected into either the left or right carotid artery in order to temporarily knock out the hemisphere on that side. The physicians or researchers must then act quickly to test the language ability of the remaining hemisphere by asking the person questions, since the inactivated hemisphere will wake up in a matter of minutes. This procedure is used, for instance, before an operation to remove an area of cortex implicated in the generation of epileptic seizures, in an attempt to determine whether language abilities will be affected. Those anxious to try this procedure themselves in order to see what a purely right hemisphere state of mind is like should think twice – the procedure is dangerous since there is a chance a blood clot will be produced.

6.3.1 Wernicke's and Broca's areas

Wernicke's area, located in the posterior temporal lobe near the auditory cortex, seems to be an important receptive center for language, while Broca's area, on the left side of the frontal lobes, seems to be an important language production center. *Wernicke's area* may prove to be a more enduring concept than *Broca's area*. Broca's primary patient seems to show a neat lesion only in Broca's area from the side view. But from a more frontal view, one can see that the lesion proceeds across and to the back of the brain in a way which clearly involves other large brain systems. There is also evidence that even damage restricted to Broca's area alone, if it occurs early enough in life, does not destroy language production abilities. The brain is able to compensate for damage to Broca's area by employing other, probably adjacent cortical areas to achieve the output tasks of Broca's area. Sometimes in children a brain with a damaged Broca's area on the left-hand side switches those functions to the analogous area in the right hemisphere. Damage to Broca's area on both the left and the right, however, does not prevent the development of normal language, while similar damage to both Wernicke's areas does, indicating its criticality.

Other brain areas have been found to be involved in language, including the thalamus and the basal ganglia. Also, the cingulate gyrus seems important for word retrieval, mainly because of the central role it plays in the directing of attention to the task at hand. The anterior superior temporal gyrus, which is located directly in front of the primary auditory cortex, is involved in word and sentence comprehension: it has numerous connections with hippocampal structures that are involved in memory. These recent results also confirm that the classic Wernicke-Geschwind model is far too simple and that language is a process much more distributed across many parts of the brain. This raises the additional new difficulty of trying to understand how so many different, independently functioning structures could have evolved in tandem to produce the synchronized activity necessary for language.

Thus, in spite of reasonable success in localizing language functions to different areas of the brain, there is a trend in the current thinking away from what is seen as a sort of localizationalist fallacy, that is, too much reliance on the idea that functions pair up neatly with spatially contiguous brain areas. It is perhaps better to think of brain systems spanning multiple areas as the fundamental working unit of the brain. It also may be fallacious to think of language processing as involving step-by-step procedures one sees in the boxes-and-arrows diagrams of the cognitive psychologists. The brain has all kinds of tricks to perform tasks in parallel, or in ways which we cannot now fathom. For instance, when we listen to someone speak, we tend to create what is called a "forward model" of what the person is about to say. As the person speaks, we form a hypothesis as to what he or she will say next, probably as a method of understanding what the person is saying. This technique sometimes shows itself in the listening errors that we make – those times when we hear what we expected to hear rather than what the person actually said. These are cases where processing is "top-down," rather than "bottom-up." A hypothesis is formed, then data are (we hope) collected, as opposed to the orderly march upward from box to box depicted in some old-style cognitivist theories. As usual, the two approaches are not contradictory, and the brain, in its relentless pursuit of meaning and pattern, uses them both at the same time.

6.3.2 The neuropsychology of language

According to one model of semantic representation, we have in our heads a set of concepts that are structured into a densely interconnected net. Each concept is a sort of file of information about the things the concept stands for (or really, a set of references to other concepts or perhaps to non-conceptual analog representations); the file itself need not contain any information. Then when we learn language, we simply add to each file information about a word which is used in our culture to express that concept. So for instance, I have a concept of Bill Clinton, which contains an analog representation of the way Clinton looks, conceptual information about the fact that he was the US president, that he is married to Hillary, and so on. But suppose I also add to the concept an analog sound representation of the name "Bill Clinton," and a visual representation of the way the name "Bill Clinton" appears in its different written or printed forms. This gives a rather coherent, if greatly oversimplified, picture of how thought and language relate. Thought is not inherently linguistic, thought occurs in concepts – witness the fact that people who have never learned a language can surely still think about things. Speaking, then, involves the use of these word representations contained in the concepts. Listening involves identifying word representations. Understanding involves activating the concepts associated with those words. Of course this is just a schema of an account of how language comes together with thought. It has received some verification from psychological studies, but we are long way from understanding how the brain accomplishes the manipulation of words and concepts.

6.3.3 Disorders of language

Broca's aphasia involves difficulty producing language. Patients with Broca's aphasia may take several seconds to say each word, or struggle mightily to come up with the appropriate word. Their speech may also be difficult to understand, or may involve syntactic problems – words out of order, ungrammatical constructions, and so on. Curiously, patients with Broca's aphasia may be able to sing easily and articulately, something which may indicate that singing is a right hemisphere function. Patients with Wernicke's aphasia, on the other hand, have trouble comprehending language but no trouble producing fluent-sounding speech. Their speech may lack meaningful content, however, or it may contain non-words (neologisms), or words with their syllables out of order. Sometimes Wernicke's patients will simply talk complete nonsense without realizing it, due presumably to an inability to understand their own speech.

6.4 LANGUAGE ACQUISITION

Part of the difficulty in studying language acquisition has to do with the way children learning language for the first time can use a word in one context and apply it to another, as well as the apparently innate ability to construct new sentences never before heard or uttered by them, to express themselves. Moreover, all this is attained by the age of 4, almost universally, regardless of the sort of environment that children are brought up in; the child of a linguistics professor, for instance, and the child of a carpenter will acquire language almost invariably at the same level by that age – and regardless of which language they are taught. Thus 4-year-old children in China, India, the United Kingdom, and so on have all the same basic language skills in their respective languages, despite the huge differences between those languages. Most importantly, language is a skill that is not taught to children but nevertheless still learned by them, simply by listening and interacting with their parents, other children, and the environment. As far as we know, human children are the only creatures capable of such autonomous learning.

Most language acquisition theorists agree that language acquisition begins at birth, or even before birth. For instance, a 2- or 3-day-old child can already distinguish its native language from a foreign one, based simply on hearing its parents' voice modulations, cadence and phonetics. Up to the first few months infants can distinguish all known phonetic sounds that exist in all known natural languages, an ability that they lose abruptly by the time they are 1 year old. After the age of 1 they can distinguish the phonetic structures only of the language to which they have been exposed. One remarkable feature of this early language acquisition is that both normal and deaf children begin to babble at the same time – the deaf ones with sign-language versions that resemble the syllabic elements of vocal babbling, which strongly suggests that language acquisition is achieved not simply by speech but is implemented at the level of abstract symbolic representations of linguistic patterns in developing neural structures. Findings made on children who were not exposed to language at the normal times seem to indicate that there are critical periods in development during which language must be picked up. Language may still be learned after these critical periods, but learning becomes much more difficult.

6.4.1 Linguistics

One of the primary goals of linguists is to devise a grammar, or a formal theory of the knowledge which language speakers have. The rules of grammar are often compared to the rules of a game, since they delineate the set of allowable sentences in a language. These grammars are descriptive rather than prescriptive, that is, they represent an attempt to describe the formal structure of a language as it is spoken, rather than an attempt to prescribe the way a language should be spoken. The ultimate judge of the grammaticality of a sentence is what we might call the *grammaticality intuitions* of the speakers of that language. We all know, more or less intuitively, whether a sentence is grammatical or not, even though we may not know how we do this. For instance, we may be quite certain that a sentence is ungrammatical yet have no idea what exactly is wrong with it (i.e., what grammatical rule it violates). Exposing these intuitions to sample sentences is a time-honored way to test hypotheses about grammatical structure. A successful hypothesis produces sentences which pass according to the grammaticality judgments of speakers.

Grammarians have chosen what are called generative grammars in their attempts to describe the regularities in languages. A generative grammar is able to generate syntactical structures by applying and reapplying simple rules. For instance, a sentence consists of a noun phrase followed by a verb phrase. A noun phrase consists of an optional determiner and a noun. The verb phrase itself consists of a verb and another noun phrase. Each noun phrase may be modified by an indefinite number of adjectives. This simple set of rules can generate a huge number of English sentences. Generative grammars are considered to be psychologically realistic, in that our production of sentences seems to involve a sort of generation process, rather than the simple saying or writing of a prepared sentence. It is often taken for granted that we are constantly creating completely new sentences, but it is not often appreciated how much individual variation there is in this process. Some people seem to say pretty much the same things every day, while others are much more creative, sometimes intentionally. Again, notice that the ability to produce a grammatical sentence seems to involve more procedural memory than declarative memory, since we are not consciously aware of the rules of grammar, or of following them in producing a sentence. When we speak we might think briefly about the meaning of the sentence, but our brains seem to automatically handle the task of making what comes out grammatical, like driving a car, or riding a bicycle.

Noam Chomsky, for one, believes in a universal grammar – that is, a core grammatical structure which all natural languages share. He claims that the basis for this universality is that all humans have an innate ability to learn language, due to something in their brains called a *language acquisition device*. There are actually several pieces of evidence that would support such a claim. First, as we saw in the early part of this chapter, the brain seems to have areas devoted especially to language, such as Broca's and Wernicke's areas. It is not clear, however, that these areas evolved specifically for language use, rather than, say, for the production and comprehension of sequential behaviors in general. A second argument for the existence of an innate language acquisition device is the idea that children's brains seem able to extract the grammatical structure from the language they hear before they even have enough input to determine that structure. It is as if the language they are hearing is activating a pre-existing structure, rather than simply being used as data to construct a new theory of the structure of that data. Another interesting argument for a language acquisition device common to all people is the truism that a child of any race or nationality can be brought up in any language-using culture and will acquire that language with an ease equal to that of children native to that culture. A final argument for the claim that all human languages have a common underlying structure is the idea that anything expressible in one language can be translated and expressed in any other human language (though perhaps not as easily).

6.4.2 Language use by non-humans

Of all the naturally occurring means of communication (that we are aware of), only human languages have both a highly complex morphology and syntax, and only human languages exhibit full-blown productivity. Add to this findings concerning the localization of systems implicated in comprehension and production and the ease with which children learn language, and one has a persuasive argument that we humans are unlike the rest of the animals in that we have an innate capacity that enables us to master the complexities of human languages. We would be remiss, however, were we to neglect mentioning that human language acquisition has an important social dimension to it as well. In some ways, learning language is like learning to knit. Knowledge of how to knit is transmitted from one generation to the next, and without this social transmission there would not be any knitting (or, at the very least, there would be very little knitting). The same can be said of natural language use. On the other hand, though we have the ability to learn how to knit, no one claims that we are innately predisposed to learn how to knit.

Other creatures presumably do not have an innate ability to use language. After all, no other animal employs a grammatically structured communication system. Thus, one way to bolster the claim that our ability to master natural language is like knitting in that it depends more on social transmission than on an innate ability would be to show that other animals can learn to use language. For about the past hundred years, investigators have been trying to show precisely that. Specifically, attempts have been made to teach our closest cousins, the apes, to use a grammatically structured symbol system in order to communicate.

Early efforts at teaching language to apes were actually directed towards teaching them to talk. Surprisingly, these attempts met with some limited measure of success. Chimps and orangutans were taught to say, though their pronunciation was far from stellar, words such as "mama," "papa," and "cup." Though early attempts to teach apes to speak met with only limited success, comprehension was another matter. In the 1930s, Winthrop and Luella Kellogg raised a young chimpanzee Gua (9½ months old) alongside their infant son Donald (7½ months old) for a period of nine months. Though Gua never learned to speak, when the nine months were up, he seemed capable of understanding even more words than Donald.

One of the obstacles in the way of ape speech is the fact that they simply do not have the appropriate physical equipment. Most notably, apes have great difficulty pronouncing consonants. In order to circumvent this limitation, researchers began to investigate whether or not apes are capable of using other, non-vocal forms of communication. One chimpanzee, Washoe, was reared for four years in an environment where the only form of communication to which she was exposed was American Sign Language (ASL). Washoe eventually learned to use over a hundred signs.

One of the theoretical worries about this line of research is that apes never really understand the signs they are using, but have instead merely been conditioned (see Chapter 1) to use symbols in the context of certain environmental stimuli. Moreover, even when apes have learned to use ASL, they have not shown any clear-cut appreciation of the complexities of morphology and syntax. Finally, a more practical worry about such research is that American Sign Language may place too heavy a burden on the limited short-term memory capacity of apes. In other words, it may be difficult for an ape to maintain information about the early parts of the sentence as the later parts are being produced. In an effort to deal with these criticisms and worries, a new line of research was begun, the culmination of which was the surprising achievements of one Kanzi.

As an alternative to ASL, researchers at Georgia State University pioneered the use of a computer-driven keyboard interface, which contains a set of symbols, or lexigrams, corresponding to particular words. The hope was that apes would be able to communicate by pressing the appropriate sequence of lexigrams (which then appear on a kind of monitor over the keyboard) or follow instructions encoded in the form of lexigram sequences. Using the lexigram interface, an attempt was made to teach a species of ape, pygmy chimpanzees (or bonobos), that had previously received little attention (in large part because they are becoming quite rare). One bonobo, Matata, seemed to have a natural inclination to communicate through gestures and vocalizations, but was unable (or unwilling) to learn how to use the lexigram system. At only a few months of age, however, Matata's child Kanzi picked up on the use of the lexigram system. Kanzi frequently used the keyboard of his own accord, and became quite proficient at understanding both spoken and lexigram sentences. What is so interesting about Kanzi is that, because he was not explicitly taught, the conditioned-response criticism loses much of its force.

Like a young child, Kanzi is better at comprehending than at producing language. When it comes to comprehension, he displays an impressive grasp of syntax – comparable to a 2½-year-old child. For instance, he seems able (evidenced by his ability to follow instructions) to understand sentences that he has never heard before. Moreover, he is proficient at distinguishing pairs such as (1) and (2) or (3) and (4) while treating pairs like (5) and (6) as indistinguishable.

(1) Put jelly in milk.
(2) Put milk in jelly.
(3) Make the dog bite the snake.
(4) Make the snake bite the dog.
(5) Give Sue the pillow.
(6) Give the pillow to Sue.

Kanzi's achievements might be viewed as lending support to the view that our ability to use language depends merely on some rather general learning mechanisms. After all, if a creature that doesn't normally exhibit mastery of grammatical rules can learn them nonetheless, then perhaps no special-purpose language mechanisms are required in the human case either. Of course, Kanzi's mastery of language is limited, and questions arise as to where, precisely, the line between success and failure in ape language research should be drawn.

6.4.3 The connectionist challenge

One of the claims frequently advanced by linguistic nativists is that nothing short of innate pre-programming is required in order to master the complexities of a natural language. Thus, a possible way of falsifying this claim would be to show that a device that is not pre-programmed can nevertheless learn to navigate the complex grammatical constraints of natural language. For this reason, many researchers have become interested in determining whether or not connectionist systems can learn to master the complexities of natural language morphology and syntax. As noted in Chapters 1 and 2, one of the most interesting properties of connectionist systems is that they are able to learn. While the gross structure of a given network is usually determined by the modeler, the strengths of the connections between units are altered over the course of training by the network itself. In this latter respect, then, networks lack the kind of pre-programming that many consider essential for language acquisition.

If you will recall from the previous section, one of the limitations of ASL was that it placed too heavy a burden on the apes' limited short-term memory capacity. In order to generate grammatical speech, one must have access to prior linguistic context. After all, one can't very well supply an appropriate direct object if one doesn't remember what the subject and verb are. Memory for context becomes even much crucial once factors such as tense, number, and role are thrown into the mix (see section 6.1). Connectionists thus faced a similar challenge to the one confronting primatologists. Indeed, early back-propagation networks had no memory for context at all. One option open to connectionists is to mimic the lexigram approach adopted by primatologists to allow for the input and output of complex linguistic stimuli in their entirety (i.e., in parallel rather than sequentially). As discussed below, this approach was in fact adopted in certain quarters. The alternative is to do what primatologists could not – that is, build short-term memory into the language-learning system. Jeffrey Elman (1991), an outspoken critics of linguistic nativism, has opted for the latter approach.

Elman trained his networks to learn what kinds of words are potential successors to a given sequence. For instance, when presented with the incomplete utterance (7), you and I can imagine many permissible words that might follow (e.g., "ball," "rock," etc.) and we also know that many words would not be permissible (e.g., "that," "eat," etc.).

(7) The boy threw the . . .

In making such judgments, we seem to be drawing upon our vast knowledge of the complexities of grammar. As it turns out, Elman's models became quite successful at generating plausible successor items. His models did, in the early phases of this research, have difficulty with highly complex grammatical constructions. However, by mimicking the manner in which short-term memory capacity increases over the course of human development, he found that the complexity of the grammatical constructions that his models could handle was increased dramatically. Elman's research with systems lacking pre-programmed knowledge of grammar thus provides another challenge to those who think that humans have an innate grammatical competence.

6.4.4 Cognitive linguistics

Chomsky and Elman, though worlds apart in many respects, are alike in one very important respect: both treat grammatical knowledge as if it existed in isolation from semantic knowledge. This implicit thesis has been termed (by its antagonists) the *autonomy thesis*. There is, however, an alternative way of viewing grammatical knowledge that has been gaining attention in recent years. According to this approach, grammar and semantics are inextricably related. According to this nascent school of linguistics, known as *cognitive linguistics*, grammatical knowledge is bound up in procedures for mapping between natural language and semantics, and it therefore makes little sense to speak of grammatical knowledge as if it existed in isolation. As an alternative to the autonomy thesis, cognitive linguists tout their own *content requirement* – which claims that every grammatical difference is associated with some semantic difference.

Instead of specifying rules that express the cognitive principles underlying the production of grammatical sentences, cognitive linguists look to find the semantic import of specific grammatical structure. According to one analysis, for instance, the semantic import of the Subject Verb $Object_1$ $Object_2$ construction (known as the di-transitive construction) illustrated by (8) is said to be the signification of a relationship whereby some entity X causes entity Y to receive object Z. Because the function of the di-transitive construction is to signify this kind of relationship, only certain words can appear in this construction. Thus, while (8) is well formed, (9) seems anomalous.

(8) William threw Tammy the ball.
(9) William threw the wall a dart.

In other words, according to cognitive linguists, (9) is not anomalous because it violates some abstract rule of syntax but rather because the function of the di-transitive construction is to specify a relationship that occurs between particular kinds of entities – for instance, Object$_1$ has to be the kind of entity that can act as recipient (e.g., it has to be animate).

According to cognitive linguists, constructions such as the one just described provide templates for the construction of grammatical sentences. Moreover, these templates can be combined in various ways so long as the relevant semantic constraints are satisfied. In (10), for instance, the di-transitive construction has been combined with the possessive (i.e., Object$_1$'s Object$_2$) construction.

(10)   William threw Tammy Cynthia's cap.

Grammatical knowledge therefore becomes, according to cognitive linguists, knowledge of the procedures for mapping back and forth between natural language representations and semantic ones.

6.4.4.1 *Connectionism and syntax/semantics mappings*

Cognitive linguists have found a ready-made ally in connectionism. As Langacker (1991) notes:

> the acquisition of a grammar . . . becomes a matter of establishing form–meaning mappings, which [neural networks] handle straightforwardly as associations between input and output patterns.

(Langacker 1991, p. 122)

Indeed, the mapping between language and semantics seems rich with interacting constraints, and neural network models excel at learning to respect the various constraints that govern an input/output mapping.

The project of investigating whether or not neural networks are up to the task of learning the complex constraints that govern the mapping from linguistic to semantic representations is already well under way. One of the early models of the comprehension process was designed by McClelland and Kawamoto (1986).

The general task McClelland and Kawamoto set for their model to learn was the mapping from sentences to semantic representations. Sentences input to the network included (11)–(15).

(11)   The boy broke the window.
(12)   The rock broke the window.
(13)   The window broke.
(14)   The boy broke the window with the rock.
(15)   The boy broke the window with the curtain.

What is interesting about this set of sentences is that it reveals how context sensitive the mean-ing of a particular word can be. For instance, notice how the final noun in (14) designates an instrument used to break something, while the final noun in (15) designates a modifier of "the window." Notice, moreover, how the first noun in (11) designates the instigator of the event (the agent) while the first noun in (13) designates the thing that the event happened to (the patient). In light of the context-sensitive nature of the process, effecting the appropriate mappings between sentences and semantic representations is clearly no simple feat.

Whereas the input units of McClelland and Kawamoto's (1986) model were capable of representing particular sentence constituents in their proper order, the units at output layer represented, in terms of a set of features, the nature of the event and the properties of each of the designated items (including the role played by the entity in the event). The output units represented such features as softness, volume, fragility, gender, which entities (if any) are in contact, what kind of change is undergone by the patient, what kind of movement (if any) characterizes the agent, and so on. Thus, the proper output to a given input sentence would be a complex pattern of active and quiescent output units.

In spite of the tremendous complexities involved, the network eventually learned how to generate the appropriate semantic representation for a given sentence. Consider, for example, the network's behavior when presented with an input sentence such as "The boy broke the window." The activation pattern at the output layer indicated that, among other things, the boy was the agent in the action of breaking; there was a causal interaction instigated by the agent; the state of the patient changed to one of being in pieces; the agent was in contact with the patient; and the agent was partially in motion while the patient was immobile. Not only could the network generate sensible semantic representations for sentences that it had been trained on, but also it could "understand" sentences it had never before "seen."

The network was also able to interpret ambiguous words (e.g., "bat" in "The boy broke the vase with the bat") nearly as well as it interpreted non-ambiguous words. In addition, shades of meaning were sometimes captured unexpectedly. For instance, every occurrence of "ball" in the training data referred to a soft object, but when novel sentences in which "ball" designated an instrument of breaking were presented, the model understood "ball" to mean a hard item.

McClelland and Kawamoto's model was presented with sentences in their entirety. This is not unlike the lexigram interface devised by primatologists' research in order to circumvent problems associated with limited short-term memory capacity. As noted above, however, unlike primate researchers, connectionists have the option of building a short-term memory into their systems. A strategy similar to the one employed by Elman (1988) was eventually used in order to create the successor to McClelland and Kawamoto's (1986) model.

With the addition of memory, St. John and McClelland's model was able to deal with the sequential input of linguistic stimuli. Their model could also process sentences of far greater complexity – including sentences containing prepositions, adverbs, auxiliary verbs (for representing passive sentences), and a wider range of nouns and verbs. This added to the repertoire of sentence forms that the model learned to understand, but it also meant that the model had to learn how to deal with an even larger set of contextual factors. In the end, the model was very successful at learning to generate sensible interpretations of linguistic stimuli. In fact, because it was able to deal with the sequential input of sentence constituents, it was able to generate expectations about subsequent inputs and to modify its semantic representations as new evidence was encountered. For instance, the role filled by "hammer" is uncertain in the partial utterance "The hammer broke" until followed, for example, by "into pieces" or "the window." Much like a human, the model was able to generate a sensible interpretation for such words – an interpretation that could be revised as additional sentence constituents were provided.

7 Consciousness

7.1 INTRODUCTION

What is consciousness? What makes this question so perplexing is that the answer seems close at hand, hovering invisibly just beyond the horizon of our immediate experience, and yet when we reach out to grasp it the answer eludes us. Taking a familiar and obvious path leads straight into a labyrinth so puzzling that the problem seems utterly insoluble. How can something so familiar – ourselves, our own consciousness – appear so utterly ineffable?

The familiarity of the question stems from the fact that it is about us, the questioners. Since *we* are close at hand, the answer, it seems, must also be close at hand. Surely, it would seem, if we know anything, we must know that which is most directly accessible to us as conscious beings – our own consciousness. But as soon as we examine the facts and assumptions underlying the concept of consciousness, we realize we are further from knowing ourselves than we think. Paradoxically, the more we learn about consciousness, the more puzzled we become. How can we who know so much about so many things know so little about our own consciousness, about what it is, where it comes from, what the underlying mechanisms are that make it possible?

7.2 KINDS OF CONSCIOUSNESS, ASPECTS OF CONSCIOUSNESS

Much of what is problematic about consciousness stems from the fact that the terms "conscious" and "consciousness" are applied to so many diverse phenomena. To name just a few, one might speak of whether a recently pummeled boxer is conscious, or of whether a driver talking on a cell phone is conscious of the other cars on the road, or of whether Americans have raised their consciousness of domestic human rights violations. Not only are there multiple uses of the word "conscious" but also there are multiple aspects of consciousness that researchers are curious about. For instance, there is the subjective character of conscious experience, and the problem of what it is to be conscious of something.

7.2.1 Creature consciousness, transitive consciousness, state consciousness

• *Creature consciousness:* People are conscious (most of the time). Rocks are not conscious (ever). What about dogs and cats? Their owners and trainers are likely to agree that dogs and cats are conscious. How about fish? Bacteria? Ferns? Worms? These questions about which creatures are conscious employ the sense of the term "conscious" that we call "creature consciousness." To say of a human that they are conscious is to ascribe creature consciousness to them. Humans frequently go in and out of creature consciousness: the boxer face down on the mat and the patient on his back in surgery are temporarily (we hope) devoid of creature consciousness.

• *Transitive consciousness:* Having transitive consciousness is being conscious *of* something. Right now you are conscious of the words on the page. Prior to reading this sentence, you probably were not conscious of the feel of your clothing against your skin. Now you are. There are some things that you can become conscious of quite easily: you can become conscious of the objects in the right edge of your visual periphery just by shifting your attention. However, there are some things that you cannot become conscious of so easily. You cannot simply introspect and find out the number of neurons in your occipital lobes. You are not conscious of the computations involved in processing speech.

• *State consciousness:* Some of your mental states are conscious, some are not. Many of your memories are, right now, unconscious memories, although they can become conscious. Until you read the following sentence:

  The moon is closer to the earth than the sun,

this was a memory of yours that was not conscious, but now it is. Later in the day, when you go on to think about something else, it will return to being an unconscious memory.

What are the relations between state consciousness, creature consciousness, and transitive consciousness? An interesting related question is which of these three kinds of consciousness, if any, is most basic – is there one kind of consciousness that the other kinds may be explained in terms of? One possible way of spelling out these relationships is one that is highly compatible with the representational theory of mind, the theory by which all things mental are explained in terms of representations. Most basic, then, is transitive consciousness: *consciousness of*, which always involves *representation of*. If you are conscious of what is in your hand, then you are mentally representing what is in your hand. Next, we can explain creature consciousness in terms of transitive consciousness. All and only conscious creatures are conscious *of* something. The person who is knocked out (devoid of creature consciousness) is not conscious *of* anything, and thus devoid of transitive consciousness. Last to be explained is state consciousness: what makes some of my states conscious states and others unconscious states? We will return to this question, but a plausible account is that having a conscious state involves having a higher-order representation of that state.

7.2.2 Phenomenal consciousness: qualia and "what it is like"

Qualia are the introspectible properties of sensory experiences. ("Qualia" pronounced /KWAH-lee-uh/ is plural, "Quale" pronounced /KWAH-lay/ is singular.) They are not the experiences themselves, nor are they just any properties of the experiences, but only the introspectible ones. They are that in virtue of which we are able to discern by introspection similarities of and differences between our experiences. I may know by introspection that my visual experience of an orange is more like my visual experience of a grapefruit than my visual experience of a lime. I may also know by introspection that my visual experience of an orange is more like my visual experience of a lime than my experience of tasting a lime. My experiences also have properties that I may be unable to know by introspection, like whether my experience of pain is neurally instantiated by my c-fibers, or whether my visual experience of my coffee mug is the fifty-first visual experience of the mug that I have had today.

Bats fly around under the guidance of a sonar system. What is it like to perceive the world using sonar? What is it like to be a bat? The presumption that there is something it is like to be a bat is the presumption that bats are conscious. All and only subjects of creature consciousness are things for which there is something it is like to be. Things that are never conscious, like rocks, are things for which there is nothing it is like to be.

Qualia, the introspectible qualities of our experiences, are the features of our mental lives that determine what it is like to be us. If what it is like to be a bat is very different from what it is like to be a human, then this is due to bats' having very different qualia than we do. Thus, being a subject of qualia and being something for which there is something it is like to be go hand in hand. They are, perhaps, even synonymous. Another related, if not synonymous, concept is that of phenomenal consciousness. When you have a state with qualia, you are the subject of phenomenal consciousness.

One interesting question that we will return to is the question of the adequacy of the representational theory of mind in accounting for qualia. Representationalism is the view that qualia are representational contents. On this view, my visual experience of a red rose is a mental representation of a red rose – a representation of a thing as being red, as having a certain shape, a certain visual texture, etc. The introspectible properties of the experience are exhausted by the representational contents of the experience. Thus, the (introspectible) difference between my visual experience of a red rose and my visual experience of a white rose has to do with the fact that the former experience represents a red thing in my visual field and the latter experience represents a white thing in my visual field. But perhaps there are qualia that outstrip representational contents. There are qualia associated with feelings of pleasure and pain, with depression and free-floating anxiety. What, if anything, do these mental states represent?

7.2.3 Subjectivity and points of view

Our conscious experiences are subjective, which seems to set them apart from the rest of nature, which is objective. We have an access to our own consciousness that we do not have to the rest of nature: we consciously experience our own mental states. We thus learn subjectively – "from the inside" – what colors we see, what feelings we feel, whether we are hungry or bored, and so on. We cannot experience the rest of nature, not even other people, this way. We must experience nature and other people "from the outside," through our external sense organs – "objectively."

But we, too, have an outside. We are objects in nature. So we also learn about ourselves objectively. This dual access to ourselves gives rise to the problem of how to integrate both subjective and objective perspectives – which often conflict and sometimes may even contradict each other – into a single, coherent vision.

For instance, when you decide to do something, do you decide to do it because you want to achieve some goal – something you may know only subjectively – or because of chemical changes in your brain – something you can know only objectively? If both, how does one affect the other? Does consciousness push chemicals around or do chemicals give rise to conscious states that only make it seem as if consciousness is in control? Or does consciousness just reduce to chemicals in action, so that the apparent differences between them are merely consequences of the alternative conceptual schemes we use to describe and explain behavior? If such mentalistic and physicalistic explanations of consciousness are merely two ways of describing the same phenomena – ways that conceptualize the phenomena differently – what accounts for the radical differences between these conceptualized schemes and what is their relationship to each other?

Regardless of the ultimate ontological status of these two different perspectives on our own consciousness – the subjective and the objective – of ourselves, since we neither should, nor are likely to, abandon either of them, we must integrate them somehow if we are to understand consciousness fully. At the same time, a variety of disciplines – philosophy, psychology, neurophysiology – generate illuminating concepts, insights, and empirical data that increase our knowledge about consciousness, but often from radically differing perspectives, raising again the problem of integration. Thus, if we are to understand consciousness fully, not only must we integrate the subjective and objective perspectives on consciousness but also we must integrate the various perspectives on consciousness from within the different cognitive disciplines. That is one of the main goals of cognitive science nowadays.

7.3 IS CONSCIOUSNESS PHYSICAL?

7.3.1 Leibniz's fantastic voyage

In the *Monadology*, Leibniz asks what would happen if you stepped inside a "machine whose structure produced thought, sensation, and perception," for instance, the brain.

And supposing that there were a machine so constructed as to think, feel, and have perception, we could conceive of it as enlarged and yet preserving the same proportions, so that we might enter into it as into a mill. And this granted, we should only find on visiting it, pieces which push against another, but never anything by which to explain perception. This must be sought for, therefore, in the simple substance and not in the composite or in the machine.

(*Monadology*, para. 17)

Or suppose we shrink down, as in the science fiction film, Richard Fleischer's *Fantastic Voyage* (1966), to microscopic size and enter. When this happens to the scientists in the movie, they travel into the brain and see electrical discharges along the neurons which they conclude must be the thoughts which are occurring in that brain. But thoughts as thoughts, images as images are not experienced as flashes of electrical discharge along neurons! If we looked thus inside your brain and saw neurons firing, we would not see the images you see or hear the thoughts you hear. Likewise, if we shrank even further, until we saw the atoms themselves out of which the neurons are composed, what we would see, according to such a materialist picture of reality, is lifeless clumps of atoms floating in empty space. It would look like a constellation of stars. Where are the thoughts, ideas, images that are supposed to exist at some macroscopic level where these lifeless little pieces of matter give rise to them? Where is the consciousness? Where are the qualia? Where is the "what it is like"?

Imagining Leibniz's fantastic voyage makes salient the point that brain processes do not seem like experiences and experiences do not seem like brain processes. The apparent distinction may tempt one into thinking that the distinction is *actual* – that consciousness is actually non-physical. Leibniz's considerations alone are insufficient to cement this conclusion. Just because experiences do not seem like brain processes does not mean that experiences are not brain processes. If consciousness is to be proven non-physical, more sophisticated arguments must be given.

7.3.2 Subjectivity and the knowledge argument

One set of considerations against physicalism hinges on the subjectivity of conscious experience. These considerations have been most acutely developed in the Knowledge Argument against physicalism. What subjectivity is and why it poses problems for physicalists emerges most vividly in discussions focusing on the work of philosophers Thomas Nagel and Frank Jackson. Nagel (1974) famously asked, "What is it like to be a bat?" and urged that humans, not being bats, could never know. Most importantly in his criticism of the limits of physicalism, Nagel argued that no amount of knowledge of the objective physical facts about bat brains could yield knowledge of the subjective character of bat experience. What is known from the objective point of view cannot bridge the gulf to yield what is known from the subjective point of view: knowledge of *what it is like*. Imagination and extrapolation are of little help. Even imagining flapping around and hearing our own voices reflected off of the surfaces of objects serves only to tell us what it would be like to be *us* under altered circumstances – such imaginings bring us no closer to knowing what it would be like for *bats*. What we can know about bats come from the deliverances of objective physical sciences: facts and properties knowable from multiple points of view – objective facts. The facts about bats beyond our purview are the subjective facts: facts known, if at all, only from the point of view of bats.

Nagel casts his criticism toward pointing out the limits of current physicalistic understanding, but he does not see it as falsifying physicalism. While he has no doubt *that* physicalism about subjectivity is true, Nagel says that we cannot currently understand *how* it is true.

Frank Jackson (1986), in contrast, cultivates Nagelian themes into an argument against physicalism: the knowledge argument. He imagines the following scenario: Mary is a brilliant neurophysiologist who knows all the objective physical facts about color perception, including the types and sequences of brain states and processes that would take place in a normal human perceiver when she sees something red. But the unusual aspect of the story is that Mary herself has never seen any colors: her world has been limited to black and white – everything she has ever seen has been either through a black-and-white video monitor or on a white page printed in black ink, and so on. (One must also assume that she has not seen her skin or cut herself, that her clothes as well as the walls of her living space are white, gray, or black, etc.) Finally, Mary is taken out of her achromatic prison and allowed to see the multihued world for herself. Jackson's point is that Mary learns a new fact when she sees red, a fact she did not know, even though she was aware of every physical aspect of such events. Hence knowing all the facts available to physical theory is not knowing all the facts.

Physicalists have been eager to find flaws in the knowledge argument. Before considering physicalist responses, it will be useful to have a schematic version of the argument before us:

- *First premise:* prior to having a red experience, Mary can know all of the physical facts.
- *Second premise:* upon having a red experience for the first time, Mary comes to know for the first time what it is like to see red.
- *Third premise:* knowledge of what it is like to see red is knowledge of a fact.
- *Conclusion:* since Mary knew all of the physical facts prior to seeing red, the new fact she comes to know upon seeing red is a non-physical fact.

Most physicalists responding to the knowledge argument have granted the argument's validity while questioning its soundness. The major kinds of physicalist responses may be grouped by which of the premises they question the truth of. One premise that has been subjected to quite a bit of physicalist pressure is the third premise stating that knowledge of what it is like is knowledge of a fact: propositional knowledge or knowing-that. (Recall our discussion of the kinds of knowledge in Chapter 4.) Nemirow (1990) and Lewis (1990) have defended the "ability hypothesis": the hypothesis that knowledge of what it is like is constituted not by knowing-that but instead knowing-how, procedural as opposed to propositional knowledge. The abilities that Mary gains in learning what it is like to see red are the abilities to remember seeing red and to imagine seeing red. Intuitively, these abilities are the sort that could be acquired only by first having the experience of seeing red, thus explaining why prior to seeing red, physically omniscient Mary did not know what it was like. The ability hypothesis itself has come under attack. The strongest objections to the ability hypothesis hinge on pointing out that these abilities are not necessary for knowing what it is like (Alter 1998; Tye 2000). Tye (2000) makes the point especially forcefully by pointing out the degree to which the specificity of experience typically outstrips our abilities to remember or imaginatively relive those experiences. We may have an experience of a particular shade of red, call it "red 35," but be incapable of reidentifying precisely that shade or calling to mind precisely that shade and not some other. Nonetheless, at the moment in which we are experiencing that shade of red, we know, at that moment, what it is like. Thus knowing what it is like cannot consist in the abilities mentioned in the ability hypothesis.

Such criticisms of the ability hypothesis highlight the appeal, even to physicalists, of viewing knowledge of what it is like as a kind of propositional knowledge. In keeping with this line of thought is perhaps the most popular kind of physicalist response to the knowledge argument: the mode of presentation response. According to the mode of presentation response, all of the premises of the knowledge argument are true, but the argument itself is invalid. The key point is that even though there is a sense in which Mary gains new propositional knowledge, it is only in the sense in which she comes to represent an old fact in a new way – she comes to subsume an old fact under a new mode of presentation. (Recall our discussion of modes of presentation and Frege's theory of sense in Chapter 6.) The acquisition of Mary's new knowledge is akin to the transition from knowing that Mark Twain wrote *Adventures of Huckleberry Finn* without knowing that Mark Twain is one and the same as Samuel Clemens to knowing both that Mark Twain wrote *Huckleberry Finn* and that Mark Twain is Samuel Clemens. In learning that Samuel Clemens is the author of that book one comes to represent in a new way a fact that one knew already: the fact that Mark Twain wrote that book.

The mode of presentation response is not without its own problems. Recall that prior to experiencing red, Mary is alleged to know *all* of the physical facts. This would include, among other things, facts about modes of presentation. Mary knows that "Mark Twain" and "Samuel Clemens" are different modes of presentation of the same person, and "Hesperus" and "Phosphorus" are different modes of presentation of the same planet. Thus, in learning something new in experiencing red, Mary cannot be learning a new mode of presentation of an old fact (similar objections are raised by Jackson 1998; Alter 1998).

7.3.3 Attack of the zombies

Do you know what a zombie is? Perhaps you have seen the shambling flesh-eaters in horror movies – the living dead that rise from their graves to feast on the brains of the living. When philosophers talk of zombies, they have something quite different in mind. A zombie, in the philosophical sense of the term, is a person who, despite utterly normal outward appearances and behaviors, is utterly devoid of qualia. More specifically, a zombie can be similar to a regular human in every way including internal physical structure but still be devoid of phenomenal consciousness.

Thus conceived, science could not discover whether someone is a zombie or not, but according to the philosophers who delight in talking about zombies, this is beside the point. The point that concerns philosophers is whether zombies are conceivable or imaginable and, if so, what follows from this. If you have phenomenal consciousness, you know it, right? You introspect your own experiences and you know what it is like to have them – you know what it is like to be you, and thus, that there is something that it is like to be you. You know that you are not a zombie.

Now imagine that you have a twin who is identical to you in all physical respects: your nervous systems including your brains are wired up in the same way. Now, can you imagine the possibility that your twin is a zombie? Can you imagine that your twin, despite being similar to you in all objective respects, is dissimilar from you subjectively? To help you, imagine taking Leibniz's fantastic voyage as a miniature explorer inside the brain of your twin: can you imagine that you would not find any consciousness in there? Can you conceive of the possibility that there is *nothing* it is like to be your twin, that all is dark inside? Might your twin, despite outward behaviors and internal physiology, have no more phenomenal consciousness than a rock? Many philosophers say that the answer to such questions should be "Yes." Zombies are possible: they are perfectly conceivable and imaginable. Worse, these philosophers hold that the imaginability of zombies entails that falsity of physicalism. How so? As follows. If consciousness is identical to some physical process – call it process P – then it should be impossible to have process P without any consciousness. Consider, by analogy, that if Mark Twain is identical to Samuel Clemens, then it is impossible to have Mark Twain enter the room without Samuel Clemens also entering. But the imaginability of zombies entails the imaginability of a creature that has process P without any consciousness. And if imaginability is a guide to possibility, then it is possible to have process P without any consciousness, thus consciousness cannot be identical to process P. This, then, is the zombie problem for physicalism: if zombies are possible then physicalism is false. Some physicalists, like Dennett 1991, have denied that zombies are imaginable. Other physicalists have responded to the above sorts of considerations by arguing that imaginability is not a guide to possibility, that just because zombies are imaginable, this does not mean that they are possible, and thus physicalism remains unscathed by the imaginability of zombies. But just how powerful is this physicalist response? We examine this question in further detail in the next section.

7.3.4 Kripke's argument against physicalism

Another argument against physicalism about consciousness is due to the philosopher Saul Kripke (1972). Consider a particular kind of conscious state, like the state of being in pain. Physicalists, let us suppose, hypothesize that there is kind of physical state or process – call it process P – that the mental state is identical to. As discussed in section 7.3.3 on zombies, some anti-physicalists have objected that being in pain cannot be the same as having process P since one can imagine pains occurring without process P. Physicalists have responded that this imaginability of pain without process P is no threat to their identification. They draw an analogy to the imaginability of heat without mean molecular energy. Heat is mean molecular energy, but one can imagine that they are not. One can imagine the presence of heat without there being mean molecular energy (because, imaginably, heat turned out to have been the substance caloric). Likewise, the imaginability of pain without process P does not entail their distinctness: they may be one and the same nonetheless.

Kripke argues that the physicalists' analogy does not hold – that there is a fundamental difference between the relation of pain to process P and the relation of heat to mean kinetic energy. The first step in understanding Kripke's argument is to understand that on Kripke's view identity statements are necessary if true. For instance, if Mark Twain is Samuel Clemens, then, necessarily, Mark Twain is Samuel Clemens. In other words, there are no contingent identity statements. So, for any *x* and any *y*, if *x* is identical to *y*, then *x* is necessarily identical to *y*. By contraposition it follows that if it is *possible* that *x* and *y* are distinct (i.e. if it is *not* necessary that *x* and *y* are identical), then *x* and *y* *are* distinct. A key part of Kripke's antiphysicalist argument, then, will be arguing that it is possible that pains are distinct from process P.

Let us reflect further on Kripke's claim that identities, if true, are necessarily true. This will help us get a feel for the relations Kripke sees between possibility and imaginability. Consider the identification of Hesperus with Phosphorus: the discovery that these are not two different heavenly bodies, but instead one and the same as the planet Venus. Could you imagine a possible situation in which Hesperus turns out to be distinct from Phosphorus? No, you cannot. You could imagine a situation in which the English phrase "Hesperus is Phosphorus" meant something different and thus turned out false, but this is different from imagining Hesperus to turn out to be distinct from Phosphorus. Nonetheless, a puzzle remains, since "Hesperus is Phosphorus" is a piece of a posteriori knowledge. How can a necessary truth be a posteriori? Part of the answer will make appeal to the notion of rigid designation (see the box on rigid designators in Chapter 6). When we initially fix the reference of "Hesperus" and "Phosphorus" we use descriptions such as "the bright body seen in the morning" and "the bright body seen in the evening" respectively. But these reference-fixing descriptions are not synonymous with the names "Hesperus" and "Phosphorus." And once the references of those names are fixed, we use those names as rigid designators: they refer to the same object in all possible worlds in which they refer at all. Thus, "Hesperus is Phosphorus" is necessarily true because "Hesperus" designates the same object as "Phosphorus" in all possible worlds in which they designate at all. "Hesperus is Phosphorus" is a posteriori however because of the reference-fixing descriptions.

Consider the case of the identity of heat with mean molecular energy. We think we can imagine their non-identity, but we are mistaken. What are we imagining when we find ourselves mistakenly saying that it is contingent that heat is the same as mean molecular energy? We are not imagining heat without mean molecular energy. We are imagining having the *sensation* of heat without mean molecular energy. This difference here is analogous to the difference between imagining that 2 + 2 does not equal 4 and "2 + 2 = 4" being used to express a falsehood: the former is unimaginable but the latter is imaginable. As Kripke puts the point,

> We use "heat" and "the motion of molecules" as rigid designators for a certain external phenomenon. Since heat is in fact the motion of molecules, and the designators are rigid . . . it is going to be *necessary* that heat is the motion of molecules. What gives us the illusion of contingency is the fact we have identified the heat by the contingent fact that there happen to be creatures on this planet . . . who are sensitive to it in a certain way, that is, who are sensitive to the motion of molecules or to heat.
>
> (p. 187)

We use descriptions like "that which causes this sensation" to fix the reference of heat, but this reference-fixing description picks out a contingent property of heat (Kripke 1972, p. 188).

So "heat is mean molecular energy" seems contingent, but this is an illusion: we cannot really imagine heat being something else. What we are imagining instead is the *sensation* of heat being caused by something else. Kripke argues that this is completely different from what happens when we imagine pain without process P. While there is a contingent relation between heat and the sensation of heat, the relation of pain to the sensation of pain is necessary. Pain *just is* the sensation of pain – it is an essential feature of pains that they be felt as painful. However, it seems contingent that pains are associated with physical process P and not some other physical process, say, process Q. In the case of the apparent contingency of heat being mean molecular energy, the appearance of contingency could be explained away as illusory. But the apparent contingency of pain's relation to process P cannot be similarly explained as illusory. Thus the best explanation of the apparent contingency is that the relation really is contingent. Since pain is only contingently related to process P, it cannot be identical to it. Relatedly it cannot be identical to any physical process, thus physicalism, according to Kripke, is false.

7.3.5 Does consciousness do anything?

Even if the assumption that consciousness is a physical brain process is granted, any given behavior can be produced by more than one process. We use consciousness to make certain visual discriminations (seemingly, although some would question this – see the discussion of zombie phenomena in section 7.3.3), but assembly-line robots make similar discriminations using simple video cameras – a process which does not involve consciousness. (At least it doesn't *seem* to. But how do we know? How can we tell whether or not the robots are actually *seeing* anything?) This seems to be true in general: any given behavior can be produced by a variety of processes. Why did evolutionary processes seize on consciousness as a way to produce certain behaviors, rather than some other process? One clue may come from careful observation of the time course of conscious intentions and decisions. The knee-jerk reflex happens too quickly for consciousness, while at the other end, the learning of golf seems to happen too slowly. Effortful driving is a good example of a conscious state: memory, perception, the need to quickly modify action plans, are all coming together. When driving becomes routine and monotonous, however, consciousness seems to go away from the driving tasks for short periods.

Another sort of attack on the efficacy of consciousness has to do with whether it really has the causal powers it appears to have. Here we need to make a distinction between what we might call ontological and functional epiphenomenalism. Ontological epiphenomenalism is a type of dualism in which body affects mind but mind has no effect at all on body. One mind state can cause another, just as one brain state can cause another, and the causal arrow between brain states and mind states is one way only, from brain to mind. The leading ontological epiphenom- enalists today hold the view that the mind states don't cause anything at all, they are just emergent properties of the brain states. The aspect of this view that is difficult to accept is that if this is true then your mental states, such as deciding to touch your nose, are not really causally effective and our mental lives, which we think are the lives of conscious causal agents, are an elaborate illusion.

Most epiphenomenalists today are not dualists. Rather, they wonder whether consciousness serves any useful function in the planning and execution of actions. They do not doubt that con- sciousness is a real physical process, they simply doubt whether that process has the causal powers it appears to have.

In experiments conducted by Libet, a subject is told to raise a finger any time within the next 15 seconds. Before the finger goes up, however, activity in the motor cortex seems to actually precede the formation of the conscious intention to raise the finger. This proves, according to the functional epiphenomenalists, that consciousness is not actually what initiates the finger movement. Something else begins the movement, and we simply do not notice that our conscious intention does not occur soon enough to be the cause.

But we must be careful here not to jump to any conclusions. We often intend to do things without intending to do them at an exact time and simply find ourselves initiating the action in an automatic way. When I get out of bed in the morning for instance, as I lie there I say to myself, "Time to get up." Often, however, I do not get up after thinking this thought. I continue to lie there, in blissful warmth until, several seconds later, I simply find myself getting up. When I initially form the intention to get out of bed, I plant a seed as it were, and I actually get up when some other events happen, outside of consciousness.

When my finger goes up in the Libet experiment, yes, the movement is intentional, but that does not mean that it must be preceded by an explicit conscious intention, something expressible as, "I will now move my finger," perhaps. When I dial a phone number, each act of pushing a button is intentional, but I obviously do not need to form an explicit intention for each one. What the Libet experiment may show is not that consciousness has no real causal efficacy but rather something about the time course over which consciousness works. Conscious decision processes take place over a span of seconds rather than milliseconds. To put it another way, perception–action cycles involving significant conscious events take place over relatively long periods of time. A conscious decision is made, then processing is turned over to more automatic processes capable of guiding behavior in real time, i.e. capable of executing much shorter perception–action cycles.

7.4 CONSCIOUSNESS AND THE BRAIN

7.4.1 Binocular rivalry

The ingenious work of Nikos Logothetis (Logothetis and Schall 1989) and his colleagues is particularly important in understanding consciousness in terms of brain processes. It is based on the phenomenon of binocular rivalry: send different visual input to each eye, but overlapping, so that one sees the visual input as received first by the left eye, then the right one, and so on. Monkeys can be trained to give a behavioral response which indicates which of the two competing inputs they see. This is important, because we are presumably getting an accurate description of what the monkey's conscious percept is, as opposed to what the stimulus itself is. Logothetis then recorded activity from neurons in the visual cortices to determine which ones were correlated with what the monkey reported. Since the percept is changing but the stimulus is not, he looked for cells whose change in activity level mirrored the changes the monkey reported. In general, the activity of neurons in the temporal cortex (the inferotemporal, superior temporal, and medial temporal regions) correlate much better with the monkey's reports than neurons in the primary visual cortex (V1) which seemed to correlate more closely with the actual stimulus, and did not change with changes in the monkey's report. This provides a hint that the conscious percept may occur in the temporal lobes. Of course, there are ways this hypothesis can be wrong: the activity in the temporal lobes may simply be correlated with some other area where the conscious event is actually occurring. There are no known motor areas in the temporal lobes, so the idea that this activity may be due to the response itself seems not to be valid. Obviously much more research is needed, but this is an encouraging start.

7.4.2 Blindsight

Certain patients with damage to the early visual cortex exhibit a phenomenon which has come to be called blindsight. "Here is the paradox," says Weiskranz (1997), "human patients in whom the occipital lobe is damaged say that they are blind in that part of the visual field that maps onto the damaged V1." These patients' experience is that of a completely blind person, but they retain certain visual abilities, apparently unconsciously.

The first clue about residual vision in people with visual cortex damage came from a study at MIT in 1973 (Pöppel et al. 1973) in which brain-damaged US war veterans were asked simply to move their eyes to the positions of a brief spot of light shone into their blind fields. The position of the light was varied from trial to trial in a random order. As they could not "see," the subjects thought the instruction odd, but it emerged that their eyes did, in fact, move to the correct position (Weiskranz 1997). They are also able to indicate with an arm movement the direction of a beam of light moving along a screen in front of them. It is known that there are several routes by which visual information leaves the lateral geniculate nucleus, and current thinking is that one of these routes must be intact in blindsight patients. In other words, their brains can apparently see things without any of the sort of conscious activity that we sighted people associate with perceiving. This raises several important questions, not the least of which is what consciousness itself is and to what degree, or whether if at all, it is necessary to the cognitive functioning of the human being. If we can respond to visual stimuli without consciousness, then why do we need consciousness? Variations of this problem are related to the problems raised by the alleged imaginability of zombies discussed in section 7.3.3.

7.5 CONSCIOUSNESS AND THE REPRESENTATIONAL THEORY OF MIND

Throughout this book we have seen the explanatory power of the representational theory of mind with regard to the diverse phenomena of memory, perception, language, etc. However, consciousness seems to pose the greatest challenges. For example, how can qualia and what it is like to have them be representational? Problems are exacerbated by the philosophical tradition that divides mental states into the representational, like beliefs, and the phenomenal, like pains. According to this tradition, conscious sensations like pain represent nothing. We turn now to a class of theories that challenge this traditional division, and argue instead that even sensations like pains can be understood representationally.

As discussed above in connection with Leibniz's imaginary voyage into the brain, conscious experiences do not *seem* like brain processes. But this raises the question of what it is they *do* seem like. One plausible answer to this question, given by G.E. Moore (1922), among others, is that experiences seem like the presentations to a subject of the instantiations of properties by objects in a world (the subject's body being among the objects so encountered). For example, my current visual experience is an experience of an array of colored objects, each bearing various spatial relations to the other, as well as myself. Further, Moore remarked, when I introspect the qualities of my visual experience, the experience is, as it were, looked right through to an apparent external world populated by colored objects – my experiences are thus transparent, so to speak. Acknowledging the transparency of experience opens the door to a promising solution to Leibniz's problem: representationalism. Representationalism is the application of the representational theory of mind to consciousness. The central idea of representationalism is that conscious experiences comprise a kind of mental representation and that the introspectible qualities of experience are exhausted by their representational contents. Recent advocates of representationalism include Fred Dretske (1995), Michael Tye (1995), and William Lycan (1996).

Treating experiences as representations and qualia as representational contents allows us to solve Leibniz's problem by appealing to the content/vehicle distinction (recall our discussion from Chapter 1). A miniaturized Leibniz cannot find qualia in the brain for the same reason that someone who cannot read English will not be able to extract the story of *Moby Dick* (1851) from even the most careful scrutiny of the paper and ink in a copy of Herman Melville's novel. Even the closest examination of a representation's vehicle need not yield any clues to the representation's content, for the properties had by the former need not be had by the latter, and vice versa. To think otherwise is to be surprised upon opening a copy of Stephen Crane's *The Red Badge of Courage* (1895) and discovering that it is not printed in red ink.

Most representationalists rely on causal covariational theories of mental representation as described in Chapter 1, section 1.4.2.3, whereby an experience represents some thing or property in virtue of having the function of causally covarying with that thing or property. One strategy that representationalists employ in arguing for their view is to tell a plausible story for each kind of experience whereby there is something it has the function of causally covarying with. The challenge is to make this strategy succeed for all sorts of experiences including afterimages, pains, tickles, itches, tingles, thirst, temperature, hunger pangs, orgasms, background feelings, emotions, and moods such as anxiety and depression.

This strategy is particularly evident and effective in the treatment of pains. What is it like to have a pain in your foot? It's like having something terrible happening in your foot. And, what does this terrible sensation have the function of causally covarying with? It covaries with damage to or disturbance of the tissue in that organ. Thus pains represent tissue damage and disturbances. Twinges of pain represent mild brief disturbances; aches represent volumes inside the body that have vague dimensions and locations; stabbing pains represent sudden damage to well-defined bodily regions. The representationalist strategy is particularly effective in the case of pains because that which introspection reveals the pains to be about fits our ideas about what the biological function of pain is. Further considerations in favor of viewing pains as representational come from the considerations of phantom limb syndrome discussed in Chapter 3 in section 3.12.2. One need not even have a hand for it to feel like one has a pain in a hand. This is explained by thinking of pains as representations in the brain: representations that something nasty is happening in, e.g., a hand.

One problem that representational theories need to deal with is to explain state consciousness. Consider the case of the long-distance truck driver. He has been driving for so long that he can let his conscious awareness wander: he is not always explicitily conscious of what is on the road. Perhaps you have similar experiences while driving or doing some other task that you know so well you can "space out" and "go on autopilot" without detriment to your performance. You may be driving for many miles in this disengaged state and then you snap out of it, and realize that you were not quite conscious of what you were doing: you were not quite conscious of the road, the color of other cars, etc. But here is where the puzzle arises. In spite of the fact that you were "on autopilot" your brain was still processing visual information about the road, your car, and other cars. You were driving quite well, much better than you would if there were a bag over your head depriving your brain of any visual information about what was going on. Thus the problem for representationalism arises: you had lots of representations of the road, the other cars, etc., but your perceptual representations were not conscious; they did not have state consciousness. Thus, the case of the driver operating on autopilot seems to be a case of transitive consciousness without state consciousness. There is a sense in which the driver is conscious of the road and other cars – this is why he did not get in any accidents. But the perceptual states are not themselves conscious, they are devoid of state consciousness. Thus, merely representing the road in perception seems insufficient for accounting for an important aspect of consciousness. How can a representational theory account for state consciousness?

According to higher order theories of consciousness, as advocated by theorists such as Rosenthal (1993) and Lycan (1996), a mental state x becomes conscious when there is a higher order state y that represents x. Depending on the theory, that higher order state may be a kind of thought or a kind of percept. We will not here get into the difference between the perception and thought versions of higher order theories. We will gloss over the differences by just talking about higher order states (HOSs). According to the HOS theories, state consciousness is explained in terms of a kind of self-directed transitive consciousness. What makes a first-order perceptual state conscious (state conscious) is that one is conscious *of* that first-order state, and one is conscious of the first-order state by having an HOS that is directed toward that first-order state. The HOS itself need not be conscious. It could be, but only if there is some yet higher – third-order – state that is directed toward the second-order HOS.

The HOS theory helps explain the long-distance truck driver case as follows. When the driver is "on autopilot" he has first-order perceptual states directed toward the road, but no HOSs directed toward his first-order states. Later, when he "snaps out of it," he becomes conscious of what he's been seeing, by forming HOSs directed at his perceptual states.

THE BINDING PROBLEM

When you have a conscious visual experience, say of a red square and a green circle you are looking at on a piece of paper, certain states in your brain may be responsible for producing the colors you apprehend, while other states form the shapes you are aware of. Your visual experience is not divided up into these two parts, however. The shapes and the colors are both present in the same experience at the same time. How then does the brain accomplish this? What process connects the colors with the shapes? This is the binding problem: how functions achieved by different parts of the brain somehow combine their output into a single conscious percept – the two colored shapes. Not only does the problem of binding occur across components of a single modality, in this case the shape and color components of the visual modality, but also the problem exists for multiple modalities: how is it that a single conscious experience contains information from vision, hearing, touch, smell, and taste, all at the same time?

Given that much of our visual information processing is done using retinotopic maps as data structures, one might speculate that one or more of these maps is simply conscious. Damage to such maps will normally be consciously detectable by the person. For instance, there is some evidence that the retinotopic map in the area known as V4 is responsible for producing the color component in vision (Zeki 1993). Damage to this area can produce a type of color blindness. We have also seen that damage to certain parts of the ventral visual-processing stream can produce a kind of shape blindness. Given that the evidence that shape and color are computed by two or more different somatotopic maps, the binding problem in this case reduces to the question of how the brain merges these two maps to produce a single percept.

As to the problem of how to bind information from the different senses, the answer might at first seem rather obvious: simply look for the place in the brain where processing streams from all of the modalities come together. One might think that the problem here is that there is no such place. But really the problem is more that there are too many such multimodal areas. There are places in the temporal lobes which receive input from all modalities (the superior temporal sulcus), and places in the prefrontal lobes which also receive input from all modalities. One candidate for the neural substrate of binding is a type of resonation or oscillation which spans all of the bound areas.

The binding problem is a problem about how the different parts of a conscious state are realized in such a way that they are parts of the *same* state. On the assumption that conscious states are realized in spatially separate brain areas, the binding problem evolves into the problem of discerning which physical process involves all of these disparate parts. Oscillation theories (Steriade et al. 1990) attempt to solve the binding problem by linking the parts of a conscious state with a process of electrical oscillation. The magical frequency seems to be somewhere around 40 times per second. Indeed, such coherent electrical oscillations can be measured across wide areas of the cortex.

References

Adolphs, R., Tranel, D., Damasio, H., and Damasio, A. (1994) "Impaired recognition of emotion in facial expressions following bilateral damage to the human amygdala," *Nature*, 372: 669–672.

Amaral, D.G., Price, J.L., Pitkänen, A., and Carmichael, S.T. (1992) "Anatomical organization of the primate amygdaloid complex," in J.P. Aggleton (ed.) *The Amygdala: Neurobiological Aspects of Emotion, Memory, and Mental Dysfunction*, New York: Wiley-Liss, pp. 1–66.

Andersen, R.A., Snyder, L.H., Li, C.S., and Stricanne, B. (1993) "Coordinate transformations in the representation of spatial information," *Current Opinion in Neurobiology*, 3(2): 171–176.

Bach-y-Rita, Paul (1972) *Brain Mechanisms in Sensory Substitution*, New York and London: Academic Press.

Baddeley, A.D. (1990) *Human Memory: Theory and Practice*, Hove, UK: Erlbaum.

Bartram, D.J. (1974) "The role of visual and semantic codes in object naming," *Cognitive Psychology*, 6: 325–356.

Bartram, D.J. (1976) "Levels of coding in picture–picture comparison tasks," *Memory and Cognition*, 4: 593–602.

Bauer, R.M. (1984) "Autonomic recognition of names and faces in prosopagnosia: A neuropsychological application of the Guilty Knowledge Test," *Neuropsychologia*, 22: 457–469.

Bauer, R.M. (1986) "The cognitive psychophysiology of prosopagnosia," in H.D. Ellis, M.A. Jeeves, F. Newcombe, and A.W. Young (eds) *Aspects of Face Processing*, Dordrecht: Nijhoff.

Bechtel, W. and Abrahamsen, A. (1991) *Connectionism and Mind: An Introduction to Parallel Processing in Networks*, Cambridge, MA: Basil Blackwell.

Bechtel, W. and Richardson, R.C. (1993) *Discovering Complexity: Decomposition and Localization as Strategies in Scientific Research*, Princeton, NJ: Princeton University Press.

Berkeley, George (1710) *A Treatise Concerning the Principles of Human Knowledge*, Dublin: Jeremy Pepyat.

Berkeley, George (1713) *Three Dialogues between Hylas and Philonous*, London: Jacob Tonson.

Biederman, I. (1987) "Recognition-by-components: A theory of human image understanding," *Psychological Review*, 94(2): 115–147.

Biederman, I. (1995) "Visual object recognition," in S. Kosslyn and D. Osherson (eds) *An Invitation to Cognitive Science*, 2nd edn, Cambridge, MA: MIT Press, pp. 121–165.

Biederman, I. and Gerhardstein, P.C. (1993) "Recognizing depth-rotated objects: Evidence and conditions for three-dimensional viewpoint invariance," *Journal of Experimental Psychology: Human Perception and Performance*, 18: 121–133.

Bizzi, E., Mussa-Ivaldi, F.A., and Giszter, S. (1991) "Computations underlying the execution of movement: A biological perspective," *Science*, 253: 287–291.

Braitenberg, Valentino (1984) *Vehicles: Experiments in Synthetic Psychology*, Cambridge, MA: MIT Press.

Bülthoff, H.H. and Edelman, S. (1992) "Psychophysical support for a two-dimensional view interpolation theory of object recognition," *Proceedings of the National Academy of Sciences USA*, 89(1): 60–64.

Chomsky, Noam (1964[1959]) "Review of *Verbal Behavior*, by B.F. Skinner," *Language*, 35: 26–58, reprinted in J.A. Fodor and J.J. Katz (eds) *The Structure of Language*, Englewood Cliffs, NJ: Prentice Hall.

Chomsky, Noam (1972) *Some Empirical Issues in the Theory of Transformational Grammar*, Wellesley, MA: A.K. Peters.

Churchland, Patricia S. (1993) *Neurophilosophy: Toward a Unified Science of the Mind/Brain*, Cambridge, MA: MIT Press.

Churchland, Patricia S. and Ramachandran, V.S. (1994) "Filling in: Why Dennett is wrong," in Bo Dahlbom (ed.) *Dennett and his Critics*, Oxford: Basil Blackwell.

Churchland, Paul M. (1979) *Scientific Realism and the Plasticity of Mind*. Cambridge: Cambridge University Press.

Churchland, Paul M. (2006[1985]) "Reduction, qualia, and the direct introspection of brain states," *Journal of Philosophy*, 82(1): 8–28, reprinted in D. Kolak and R. Martin (eds) *The Experience of Philosophy*, New York: Oxford University Press, pp. 486–494.

Clark, Austen (1993) *Sensory Qualities*, Oxford: Oxford University Press.

Clark, P. (1990) "Machine learning: Techniques and recent developments," in A.R. Mirzai (ed.) *Artificial Intelligence: Concepts and Applications in Engineering*, London: Chapman and Hall, pp. 65–93.

Congdon, C.B. and Laird, J.E. (1997) *The Soar User's Manual: Version 7.0.4.*, Ann Arbor, MI: University of Michigan Press.

Cronk, George (2003) *On Shankara*, Belmont, CA: Wadsworth.

Dahlbom, Bo (1993) *Dennett and his Critics*, Oxford: Blackwell.

Damasio, Antonio (1994) *Descartes' Error: Emotion, Reason, and the Human Brain*, New York: G.P. Putnam's Sons.

Dancy, Jonathan (1985) *An Introduction to Contemporary Epistemology*, Oxford: Blackwell.

Darwin, C.J., Turvey, M.T., and Crowder, R.G. (1972) "The auditory analogue of the Sperling partial report procedure: Evidence for brief auditory storage," *Cognitive Psychology*, 3: 225–267.

Davidson, D. (1993) "Thinking causes," in J. Heil and A. Mele (eds) *Mental Causation*, Oxford: Oxford University Press.

Davidson, D. and Hintikka, J. (1969) *Words and Objections*, Dordrecht: Reidel.

Dennett, Daniel C. (1991) *Consciousness Explained*, Boston, MA: Little Brown and Company.

Dennett, Daniel C. and Kolak, Daniel (2000) *A Dialogue on Consciousness, Self and Reality*, in Daniel Kolak (ed.) *Questioning Matters,* Mayfield.

De Renzi, E., Liotti, M., and Nichelli, P. (1987) "Semantic amnesia with preservation of autobiographical memory," *Cortex*, 4: 234–250.

Descartes, René (1970[1641]) *The Philosophical Works of Descartes*, trans. Elizabeth Haldane and G.R.T. Ross, London: Cambridge University Press.

Dretske, F. (1995) *Naturalizing the Mind*, Cambridge, MA: MIT Press.

Ebbinghaus, Hermann (1885) *Memory: A Contribution to Experimental Psychology*, trans. Henry A. Ruger and Clara E. Bussenius (1913), New York: Teachers College, Columbia University.

Ellis, H.D. and Young, A.W. (1988) *Human Cognitive Neuropsychology*, Hove, UK: Erlbaum.

Ellis, H.D. and Young, A.W. (1990) "Accounting for delusional misidentifications," *British Journal of Psychiatry*, 157: 239–248.

Ellis, H.D., Young, A.W., Quayle, A.H., and de Pauw, K.W. (1997) "Reduced autonomic responses to faces in Capgras delusion," *Proceedings of the Royal Society of London*, 264(1384): 1085–1092.

Elman, J.L. (1991) "Distributed representations, simple recurrent networks, and grammatical structure," *Machine Learning*, 7(2/3): 195–225.

Evans, Gareth (1985) "Things without the mind," in Gareth Evans (1985) *The Collected Papers of Gareth Evans*, London: Oxford University Press.

Fiorini, M., Rosa, M.G.P., Gattass, R., and Rocha-Miranda, C.E. (1992) "Dynamic surrounds of receptive fields in primate striate cortex: A physiological basis," *Proceedings of the National Academy of Science*, 89: 8547–8551.

Fischoff, B., Slovic, P., and Lichtenstein, S. (1977) "Behavioral decision theory," *Annual Review of Psychology*, 28: 1–39.

Fodor, J.A. (1983) *The Modularity of Mind: An Essay on Faculty*, Cambridge, MA: MIT Press.

Fodor, J.A. and Lepore, E. (2002) *The Compositionality Papers*, New York: Oxford University Press.

Fodor, J.A. and Pylyshyn, Z.W. (1981) "How direct is visual perception? Some reflections on Gibson's 'Ecological Approach'," *Cognition*, 9(2): 139–196.

Frege, Gottlob (1950[1884]) *Die Grundlagen der Arithmetik* (*The Foundations of Arithmetic*), trans. J.L. Austin, Oxford: Basil Blackwell.

Freud, Sigmund (1947) *The Ego and the Id*, London: Hogarth Press.

Galanter, E. (1988) "Writing *Plans . . .*," in W. Hirst (ed.) *The Making of Cognitive Science: Essays in Honor of George A. Miller*, New York: Cambridge University Press, pp. 36–44.

Galilei, Galileo (1954[1623]) *Two Kinds of Properties*, trans. A. Danto, *Introduction to Contemporary Civilization in the West*, 2nd edn, New York: Columbia University Press, vol. I, pp. 719–724.

Gauthier, I. and Tarr. M.J. (1997) "Orientation priming of novel shapes in the context of viewpoint dependent recognition," *Perception*, 26: 51–73.

Gauthier, I., Tarr, M.J., Anderson, A.W., Skudlarski, P., and Gore, J.C. (1999) "Activation of the middle fusiform 'face area' increases with expertise in recognizing novel objects," *Nature Neuroscience*, 2: 568–573.

Gentner, D. (1983) "Structure-mapping: A theoretical framework for analogy," *Cognitive Science*, 7(2): 155–170.

Geshwind, N. (1965) "Disconnexion syndromes in animals and man," *Brain*, 88: 237–294, 585–644.

Gettier, Edmund (1963) "Is justified true belief knowledge?" *Analysis*, 23: 121–123.

Ghez, Claude (1991) "The control of movement", in E.R. Kandell, J.H. Schwartz, and T.M. Jessell (eds) *Principles of Neural Science*, 3rd edn, New York: Elsevier.

Glanzer, M. and Cunitz, A.R. (1966) "Two storage mechanisms in free recall," *Journal of Verbal Learning and Verbal Behaviour*, 5: 351–360.

Goldman-Rakic, Patricia (1992) "Working memory and the mind," *Scientific American*, 267(3): 110–117.

Gordon, Robert M. (1987) *The Structure of Emotions: Investigations in Cognitive Philosophy*, New York: Cambridge University Press.

Griggs, R.A. and Cox, J.R. (1982) "The elusive thematic-materials effect in Wason's selection task," *British Journal of Psychology*, 73: 407–420.

Hardin, C.L. (1988) *Color for Philosophers: Unweaving the Rainbow*, Indianapolis, IN: Hackett.

Harman, G. (ed.) (1993) *Conceptions of the Human Mind: Essays in Honor of George A. Miller*, Hillsdale, NJ: Erlbaum.

Hearnshaw, L.S. (1987) *The Shaping of Modern Psychology*, London: Routledge & Kegan Paul.

Hebb, D.O. (1949) *The Organization of Behavior*, New York: Wiley.

Hempel, Carl (1965) *Aspects of Scientific Explanation*, New York: Free Press.

Hirstein, W. and Ramachandran, V.S. (1997) "Capgras Syndrome: A novel probe for understanding the neural representation of the identity and familiarity of persons," *Proceedings of the Royal Society of London*, B264: 437–444.

Hobbes, T. (1988[1651]) *Leviathan*, Paris, reprinted New York: E.P. Dutton.

Howden, J.C. (1873) "The religious sentiments of epileptics," *Journal of Mental Science*, 18: 491–497.

Hubel, D.H. and Wiesel, T.N. (1959) "Receptive fields of single neurons in the cat's striate cortex," *Journal of Physiology*, 148: 574–591.

Hume, David (1977[1777]) *Enquiry Concerning Human Understanding*, ed. L.A. Selby-Bigge, Oxford: Oxford University Press.

Hyde, Thomas A. and Jenkins, James J. (1973) "Recall for words as a function of semantic, graphic and syntactic ordering tasks," *Journal of Verbal Learning and Verbal Behavior*, 12(5): 471–480.

Jackson, D.H. (1866) "Notes on the physiology and pathology of language," *The Medical Times and Gazette, London*, 1: 659–662.

Jackson, D.H. (1875a) "Case of hemikinesis," *British Medical Journal*, 1: 773.

Jackson, D.H. (1875b) "Syphilitic affections of the nervous system," *Journal of Mental Science*, 20.

Jackson, D.H. (1898) "Remarks on the relations of different divisions of the central nervous system to one another and to parts of the body," *British Medical Journal*, 1: 65–69.

Jackson, D.H. (1915) "Notes on the physiology and pathology of language 6," *Brain*, 38: 65–71.

Jackson, F. (1986) "What Mary did not know," *Journal of Philosophy*, 83: 291–295.

James, William (1890) *The Principles of Psychology*, New York: Henry Holt.

Jolicoeur, P. (1985) "The time to name disoriented natural objects," *Memory and Cognition*, 13: 289–303.

Kahneman, D. and Tversky, A. (1973) "On the psychology of prediction," *Psychological Review*, 80: 237–251.

Kintsch, W. (1998) *Comprehension: A Paradigm for Cognition*, New York: Cambridge University Press.

Kolak, D. (2000) *Questioning Matters*, New York: McGraw Hill.

Kolak, D. (2001) *On Hintikka*, Belmont, CA: Wadsworth.

Kolak, D. (2004) *I Am You: The Metaphysical Foundations for Global Ethics*, Dordrecht: Springer.

Kolak, D. and Martin, R. (1991) *Self and Identity*, New York: Macmillan.

Kosslyn, Stephen M. (1994) *Image and Brain: The Resolution of the Imagery Debate*, Cambridge, MA: MIT Press.

Kripke, S. (1980) *Naming and Necessity*, Cambridge, MA: Harvard University Press.

Kuhn, T.S. (1996) *The Structure of Scientific Revolutions*, 3rd edn, Chicago, IL: University of Chicago Press.

Langacker, Ronald W. (1991) *Foundations of Cognitive Grammar*, Volume 2, Stanford, CA: Stanford University Press.

Leibniz, G.W. (1996[1705]) *New Essays on Human Understanding*, ed. Peter Remnant and Jonathan Bennett, New York: Cambridge University Press.

Lettvin, J.Y., Maturana, H.R., McCulloch, W.S., and Pitts, W.H. (1959) "What the frog's eye tells the frog's brain," *Proceedings of the Institute of Radio Engineers*, 47: 1940–1959.

Logothetis, N.K. and Schall, J.D. (1989) "Neuronal correlates of subjective visual perception," *Science*, 245: 761–763.

Longoni, A.M., Richardson, J.T., and Aiello, A. (1993) "Articulatory rehearsal and phonological storage in working memory," *Memory and Cognition*, 21(1): 11–22.

Lowe, D. (1985) *Perceptual Organization and Visual Recognition*, Boston, MA: Kluwer.

McCarthy, John and Hayes, Patrick J. (1969) "Some philosophical problems from the standpoint of artificial intelligence," *Machine Intelligence*, 4: 463–502.

McClelland, J.L. and Kawamoto, A.H. (1986) *Parallel Distributed Processing: Explorations in the Microstructure of Cognition, Volume 2: Psychological and Biological Models*, Cambridge, MA: MIT Press.

MacKinnon, D. and Squire, L.R. (1989) "Autobiographical memory in amnesia," *Psychobiology*, 17: 247–256.

MacLean, Paul (1992) "The limbic system concept: Introduction," in M. Trimble and T.G. Bolwig (eds) *The Temporal Lobes and the Limbic System*, Petersfield, UK: Wrightson Biomedical.

MacLean, Paul (2002) *The Evolutionary Neuroethology of Paul MacLean: Convergences and Frontiers*, ed. Russell Gardner and Gerald A Cory, Westport, CT: Praeger.

Mandik, P. (1999) "Qualia, space, and control," *Philosophical Psychology*, 12(1): 47–60.

Mandik, P. (2001) "Mental representation and the subjectivity of consciousness," *Philosophical Psychology*, 14(2): 179–202.

Marr, D. and Nishihara, H.K. (1978) "Representation and recognition of the spatial organization of three-dimensional shapes," *Proceedings of the Royal Society of London*, 200: 269–294.

Martin, R.C. and Breedin, S.D. (1992) "Dissociations between speech perception and phonological short-term memory deficits," *Cognitive Neuropsychology*, 9: 509–534.

Mathews, A. and MacLeod, C. (1994) "Cognitive approaches to emotion and emotional disorders," *Annual Review of Psychology*, 45: 25–50.

Mazoyer, B.M., Tzourio, N., Frak, V., Syrota, A., Murayama, N., Levrier, O. et al. (1993) "The cortical representation of speech," *Journal of Cognitive Neuroscience*, 5(4): 467–479.

Meinong, A. (1960) *On the Theory of Objects*, in Roderick M. Chisholm (ed.) *Realism and the Background of Phenomenology,* trans. I. Levi, D.B. Terrell, and R.M. Chisholm, Glencoe, IL: Free Press, pp. 76–117 [translation of *Über Gegenstandtheorie*].

Meinong, A. (1972) *On Emotional Presentation*, trans. and introduction by Marie-Luise Schubert Kalsi, foreword by John N. Findlay, Evanston, IL: Northwestern University Press, pp. lxvii–181.

Meinong, A. (1983) *On Assumptions*, ed., trans. and with introduction by James Heanue, Berkeley, CA: University of California Press, pp. xlviii–331 [translation of 2nd edition of *Über Annahmen*].

Miikkulainen, R. (1993) *Subsymbolic Natural Language Processing: An Integrated Model of Scripts, Lexicon, and Memory*, Cambridge, MA: MIT Press.

Minsky, M. (1985) *The Society of Mind*, New York: Simon & Schuster.

Minsky, M. and Papert, S. (1969) *Perceptrons*, Cambridge, MA: MIT Press.

Nagel, Thomas (1974) "What is it like to be a bat?" *Philosophical Review*, 83: 435–450.

Neisser, U. (1967) *Cognitive Psychology*, New York: Appleton-Century-Crofts.

Neisser, U. (1988) "Five kinds of self-knowledge," *Philosophical Psychology*, 1: 37–59.

Newell, A. and Simon, H. (1956) "The logic theory machine: A complex information processing system," *Information Theory, IEEE Transactions*, 2(3): 61–79.

Newell, A. and Simon, H. (1972) *Human Problem Solving*, Englewood Cliffs, NJ: Prentice Hall.

Palmer, S., Rosch, E., and Chase, P. (1981) "Canonical perspective and the perception of objects," in J. Long and A. Baddeley (eds) *Attention and Performance* IX, Hillsdale, NJ: Erlbaum.

Papez, James Wenceslas (1937) "A proposed mechanism of emotion," *Archives of Neurology and Pathology*, 38: 725–743.

Pavlov, I.P. (1927) *Conditioned Reflexes*, London: Oxford University Press.

Penfield, W. (1958) *The Excitable Cortex in Conscious Man*, Liverpool: Liverpool University Press.

Plato (1920) *Phaedo, The Dialogues of Plato*, trans. B. Jowett, New York: Oxford University Press.

Pöppel, E., Held, R., and Frost, D. (1973) "Residual visual function after brain wounds involving the central visual pathways in Man," *Nature*, 243: 295–296.

Popper, Karl (1958[1935]) *The Logic of Scientific Discovery*, London: Hutchinson.

Postman, L. and Philips, L.W. (1965) "Short-term temporal changes in free recall," *Quarterly Journal of Experimental Psychology*, 17: 132–138.

Putnam, Hilary (1975) "Minds and machines," in H. Putnam, *Mind, Language and Reality: Philosophical Papers Volume 2*, New York: Cambridge University Press.

Putnam, Hilary (1981) *Reason, Truth, and History*, Cambridge: Cambridge University Press.

Pylyshyn, Z.W. (1984) *Computation and Cognition: Toward a Foundation for Cognitive Science*, Cambridge, MA: MIT Press.

Quine, W.V. (1960) *Word and Object*, Cambridge, MA: MIT Press.

Ramachandran, V.S. (1992) "Blind spots," *Scientific American*, 266: 86–91.

Ramachandran, V.S. and Hirstein, W. (1998) "The perception of phantom limbs," *Brain*, 121: 1603–1630.

Reid, T. (1785) *Essays on the Intellectual Powers of Man*, Edinburgh.

Richard, M. (1990) *Propositional Attitudes: An Essay on Thoughts and How We Ascribe Them*, Cambridge: Cambridge University Press.

Rips, L. (1994) *The Psychology of Proof*, Cambridge, MA: MIT Press.

Rosenblatt, F. (1961) *Principles of Neurodynamics: Perceptrons and the Theory of Brain Mechanisms*, Washington, DC: Spartan.

Rosenthal, David M. (1993) "Thinking that one thinks," in M. Davies and G.W. Humphreys (eds) *Consciousness*, Cambridge, MA: Blackwell.

Russell, Bertrand (1910) *Philosophical Essays*, London and New York: Longmans.

Russell, Bertrand (1914) *Our Knowledge of the External World*, Chicago and London: Open Court.

Ryle, Gilbert (1949) *The Concept of Mind*, London: Hutchinson.

Schank, R.C. and Abelson, R. (1977) *Scripts, Plans, Goals, and Understanding*, Hillsdale, NJ: Erlbaum.

Shepard, R.N. and Cooper, L A. (1982) *Mental Images and their Transformations*, Cambridge, MA: MIT Press.

Shepard, R.N. and Metzler, J. (1971) "Mental rotation of three-dimensional objects," *Science*, 171: 701–703.

Simon, H.A. (1967) "Motivational and emotional controls of cognition," *Psychological Review*, 74(1): 29–39.

Sperling, G. (1960) "Afterimage without prior image," *Science*, 131: 1613–1614.

Steriade et al. (1990) "Neuronal activities in brain-stem cholinergic nuclei related to tonic activation processes in thalamocortical systems," *Journal of Neuroscience*, 10(8): 2541–2559.

Tarr, M.J. and Bülthoff, H.H. (1995) "Is human object recognition better described by geon structural descriptions or by multiple views? Comment on Biederman and Gerhardstein (1993)," *Journal of Experimental Psychology: Human Perception and Performance*, 21(6): 1494–1505.

Tarr, M.J. and Pinker, S. (1989) "Mental rotation and orientation dependence in shape recognition," *Cognitive Psychology*, 21: 233–282.

Tarr, M.J. and Pinker, S. (1991) "Orientation-dependent mechanisms in shape recognition: Further issues," *Psychological Science*, 2: 207–209.

Tarr, M.J., Bülthoff, H.H., Zabinski, M., and Blanz, V. (1997) "To what extent do unique parts influence recognition across changes in viewpoint?" *Psychophysical Science*, 8(4): 282–289.

Tarr, M.J., Hayward, W.G., Gauthier, L., and Williams, P. (1994) "Geon recognition is viewpoint dependent," Paper presented at the Thirty-fifth Annual Meeting of the Psychonomic Society, St. Louis, MO, November.

Thach, W.T., Goodkin H.P., and Keating, J.G. (1992) "The cerebellum and the adaptive coordination of movement," *Annual Review of Neuroscience*, 15: 403–442.

Tolman, Edward Chace (1922) "A new formula for behaviorism," *Psychological Review*, 29: 44–53.

Tolman, Edward Chace (1948) "Cognitive maps in rats and men," *Psychological Review*, 55(4): 189–208.

Tranel, D. and Damasio, A.R. (1985) "Knowledge without awareness: An autonomic index of facial recognition by prosopagnosics," *Science*, 228(4706): 1453–1454.

Tranel, D. and Damasio, A.R. (1988) "Intact recognition of facial expression, gender, and age in patients with impaired recognition," *Neurology*, 38(5): 690–696.

Trimble, M.R. (1991) *The Psychosis of Epilepsy*, New York: Raven Press.

Tulving, Endel (1995) "Introduction to section on memory," in Michael S. Gazzaniga (ed.) *The Cognitive Neurosciences*, Cambridge, MA: MIT Press.

Tye, M. (1995) *Ten Problems of Consciousness: A Representational Theory of the Phenomenal Mind*, Cambridge, MA: MIT Press.

Tye, M. (2000) *Consciousness, Color, and Content*, Cambridge, MA: MIT Press.

Ullman, S. (1989) "Aligning pictorial descriptions: An approach to object recognition," *Cognition*, 32: 193–254.

Ungerleider, L.G. and Mishkin, M. (1982) "Two cortical visual systems," in D.J. Ingle, M.A. Goodale, and R.J.W. Mansfield (eds) *Analysis of Visual Behavior*, Cambridge, MA: MIT Press, pp. 549–586.

Uttal, W.R. (1973) *The Psychobiology of Sensory Coding*, New York: Harper & Row.

Wason, P.C. (1966) "Reasoning," in B.M. Foss (ed.) *New Horizons in Psychology*, Harmondsworth: Penguin.

Watson, John B. (1913) "Psychology as the behaviorist views It," *Psychological Review*, 20: 158–177.

Waxman, S.G. and Geschwind, N. (1975) "The interictal behavior syndromes of temporal lobe epilepsy," *Archives of General Psychiatry*, 32: 1580–1586.

Wernicke, C. (1969[1874]) "The symptom complex of aphasia: A psychological study on an anatomical basis," in R.S. Cohen and M. Wartofsky (eds) *Boston Studies in the Philosophy of Science*, Dordrecht: D. Reidel, pp. 34–97.

Whitehead, Alfred North and Russell, Bertrand (1910–1913) *Principia Mathematica*, Volume 1 1910, Volume 2 1912, Volume 3 1913, Cambridge: Cambridge University Press.

Winograd, Terry (1972) *Understanding Natural Language*, New York: Academic Press.

Wittgenstein, Ludwig (1958) *Philosophical Investigations*, trans. G.E.M. Anscombe, New York: Macmillan.

Wittgenstein, Ludwig (1998) *Tractatus Logico-Philosophicus*, trans. Daniel Kolak, New York: McGraw Hill.

Yerkes, Robert M. and Morgolis, Sergius (1909) "The method of Pavlov in animal psychology," *The Psychological Bulletin*, 6: 257–273.

Zeki, S.M. (1993) *A Vision of the Brain*, Oxford: Oxford University Press.

Index

Note: References to figures and boxes are indicated as 20*f* and 22*b*.

knowledge 146–8; acquaintance knowledge
147; declarative knowledge 147; empirical
knowledge 148, 150, 155; a posteriori 147,
148; a priori 147–8; procedural knowledge
147, 188, 214; propositional knowledge 146,
147–8, 214, 215; and science 41; senses of
"know" 146–7; *see also* epistemology;
philosophy of science; self-knowledge
Knowledge Argument 213–15
Kohler, Wolfgang 138*b*
Kohonen maps 78, 128
Korsakoff's syndrome 133
Kripke, S. 194–5*b*, 216–18
Kuhn, T.S. 158–61, 159*f*

Langacker, Ronald W. 205
language 187–8, 196–9; declarative sentences
189; disorders 199; imperatives 189;
interrogatives 189; lateralization 196, 197;
morphemes 23; morphology 188, 201;
neurophysiology 196–8; neuropsychology
198–9; phonemes 23; productivity 188, 201;
semantics 52, 189, 194, 205–7; sign
language 200, 202, 203; syntax 52, 187,
201, 205–7; *see also* language acquisition;
linguistics; philosophy of language; speech
disorders
language acquisition 199–207; autonomy thesis
204; cognitive linguistics 204–7;
connectionist challenges 203–4, 205–7;
critical periods 200; language acquisition
device 201; by nonhumans 199, 201–3; sign
language 200; social dimension 201–2;
universal grammar 201
language of thought (LOT) hypothesis 138–40*b*
lateral geniculate nucleus (LGN) 82, 220
L-DOPA 170
left-/right-handedness 196
Leibniz, G.W. 11–12, 138*b*, 212–13, 220–1
Lenat, Douglas et al. 72
lens 82, 84*f*
Leonardo da Vinci 8
Lepore, E. 139*b*
Lettvin, J.Y. et al. 50
Lewis, David 214
lexigram system 202
LGN *see* lateral geniculate nucleus

libertarianism 175
Libet, E. et al. 219
limbic system 177, 178*f*, 179, 181
linguistics: behaviorism 23, 24; cognitive
linguistics 204–7; generative grammars
23–4, 200–1; grammar 200–1; poverty of the
stimulus 24; structuralism 23; universal
grammar 201
logic 34, 189
logical behaviorism *see* philosophical
behaviorism
logical formalisms 12–13
logical positivism 155–8
logical truths 148
Logothetis, N.K. 219–20
long-term memory 63, 130–3, 134, 136
long-term potentiation (LTP) 133
LOT (language of thought hypothesis)
138–40*b*
Lowe, D. 92
L.P. (encephalitis patient) 132
LSD 79, 105
Lycan, William G. 221, 222

McCarthy, John 139*b*
McClelland, J.L. 205–7
McCulloch, Warren 26, 38
MacLean, Paul 177, 179, 182
magnetic resonance imaging (MRI) 58, 58*f*;
see also fMRI
Marr, D. 92
Martin, R.C. 129
mathematical truths 12, 148
Mazoyer, B.M. et al. 69
mechanoreceptors 80
Meinong, A. 191
memory 7, 126–36; amnesia 131, 132, 133;
cellular bases of information storage 132–3;
confabulation 133; consolidation process
131; declarative memory 126, 127–34;
encoding, storage and retrieval 127; episodic
and semantic memory 131–2; experimental
psychology 18–19; frames 134; long-term
memory 63, 130–3, 134, 136; phonological
loop 127–9; primacy effect 63; procedural
memory 126, 135–6, 168; processing depth
130–1; recall scores 62–3; recency effect 63,

Related titles from Routledge

Philosophy of Psychology

José Luis Bermudez

'Philosophers of psychology and philosophically minded psychologists are in need of just this kind of introductory book. I would recommend this material both for pedagogy and as a place for scholars to turn to for a refresher.' – *Joe Cruz, Williams College, USA*

'An outstanding introductory text in philosophy of psychology that lends itself readily to use in a variety of courses. It will, in addition, constitute an independent, substantive contribution to philosophy of psychology and philosophy of mind.' – *David Rosenthal, City University of New York, USA*

Philosophy of Psychology is an introduction to philosophical problems that arise in the scientific study of cognition and behavior.

José Luis Bermúdez introduces the philosophy of psychology as an interdisciplinary exploration of the nature and mechanisms of cognition. *Philosophy of Psychology* charts out four influential 'pictures of the mind' and uses them to explore central topics in the philosophical foundations of psychology, including the relation between different levels of studying the mind/brain; the nature and scope of psychological explanation; the architecture of cognition; and the relation between thought and language.

An introductory chapter looks at what the philosophy of psychology is, tracing its historical background and exploring its relationship to philosophy of mind and to psychology itself. Further chapters cover all the core concepts and themes found in undergraduate courses in philosophy of psychology.

ISBN10: 0–415–27594–6 (hbk)
ISBN10: 0–415–27595–4 (pbk)

ISBN13: 978–0–415–27594–1 (hbk)
ISBN13: 978–0–415–27595–8 (pbk)

Available at all good bookshops
For ordering and further information please visit:
www.routledge.com

Related titles from Routledge

Logical Investigations Volume 1 & 2

Edmund Husserl

Edmund Husserl is the founder of phenomenology and the *Logical Investigations* is his most famous work. It had a decisive impact on twentieth century philosophy and is one of few works to have influenced both continental and analytic philosophy.

This is the first time both volumes have been available in paperback. They include a new introduction by Dermot Moran, placing the *Investigations* in historical context and bringing out their contemporary philosophical importance.

These editions include a new preface by Sir Michael Dummett.

Volume 1
ISBN10: 0–415–24189–8
ISBN13: 978–0–415–24189–2

Volume 2
ISBN10: 0–415–24190–1
ISBN13: 978–0–415–24190–8

Available at all good bookshops
For ordering and further information please visit:
www.routledge.com